Zinky Boys

Zinky Boys

Soviet Voices from the Afghanistan War

SVETLANA ALEXIEVICH

Translated by Julia and Robin Whitby

With Introduction by Larry Heinemann

W. W. NORTON & COMPANY
Independent Publishers Since 1923
New York   London

Library of Congress Cataloging-in-Publication Data
Alexievich, Svetlana.
[TSinkovye mal'chiki. English]
Zinky boys : Soviet voices from a forgotten war / Svetlana
Alexievich ; translated by Julia and Robin Whitby.
p. cm.
1. Afghanistan—History—Soviet occupation, 1979–1989—Personal
narratives. 2. Soldiers—Soviet Union—Biography. I. Title.
DS371.2.A4513 1992
958.104'5—dc20 92-17855

ISBN: 978-0-393-33686-3

W. W. Norton & Company, Inc.
500 Fifth Avenue, New York, N.Y. 10110
www.wwnorton.com

W. W. Norton & Company Ltd.
Castle House, 75/76 Wells Street, London W1T 3QT

1 2 3 4 5 6 7 8 9 0

Contents

Introduction   vii

Translators' Preface   xv

Short Glossary   xix

Notes from my Diary   1

The First Day   13

The Second Day   69

The Third Day   131

Postscript: Notes from my Diary   181

Introduction

by Larry Heinemann

The stories of soldiers in war are painfully difficult to read, intriguing and bothersome. Oral testimony, simply expressed, is always the first wave of 'story' that emerges from any war. Until recently, the publication of a book of stories about the Soviet war in Afghanistan would have been virtually impossible. I have no doubt that novels, poetry, theatre, and films will follow in the years to come when the soldiers find the language and the 'way' to tell the story. But for now we have the testimony of ordinary soldiers and platoon officers, women volunteers and gulled civilians who spent time in Afghanistan. And if you don't mind my saying so, these stories in Svetlana Alexievich's *Zinky Boys* read remarkably like the stories that first emerged from American troops returning from Vietnam – this is what I saw, this is what I did, this is what I became.

If the war in Vietnam was a benchmark of American history, then the war in Afghanistan can rightly be called an equally dramatic watershed for the Russian empire. (I think we can call it that with a straight face, don't you?) The contrasts and comparisons between the two wrenching political and historical events will have lasting reverberations for both countries. Though, I suppose we could say that the results of the Soviet Union's war in Afghanistan were more dramatic, to put it mildly.

In late 1989, while the fighting continued, I was fortunate enough to travel to the old USSR with a group of Vietnam veterans and psychologists expert in post-war trauma. We were going to meet and talk with young veterans of the Soviet war in Afghanistan – Afgantsi, they call themselves.

We flew into Moscow airport through 10,000 feet of solid overcast. Now, I don't know about anybody else on the plane, but I felt mighty strange. Flying into Moscow I was literally coming down from a lifetime's propaganda about the USSR as a place and the Soviets as a people; stories of a bloody, hateful revolution; cycles of crushing famines and virtually endless economic depressions; Communist suppression at least as viciously brutal as life under the tsars; stories of sour-faced and lazy, fat, and selfish commissars ready to grab any good thing out of the hands of ordinary working stiffs, and if they *dare* criticize anything or speak their minds, throw them into the grinder of the labor camp gulags and work them to death or condemn them to an insane asylum to keep them docile and stupid with plenty of State-approved psychotropic drugs. This was the Soviet Union of my childhood; the paranoid and hideous Stalin purges; the doomed Hungarian revolution of 1956, when the people of Budapest attacked Soviet tanks with their bare hands, Molotov cocktails and small arms captured from the despised secret police; the ever-present threat of tens of thousands of mad-dog troops atop tens of thousands of invincible tanks waiting on the other side of the Iron Curtain just *itching* to sweep across Europe to enslave a continent, leaving in its wake a devastation of rape, pillage, and murder. Tens of thousands of tactical and strategic nuclear weapons atop launch-ready ICBMs; supersonic bombers poised at the end of runways, their sweptback wings drooping to the tarmac with 'payload', ready to leap into the air at a moment's notice with enough megatons to render the planet dead at the start of a long nuclear winter.

I was on the trip because I'd been a soldier once, in Vietnam. I had written about that war, and have since become intimate with the personal reverberations of what being a soldier means. And, too, I'd heard that the Afgantsi had to endure the same military grind as American soldiers in Vietnam, and would no doubt have to endure the same personal reverberations when they got home. I wanted to see for myself what effect the war had on them, and perhaps save them some of the grief I have had to endure.

They met us at the airport with astonishing warmth and hospitality, and told us more than once that finally, *finally*, they had someone to talk to who would understand. I couldn't help but wonder, hadn't they been talking to their fathers? But then I remembered the struggling conversations with my own father when I came home from overseas – trying to make sense to him about what had just happened to me. I was surprised and gratified to hear the Afgantsi say, after we'd hung out together for the better part of two weeks, that the only difference between Afghanistan and Vietnam was that Afghanistan was brown and Vietnam was green. We shared the large similarities and the peculiar differences. For instance, the Soviet army did not issue dog tags, so many of the Afgantsi tattooed their blood type on their wrists or shoulders, or carried an empty AK-47* cartridge on a string around their necks with a piece of paper inside with the name, address, and phone number of their next of kin. Such homemade solutions were commonplace.

We met and talked many times in those weeks, the conversations lasting well into the night, lubricated by liter bottles of vodka (an ice-cold it poured like liqueur). More than a few talked as radically as any angry, bitter, pissed-off Vietnam GI from the late 1960s and early 1970s. They took us to a 'private' museum, where among the military artefacts were booby-trapped rag dolls with plastic hands and faces. Who would pick them up? Children, of course. Who would make such a thing? KGB or CIA? Who, indeed?

What amazed me and touched me most deeply about the visit, the meetings, and the private talks was that I was talking to men who were young enough to be my own sons.

What came through most forcefully was that no matter the nationality – Americans fighting in Vietnam, Soviets in Afghanistan, South African conscripts in Angola, British troops in Northern Ireland, Israelis and Palestinians in the Middle East – the reality of being a soldier is dismally and remarkably the same; gruelling and brutal and ugly. Regardless of the military or political reason (always decisions made by politicians and 'statesmen' far removed from the realities of the field), for ordinary everyday grunts the

---

* Automatic Kalashnikov, the standard issue assault rifle of the Soviet armed forces. An excellent weapon.

results are always the same; it is soul-deadening and heart-killing work.

The eighth-century Chinese poet Li Po probably said it the best of all:

> . . . sorrow, sorrow like rain.
> Sorrow to go, and sorrow, sorrow returning.

The similarities of the United States' war in Vietnam and the Soviet war in Afghanistan are striking and ironic, and prove to me that we as people have a lot more in common than we might think.

Both wars were fought without the full support or involvement of their country's citizens. Indeed, before 1985 the Soviets were told their troops were in Afghanistan fulfilling their 'international duty' building hospitals and schools, planting trees, and generally helping the Afghans build a socialist state. Letters were heavily censored and photographs were not permitted. Indeed, so thorough was the censorship that few battlefield photographs by the soldiers survive (in contrast to Americans in Vietnam who took pictures of anything and everything). The Afgantsi mustering out of the army were told bluntly and firmly not to talk about what was going on – a pall of denial by the government not unlike the experience of Vietnam GIs. The corpses of Soviet soldiers were sent home in sealed zinc coffins, accompanied by military escorts with orders that the coffins not be opened. The families, in their bottomless grief, could never be positively certain that their sons and brothers and husbands were actually dead and their bodies actually present in the coffins. No explanation for the deaths was given; the funerals were conducted at night to keep down the crowds; and the tombstones were inscribed with the words 'Died fulfilling his international duty', which became the euphemism for Killed-in-Action.

Both wars are now clearly understood to be foreign policy disasters, regardless of the considerable revisionist thinking about Vietnam. In the fall of 1988, when the Soviets announced they were pulling out of Afghanistan, a Soviet general was asked if the war was a mistake, and like flag officers everywhere he wouldn't come right out and say no – military lifers being who and what they are. Rather, he paused for a moment, and then responded by saying there was an old Russian proverb that a tailor should measure his cloth seven times before he cuts it. It was as close to an apology as the Soviet people are ever going to get. Can you imagine William Westmoreland saying such a thing?

Both were civil wars fought by uninspired and lacklustre government troops (the 'host' government itself bought and paid for) with the help of main force battle troops from a powerful (if not *over*powering) ally. The Soviet veterans spoke of the Afghan troops with undisguised derision in the same way Americans spoke of South Vietnamese ARVN troops – the last to join the battle; the first back at camp when it was over; plenty of nap time in between. Both wars were fought against well-armed and supplied, highly motivated guerrillas. In Afghanistan it was the mujahedin, whom the Afgantsi called bandits.

Both the Viet Cong and the mujahedin were absolutely committed to national liberation and used classic guerrilla terror tactics of hit-and-run fire fights, ambushes, road mines, and booby traps, utilised the safety of abundant border sanctuaries; and obtained plenty of military aid from supportive foreign governments.

Both the American and Soviet veterans were overwhelmingly 'working class'. In the United States, if you didn't have the money or the savvy for a leisurely college deferment or the family influence to obtain a slot in the National Guard (or some other artful dodge), you were likely to be scooped up in the draft; not for nothing was it called Selective Service. In the USSR it was the children and grandchildren of ordinary working stiffs and outright peasants who served – not the sons of intellectuals, high-ranking executives, or Party officials. 'Twas ever thus.

In both wars the average age of the soldiers was nineteen, and both served a fixed combat tour of duty: GIs one year and Soviets two years. There is an important difference here. With the exception of the first arrival of entire divisions, the American troops arrived and departed individually. You arrived in-country as a 'cruit, a newbee, a Fucking New Guy. When you finished your tour as a 'short-timer', you said your goodbyes around, turned in your gear, got on your plane and came home – often turned loose at Oakland Army Terminal with a discharge. There are any number of stories about being in the bush one day, and home the next – and by home I mean *the house where you grew up* – with no one to commiserate or empathize with; your isolation was sudden and extreme; and as you travelled closer to home your isolation became deeper and more complete. You arrived amidst a personal celebration of survival, followed quickly and inevitably by a crushing depression that could linger for years. Soviet troops served a two-year combat tour, but they were rotated by unit. The units were often composed of men who grew up and went to school together, and then into the army. Unit rotation provided the structure for the Afgantsi 'clubs' that gave them close mutual support and a ready-made structure for a national organization, which was illegal outside the Party before the disintegration of the Soviet states.

In Afghanistan and Vietnam the medical evacuation by helicopter and advances in frontline medical care saved many lives, but has produced thousands of bedridden and disabled veterans who need serious, lifelong medical care – prosthetics, wheelchairs, and treatment for alcoholism, drug abuse, and psychological problems. These are the inevitable and virtually irremediable results of the ordinary horrors of everyday life among soldiers in war.

In the 1960s and 1970s the Veterans Administration in the US was ill-equipped to deal with Vietnam's GIs, as Ron Kovic's memoir *Born on the Fourth of July* amply testifies. American GIs have come to understand that the VA is not an advocate of their health. But the Soviet Union has no VA, and their medical facilities are appallingly inadequate and woebegone – there is not enough of anything. There are no special facilities for wheelchairs or the blind, and the engineering for artificial limbs – prosthetics – is abysmal, not to say medieval; though this has changed for the better in recent years. If you've had your leg blown off and are fitted with a lousy artificial leg, then by the time you're forty you'll probably need the stump trimmed a couple of times, and at the very least might well wind up with a bad back in a wheelchair. Is it any wonder that the Afgantsi were bitter towards the Communist Party and their endless bureaucratic jive? Several weeks before I arrived in Moscow eighty wheelchair Afgantsi gathered in Red Square, that area by Lenin's tomb between the GUM Department Store and the Kremlin wall, to protest the lack of decent health care and handicapped access.

They were beaten up by the cops.

Both American and Soviet veterans have experienced pro-longed emotional problems in the years following military service – Post-Traumatic Stress Disorder, delayed stress, or what used to be called battle fatigue and shell-shock (after the American Civil War it was called 'soldier's heart'). Simply put, because of the destructive nature of armed combat the effects of delayed stress are irresistible and irremediable. The list of important symptoms includes: recurring dreams and nightmares; a survivor's guilt that is most often expressed as an unshakable, debilitating depression; hyper-vigilance and an exaggerated startle response; and a purposeful self-destruction that might take the form of out-and-out suicide or the more punishing form of drug and alcohol abuse – what the VA refers to as self-medication. (Though 58,000 Americans were killed in Vietnam, an equal number have since died by their own hand, most through alcohol or drugs.)

There was no preparation by the Americans or the Soviets for the emotional upheaval experienced by the returning soldiers, as well as their families. Americans typically got their discharge at Oakland Army terminal, then were literally shown the door and the waiting cab line for the ride to the airport. The Soviets were turned loose at Tashkent in Central Asia and had to make their way home as best they could, with the added *caveat* not to talk about where they'd been or what they'd seen. So long, *pal*, and good luck. Don't call us, we'll call you.

Indeed, before 1980, meaningful, sensible treatment for PTSD by the VA was simply unheard of. If a veteran went to the VA he was diagnosed as a paranoid schizophrenic, invited to enter the Psychiatric Ward and join the Thorazine shuffle.

Until 1988, Soviet psychologists had never heard of PTSD, until American psychologists expert with post-war trauma visited and told them. Up till then their answer was behaviour modification with drugs – the way Soviet psychiatry had always dealt with mental illness.

Soviet government policies dictated that local communities conduct 'Welcome Home' ceremonies, no doubt to the bafflement of officials since the troops were in Afghanistan engaged in 'public works'. The Afgantsi I spoke to called these largely meaningless, empty rituals the 'false face of welcome'. If Vietnam veterans were not literally spit on and called baby killers – and most were not – at the very least there was an aggressive indifference. 'Been to Vietnam? So what?' Or the more blunt, 'Lost your arm? Serves you right, mother fucker!' The 'Welcome Home' parades and monuments (eloquent though they may be) that have become fashionable in the last ten years are, basically, a day late and a dollar short.

But of all the comparisons between the American GIs who fought in Vietnam and the young Soviets who fought in Afghanistan, perhaps the most remarkable and consistent is their bitterness towards their governments. Both groups of men feel profoundly betrayed, and it is having been lied to that most sticks in the craw. If we can metaphorically speak of the government as a 'father' – who you assume loves you and wishes you only the best – then being betrayed by your father not once but day after day after day is a powerful, unforgettable lesson. It is the sort of reverberating resentment that will soften over the years, but will never be ameliorated. In 1971, it showed itself on the Capitol steps in Washington, DC, when one Vietnam veteran after another stepped up to the hastily erected fence and threw his medals back at the government that awarded them. In the autumn of 1991, young Afgantsi gathered from all over Moscow, Russia, and the rest of the former Soviet states to defend the Russian parliament building (called the 'White House') and the emerging leader of Russia, Boris Yeltsin. The Afgantsi quickly organized to prevent provocateurs, just plain drunks, and hotheads from starting trouble with the armoured personnel carriers and tanks that surrounded them; to isolate conflicts and minimize casualties if they did break out; and if a clear-cut attack did happen, to fight to the death. The night that an attack by the coup leaders was expected, and priests were baptizing Afgantsi wholesale, there were Afgantsi by the thousands ready, willing, and certainly able to fight back, and they were not helpless or unarmed. The presence of the Afgantsi helped prevent a blood-bath.

After the danger of the coup had passed, one of the Afgantsi leaders said, 'We don't think that democracy has yet been won.' But the Afgantsi I met and talked with impressed me as being capable and savvy, young and tough enough not to take no for an answer.

Translators' Preface

The voices in this book speak against two different backgrounds: the ten-year war in Afghanistan, and a great turbulence at the heart of Soviet society.

The roots of the war go back at least 150 years, to the struggle between Russia and Britain for influence in Central Asia. In the nineteenth century, after two wars with Britain, Afghanistan became a buffer state between British India and Russia. A third war led to independence in 1921. A monarchy, established in 1926, was overthrown in 1973 by Mohammed Daud, who was assassinated in 1978. The new government was headed by Nur Mohammed Taraki and his Marxist People's Democratic Party. The following year, after two further coups, Babrak Karmal came to power with Soviet backing. This event effectively marked the outbreak of war between the rebels (mujahedin) on one side and the Soviet and Afghan government forces on the other. Mohammed Najibullah, who became President in 1987, has to date survived the complete evacuation of Soviet forces in 1989 and the continuing determination of the rebels to establish an Islamic state. Soviet economic and military aid continues to succour the Najibullah regime on a massive scale.

It has been estimated that the conflict has cost approximately one million Afghan lives.

The men and women who express their thoughts and experiences in the following pages need no introduction – they must speak for themselves. The confusion and contradictions displayed by some are as revealing as the honesty and insight of others. As we listen to them, however, we need to bear in mind certain aspects of Soviet life with no immediate parallel in the West. To begin with, we may find it difficult to envisage the almost complete ignorance in which the Soviet public was kept about the war, at least until the advent of some measure of media freedom (the celebrated *glasnost*) in the mid-1980s. The information available to ordinary people amounted to a few pat phrases about the 'limited contingent' of Soviet troops and the 'fulfilling of international obligations', together with much anti-American propaganda. True public debate and political opposition of the sort which, at the very least, provides some counterweight to the government version of events in more open societies, simply did not exist.

Another factor, related to this ignorance, was the ruthless secrecy with which news of casualties was treated. This applied not only to the press, but to society in general. To take just two examples: in the hope of obscuring the true impact of the war, some local authorities refused to allow special areas in cemeteries to be set apart for the graves of soldiers killed in Afghanistan; while others forbade the cause and place of death to be stated on gravestones or memorial shields.

Soviet army sources recently stated that the war claimed the lives of some 15,000 military personnel, with more than double that number seriously wounded. In a country of 280 million, and over a ten-year period, this might seem 'acceptable' in the dreadful calculus of modern conflict. Three factors in particular, however, give the lie to any such complacency. First, this was, in the main, a war fought not by professional soldiers but by conscripts aged between 18 and 20, and it was they who suffered the brunt of the casualties (and the dreadful institutionalised bullying inseparable from Soviet army life). Second, the total lack of government accountability meant that there was hardly any informed public discussion of, let alone support for, the war. Third, for obvious reasons of political and military reliability, Soviet forces in Afghanistan were disproportionately – some would say almost entirely – drawn from the non-Islamic republics of the USSR, i.e. Russia, Belorussia, Moldavia, Ukraine, Georgia, Armenia and the Baltic states. (Many of those who speak to us in the following pages are

Belorussian, as is Svetlana Alexievich herself.) An additional cause of resentment was the rumoured ability of certain privileged members and sections of society to buy their sons out of danger.

Finally, readers without first-hand experience of the Soviet Union may be struck by the almost obsessive interest in imported goods and clothes revealed by a few of the speakers. This simply reflects the fact that in an economy where almost any item used in daily life may be impossible to find, or appallingly shoddy, or just plain drab, such scarce articles can command enormously high prices and confer prestige on their owners.

The men and women who make up this book are very diverse; perhaps all they have in common is that they were affected by the war in Afghanistan. It is no exaggeration to say that they offer us a unique insight into the Soviet condition at a turning-point in the country's history; but they also have something to tell us about our common humanity – and inhumanity.

Post coup postscript, September 1991:

The infamous attempt to overthrow Gorbachev occurred while this book was in preparation. The whole world saw the TV pictures of the popular resistance to the KGB and Interior Ministry troops who had been ordered to surround and storm Boris Yeltsin and his supporters in the Russian Parliament (the 'White House'). It is fitting to record here that this resistance was immeasurably stiffened by the presence of several hundred Afghan veterans (Afgantsi) who gathered at the scene. Indeed, two of the three young men killed on the night of 20 August were decorated veterans of the Afghanistan war; after the coup was defeated they were honoured by Gorbachev and Yeltsin as heroes and martyrs of the new democracy.

Those earthshaking days and their aftermath lend a wholly new and unexpectedly relevant perspective to this book and go some way to temper the almost fascist image with which the Afgantsi have been saddled (to some extent with their own connivance).

JULIA & ROBIN WHITBY

Short Glossary

Afgani (slang: *afoshki*): units of local currency.
Afgantsi (singular *Afganets*): Soviet veterans of the war.
APC: armoured personnel carrier.
cheki: foreign currency vouchers paid to Soviet personnel abroad
   as part of, or in addition to, their salaries.
dembel (from Russian *dembel, demobilisatsiya*): conscript nearing
   the end of his two years' service.
dukh (abb. of *dukhman*): member of the mujahedin.
'grandad' (Russian *ded*): conscript with some considerable part
   of his two years' service behind him.
'vets': war veterans.

Asterisked footnotes, and explanatory notes between square
brackets, have been added by the translators. The verse render-
ings of Russian songs and poems are also our own.

JW & RW

Zinky Boys

Notes from my Diary

I never want to write another word about the war, I told myself. Long after I'd finished *War is not a Woman*, a book about World War II, I could still be upset by the sight of a child with a nose-bleed. Out in the country I couldn't bear to watch the fishermen cheerfully throwing their catch on to the sandy river-bank. Those fish, dragged up from the depths of God knows where, with their glassy, bulging eyes, made me want to vomit. I dare say we all have our pain threshold – physical as well as psychological. Well, I'd reached mine. The screech of a cat run over by a car, even the sight of a squashed worm, could make me feel I was going mad. I felt that animals, birds, fish, every living thing had a right to a life of its own.

And then all of a sudden, if you can call it sudden for the war had been going on for seven years . . .

One day we gave a lift to a young girl. She'd been to Minsk to do some food shopping for her mother. She had a big bag with chicken heads sticking out, I remember, and a shopping-net full of bread, which we put in the boot.

Her mother was waiting for her in the village. Or rather, standing at her garden gate, wailing.

'Mama!' The little girl ran up to her.

'Oh, my baby. We've had a letter. Our Andrei in Afghanistan. Ohhh . . . They're sending him home, like they did Ivan Fedorinov. A little child needs a little grave, isn't that what they say? But my Andrei was as big as an oak and over six foot. "Be proud of me Mum, I'm in the Paras now," he wrote to us. Oh, why? Why? Can anyone tell me? Why?'

'Each substance of a grief hath twenty shadows.' (Richard II)

Then, last year, something else happened.

I was in the half-empty waiting-room of a bus station. An officer was sitting there with a suitcase, and next to him there was a skinny boy who you could tell from his shaved head was a soldier. The young soldier was digging in a plant pot (a dry old ficus, I remember it was) with an ordinary kitchen fork. A couple of simple country women went and sat next to them and, out of sheer curiosity, asked where they were going, and why, who were they? It turned out the officer was escorting the soldier home. He'd gone mad: 'He's been digging ever since we left Kabul. Whatever he can get hold of he starts digging with. Spade, fork, stick, pen . . . you name it he'll dig with it.' The boy looked up, muttering: 'Got to hide . . . I'll dig a trench . . . won't take me long . . . brotherly graves we called them . . . I'll dig a nice big trench for you all . . . '

It was the first time I'd seen pupils as big as the eyes themselves.

What are people talking about at this moment, seven years into the war? What are they writing about in the press? About our trade deficit and such geopolitical issues as our imperial interests and our southern borders. We do hear whispered rumours about those letters being sent to jerry-built flats in towns and to picturesque peasant cottages in the villages . . . followed, a little later, by the zinc coffins themselves, too big to fit into those rabbit-hutches they built in the 1960s. (*Khrushchevki*, they call them.) Mothers, prostrate with grief over the cold metal coffins, are expected to pull themselves together and give speeches in their collectives, even in schools, exhorting other boys to 'do their patriotic duty'. Newspaper reports with any mention of our casualties are ruthlessly censored. They want us to believe that 'a limited contingent of Soviet forces is helping a fraternal people build the way forward', that they are doing good work in the *kishlaks* (the local word for villages), that our army doctors are helping the Afghan women to have their babies. Many people believe it. Soldiers on leave take their guitars to the schools and sing of things they should be weeping about.

I had a long talk with one of them. I was trying to get him to admit the awfulness of the choice: to shoot or not to shoot. But we didn't get anywhere: the problem didn't really seem to exist for him. What's good? What's bad? Is it good to 'kill in the name of socialism'? For such young men the limits of morality are defined by the military commands they receive.

Yur Karyakin once wrote: 'We should not judge a man's life by his perception of himself. Such a perception may be tragically inadequate.' And I read something in Kafka to the effect that man was irretrievably lost within himself.

But I don't want to write about war again . . .

5–25 September 1986

Tashkent Airport. An overpowering smell of melons. More like a melon-field than an airport. Two o'clock in the morning. The thermometer says 30 degrees Celsius. Fat, half-wild cats, Afghans they're called, dive fearlessly under the wheels of taxis. Young soldiers, no more than boys, hop about on crutches amidst the suntanned holiday crowds, the piles of suitcases and crates of fruit. Nobody seems to notice them – they're a familiar sight here, apparently, sleeping and eating on old newspapers and magazines, trying for weeks on end to get a ticket for Saratov, Kazan, Novosibirsk, Voroshilovograd, Kiev, Minsk . . . How were they crippled? What were they supposed to be defending? Nobody cares. Except one little boy, who can't take his huge eyes off them, and a drunken beggar-woman who goes up to a soldier. 'Come here, love . . . I'll look after you . . . ' He waves her away with his crutch, but she doesn't seem to mind, just murmurs something sad and womanly.

Some officers are sitting by me, talking about the poor quality of our Soviet-made artificial limbs. And about typhus, cholera and malaria. About how, early on in the war, there were no wells, no field-kitchens, no baths, nothing to wash up with. And about who's taking what home: who's got a video-recorder, and whether it's a Sharp or a Sony. There's a saying, 'War is a stepmother to some and a real mother to others.' I can't forget the way those officers eyed the pretty girls in their low-cut blouses, relaxed and happy after their holidays . . .

Dostoevsky described military men as 'the most unthinking people in the world'.

The stench of a broken lavatory in the little waiting-area for the Kabul flight. It was a long wait. And I'm amazed to see so many women.

Snatches of conversation:

'I'm going deaf. First thing I noticed, I couldn't hear birdsong. For example, I can't hear the yellowhammer properly. I taped it, you know, and I turn it on full blast, but . . . It's the result of my shell-shock.'

'You shoot first, and then you find out if it was a woman or a kid . . . We all have our nightmares . . . '

'The donkeys over there, they lie down during the shelling, and when it's over, they get up again.'

'What would I be back home? A prostitute? That's what it amounts to. I just want to get enough dough together to buy a flat of my own. Men? What about them? All they do is get drunk.'

'This general was talking about the external deficit and the need to defend our southern borders. He was almost in tears.'

'Bring them sweets. They're just children. That's what they like best – sweets . . . '

'There was this young officer. When he found out that his leg had been amputated he began to cry. He had a face like a little girl, all rosy and white. I was scared of bodies at first, especially the ones with arms or legs missing, but in the end I got used to them.' That was a woman talking.

'They do take prisoners. They cut off their limbs and apply tourniquets so they won't bleed to death. They leave them like that for our people to pick up the stumps. The stumps want to die, but they're kept alive.'

'The customs people noticed my bag: "What are you taking home?" – "Nothing." – "Nothing!?" They didn't believe me. Made me strip down to my underwear. Most people bring home two or three suitcases full of stuff.'

'Wake up. You don't want to miss the show, do you? We're over Kabul.'

We're landing.

. . . The sound of gunfire. Patrols with automatics and flak-jackets inspect our papers.

I didn't want to write about war again, let alone one actually in progress.

There's something immoral, voyeuristic, about peering too closely at a person's courage in the face of danger. Yesterday we had breakfast in the canteen and said hello to the young man on guard-duty. Half an hour later he was killed by a stray fragment of mortar-shell that exploded in the barracks. All day long I tried to recall the face of that boy.

'Fairy-tale merchants.' That's what they call the journalists and writers here. I'm the only woman in our group. The men can't wait to get to the front. 'Why are you so keen?' I ask one of them. 'It's interesting. I'll be able to say I've been to Salanga. Do a bit of shooting.'

I can't rid myself of the feeling that war is a product of the male nature. I find it hard to fathom.

Stories:

'I fired point-blank and saw how a human skull explodes. I thought to myself: that's my first. After action there are always dead and wounded lying about. No one says anything. I dream of trams here. I dream I'm going home by tram . . . My favourite memory is of my mother baking pies, and the whole house smelling of sweet pastry . . . '

'I had a good friend, one I got to know here. One day I see his guts trailing over the rocks . . . I want revenge.'

'We were waiting for this caravan. We waited for two or three days, lying in hot sand, had to shit wherever we could. After three days you go crazy. That first burst of firing, you give it to them with such hate . . . After the cease-fire, we discovered the caravan was carrying bananas and jam. We ate ourselves stupid . . . '

To write (or tell) the whole truth about oneself is a physical impossibility, according to Pushkin.

'Revenge for Malkin!' scrawled in red paint on a tank.

In the middle of the road a young Afghan woman kneels by

5

her dead child, howling. I thought only wounded animals howled like that.

We drive past devastated villages. They remind me of ploughed fields. The shapeless mounds of mud, family homes not long ago, frighten me more than the darkness which may be concealing enemy snipers.

At the hospital I watched a Russian girl put a teddy bear on an Afghan boy's bed. He picked up the toy with his teeth and played with it, smiling. He had no arms. 'Your Russians shot him,' his mother told me through the interpreter. 'Do you have kids? A boy or a girl?' I couldn't make out whether her words expressed more horror or forgiveness.

There are many stories of the cruelty with which the mujahedin treat our POWs. It is, literally, a different era here – the fourteenth century, according to their calendars.

In Lermontov's *A Hero of Our Time*, Maximych says of the mountain-tribesman who has killed Valla's father: 'Of course, according to their lights he was completely in the right' – although from the Russian's point of view the deed was quite bestial. Lermontov here pinpointed the amazing ability of Russians to put themselves into other people's shoes – to think according to 'their' lights, in fact.

Stories:

'We captured some terrorists and interrogated them: "Where are your arms dumps?" No answer. Then we took a couple of them up in helicopters: "Where are they? Show us!" No answer. We threw one of them on to the rocks . . . '

'They killed my friend. Later I saw some of them laughing and having a good time. Whenever I see a lot of them together, now, I start shooting. I shot up an Afghan wedding, I got the happy couple, the bride and groom. I'm not sorry for them – I've lost my friend'.

In Dostoevsky's novel Ivan Karamazov observes: 'No animal can be as cruel, so exquisitely and artistically cruel, as man.'

Yes, and I suspect we prefer to shut our eyes and ears to such truth. In every war, whether it's fought in the name of Julius Caesar or Joseph Stalin, people kill each other. It's killing, sure enough, but we don't like to think of it as such: even in our schools, for some reason, the education is officially described not as patriotic but as *military patriotic* education. I say 'for some reason', but there's no secret about it: the aim is military socialism and a militarised country. And do we really want it any other way? People shouldn't be subjected to such extremes of experience. They just can't take it. In medicine it's called 'sharp-end experience' – in other words, experimenting on the living.

Today someone quoted Tolstoy's phrase that 'man is fluid'.

This evening we switched on the cassette-recorder and heard Afgantsi songs – written and sung by veterans of this war. Childish, unformed voices, trying to sound like Vissotsky*, croaked out: 'The sun set on the *kishlak* like a great big bomb'; 'Who needs glory? I want to live – that's all the medal I need'; 'Why are we killing – and getting killed?'; 'Why've you betrayed me so, sweet Russia?'; 'I'm already forgetting their faces'; 'Afghanistan, our duty and our universe too'; 'Amputees like big birds hopping one-legged by the sea'; 'He doesn't belong to anyone now he's dead. There's no hatred in his face now he's dead'.

Last night I had a dream: some of our soldiers are leaving Afghanistan and I'm among those seeing them off. I go up to one boy, but he's got no tongue, he's dumb. I can see hospital pyjamas under his army jacket. I ask him something but he just writes his name: 'Vanechka, Vanechka . . .' I remember that name, Vanechka, so clearly. His face reminds me of a young lad I'd talked to that afternoon, who kept saying over and over again: 'Mum's waiting for me at home.'

For the last time we drive through Kabul's dead little streets, past the familiar posters adorning the city centre: 'Communism – Our Bright Future': 'Kabul – City of Peace'; 'People and Party United'. *Our* posters, printed on *our* presses, and *our* Lenin standing here with his hand raised . . .

At the airport we came across a film-crew we knew. They'd been filming the loading of the 'black tulips', as they're known

---

* Vladimir Vissotsky, a dissident singer and song-writer who dared to express what millions thought. He died in 1980, but is still vividly remembered.

here. They wouldn't look into our eyes as they described how the dead 'sometimes have to be dressed in ancient uniforms, even jodhpurs and so on from the last century; sometimes, when there aren't even enough old uniforms available, they're put in their coffins completely naked. The coffins are made of shabby old wood, held together with rusty nails. Casualties waiting to be shipped are put in cold storage, where they give off a stench of rotting wild boar.'

Who'll believe me if I write of such things.

15 May 1988

My calling as a writer involves me in talking to many people and examining many documents. Nothing is more fantastic than reality. I want to evoke a world not bound by the laws of ordinary verisimilitude but fashioned in my own image. My aim is to describe feelings about the war, rather than the war itself. What are people thinking? What do they want, or fear? What makes them happy? What do they remember?

All we know about this war, which has already lasted twice as long as World War II, is what 'they' consider safe for us to know. We have been protected from seeing ourselves as we really are, and from the fear that such understanding would bring. 'Russian writers have always been more interested in truth than beauty,' wrote Nikolai Berdyaev. Our whole life is spent in the search for truth, especially nowadays, whether at our desks, or on the streets, at demos, even at dinner parties. And what is it we literary people cogitate upon so interminably? It all comes down to the question, Who are we, and where are we going? And it dawns on us that nothing, not even human life, is more precious to us than our myths about ourselves. We've come to believe the message, drummed into us for so long, that we are superlative in every way, the finest, the most just, the most honest. And whoever dares express the slightest doubt is guilty of treachery, the one unforgivable sin!

From a history book I've been reading:

'On 20 January 1801 a Cossack expeditionary force, under the command of Vassily Orlov, was ordered to spearhead the conquest

8

of India. They were given one month to reach Orenburg [in the Urals], and a further three to gain the Indus River via Bukhara and Khiva. These 30,000 Cossacks crossed the Volga and penetrated deep into the Kazakh steppes.'*

From Pravda, *7 February 1989:*

'The almond trees were in blossom in Termez [a Soviet town on the Afghan border]; but even without so generous a gift from Nature the inhabitants of this ancient town could never forget these February days as the most joyful and splendid of their lives.

'An orchestra played as the Nation welcomed the return of her sons. Our boys were coming home after fulfilling their international obligations. For ten years Soviet soldiers in Afghanistan repaired, rebuilt and constructed hundreds of schools, technical colleges, over thirty hospitals and a similar number of nursery schools, some 400 blocks of flats and 35 mosques. They sank dozens of wells and dug nearly 150 kilometres of irrigation ditches and canals. They were also engaged in guarding military and civilian installations in Kabul.'

Berdyaev again: 'I have always been my own man, answerable to no-one.' Something which can't be said of us Soviet writers. In our day truth is always at the service of someone or something – either the interests of the Revolution, or the dictatorship of the proletariat, or some brutal dictator himself, or the Party, or the first or second five-year plan, or the latest Congress . . . Dostoevsky insisted: 'The truth is more important than Russia'.

'Take heed that no man deceive you. For many shall come in my name, saying, I am Christ' (St Matthew, 24:4,5). Russia has had to suffer so many false Messiahs – too many to mention.

I ask myself, and others too, this single question: how has the courage in each of us been extinguished? How have 'they' managed to turn our ordinary boys into killers, and do whatever they

---

* The unspoken message here is that this force never reached its destination, and that the Emperor Paul I was assassinated in a coup partly provoked by such adventurism.

want with the rest of us? But I'm not here to judge what I've seen and heard. My aim is simply to reflect the world as it really is. Getting to grips with this war today means facing much wider issues, issues of the life and death of humanity. Man has finally achieved the evil ambition of being able to kill us all at a stroke.

Nowadays it is no secret that 100,000 Soviet troops were deployed in Afghanistan every year. Over ten years, that adds up to 1,000,000. The war can be described in neat statistical terms: so many bullets and shells spent, so many armoured cars and helicopters destroyed, so many uniforms torn to shreds. How much has all this cost us?

Fifty thousand dead and wounded. A figure you may believe or disbelieve, because we all know how well officials can count. The dead of World War II are still being counted and buried . . .

Fragments of conversations:

'Even at night I'm afraid of blood, in my dreams . . . I can't even bear to step on a beetle . . . '

'Who can I tell all this to? Who'd want to listen? As the poet Boris Slutsky put it:

> 'When we returned from the war
> I saw we were needed no more.'

I have the whole Table of Elements in my body. I'm still wracked by malaria. Not long ago I had a few teeth pulled, one after the other, and in my pain and shock I began to talk. The dentist, a woman, looked at me almost in disgust: "A mouth full of blood, and he wants to talk . . . " At that moment I realised I would never be able to talk honestly about anything again. Everyone thinks of us like that: mouths full of blood, and we want to talk.'

That's why I haven't used people's real names in this book. Some asked for confidentiality; and there are others whom I can't expose to the reproach of 'a mouth full of blood, and he wants to talk'. Are we going to react to this moral crisis as we always have done in the past, by attaching blame to a few individuals in order to exonerate the rest of us? No! We are all accessories to this crime.

But I did record their names, if only in my diary, in case my cast of characters wish to be recognised one day:

Sergei Amirkhanian, Captain; Vladimir Agapov, 1st Lt., gun-crew leader; Tatiana Belozerskikh, civilian employee; Victoria V. Bartashevich, mother of Private Yuri Bartashevich, killed in action; Private Dmitri Babkin, gun-layer; Maya Ye. Babuk, mother of Nurse Svetlana Babuk, killed in action; Maria T. Bobkova, mother of Private Leonid Bobkov, killed in action; Olimpiada R. Bogush, mother of Private Victor Bogush, killed in action; Victoria S. Valovich, mother of 1st Lt. Valery Valovich, killed in action; Tatiana Gaisenko, nurse; Vadim Glushkov, 1st Lt., interpreter; Captain Gennadi Gubanov, pilot; Ina S. Golovneva, mother of 1st Lt. Yuri Golovnev, killed in action; Major Anatoli Devyatyarov, political officer of an artillery regiment; Private Denis L., grena-dier; Tamara Dovnar, widow of 1st Lt. Petr Dovnar; Yekaterina N.P., mother of Major Alexander P., killed in action; Private Vladimir Yerokhovets; Sofia G. Zhuravleva, mother of Private Alexandr Zhuravlev, killed in action; Natalya Zhestovskaya, nurse; Maria O. Zilfigarova, mother of Private Oleg Zilfigarov, killed in action; 1st Lt. Vadim Ivanov, platoon leader, engineer; Galina F. Ilchenko, mother of Private Alexandr Ilchenko, killed in action; Private Yevgeny Krasnik, armoured car gunner; Konstantin M., military adviser; Sergeant-Major Yevgeny Kotelnikov, medical instructor in an intelligence unit; Private Alexandr Kostakov, sig-naller; 1st Lt. Alexandr Kuvshinnikov, mortar-platoon com-mander; Nadezhda S. Kozlova, mother of Private Andrei Kozlov, killed in action; Marina Kiseleva, civilian employee; Vera F. K., mother of Private Nikolai K., killed in action; Private Taras Kets-mur; Major Petr Kurbanov (mountain infantry battalion); CSM Vassily Kubik; Private Oleg Lelyushenko, grenadier; Private Alex-andr Leletko; Sergei Loskutov, army surgeon; Sergeant Valery Lissichenko, signaller; Vera Lysenko, civilian employee; Major Yevgeny S. Mukhortov, battalion commander, and his son Andrei, 2nd Lt.; Lydia Ye. Mankevich, mother of Sergeant Dmitri Manke-vich, killed in action; Galina Mlyavaya, widow of Captain Stepan Mlyavy; Private Vladimir Mikholap, gunner; Captain Alexandr Nikolayenko, helicopter flight-commander; Oleg L., helicopter pilot; Natalya Orlova, civilian employee; Galina Pavlova, nurse; Private Vladimir Pankratov, reconnaissance company; Private Vitaly Ruzhentsev, driver; Private Sergei Russak, tank crew; 1st Lt. Mikhail Serotin, pilot; 1st Lt. Alexandr Sukhorukov (mountain infantry battalion); Lt. Igor Savinsky, armoured car platoon-leader; Sergeant Timofei Smirnov, gunner; Valentina K. Sanko, mother of Private Valentin Sanko, killed in action; Lt-Col. Vladimir Simanin; Sergeant Tomas M., infantry platoon commander; Leonid I. Tatarchenko, father of Private Igor Tatarchenko, killed in action; Captain Vladimir Ulanov; Tamara Fadeyev, doctor and bacteriologist; Ludmilla Kharitonchik, widow of 1st Lt. Yuri Kharitonchik, killed in action; Galina Khaliulina, civilian employee; Major Valery Khudyakov; Sergeant Valentina Yakovlova, commander of secret unit.

The First Day

'For many will come in my name . . . '

Very early one morning the phone woke me like a burst of machine-gunfire.

'Now you listen to me!' said my caller without introducing himself. 'I've read this slanderous stuff you've been writing. I'm warning you . . . '

'Who are you?'

'One of the people you've been writing about. God! How I hate pacifists! Have you ever tried climbing a mountain in full battle-dress, or sweltered inside an APC in 70 degrees Celsius? Have you had the stench of desert thorn-bushes in your nostrils all night? If you haven't, then shut up and leave us alone! This was our affair, and nothing to do with you.'

'Why won't you tell me your name?'

'Just leave it alone! My best friend, he was like a brother to me . . . I brought him back from a raid in a plastic bag. His head cut off, and his arms, and his legs, and all flayed – yes, skinned. He used to play the violin and write poetry. He should be writing now, not you . . . His mother went mad two days after the funeral. She ran to the cemetery at night and tried to lie down with him. Just leave it alone! We were soldiers. We were sent there to obey orders and honour our military oath. I kissed the flag . . . '

'"Take heed that no man deceive you. For many shall come in my name." Gospel according to St Matthew.'

'Aren't you the clever ones! With ten years' hindsight! You all want to stay squeaky clean. Motherfuckers! You don't even know the way a bullet flies. You've never shot anybody . . . I'm not

13

scared of anything. I don't give a damn about your New Testament or your so-called truth. I brought my truth back in a plastic bag . . . Head, arms, legs, all skinned . . . Go to hell!'

He slammed down the phone; it sounded like a distant explosion.

All the same, I'm sorry we didn't talk. He might have become the main character of this book, a man wounded to his very heart.

'Just leave it alone! It's ours!' he had shouted.

All of it?

Private, Grenadier Battalion

I could hear voices, but the voices had no faces attached, however hard I tried to make them out. They faded away, came back, faded again . . . I remember thinking, I'm dying – and then opening my eyes.

I came to in Tashkent sixteen days after I was wounded. My head hurt when I whispered – I couldn't speak out loud. In the hospital in Kabul they'd opened up my skull, found a lot of porridge and taken out a few bits of bone. They put my left hand back together, but with screws instead of knuckles. The first thing I felt was sad. Sad I'd never be going back there, never see my friends, never work out on those horizontal bars again.

I spent two years less fifteen days in various hospitals. Eighteen operations, four under general anaesthetic. Medical students wrote essays about me – what I had and didn't have. I couldn't shave myself, so the lads did it for me. The first time, they poured a bottle of eau-de-Cologne over me, but I screamed at them to do it again because I couldn't smell a thing. They took every damn thing from my bedside table, sausage, gherkins, honey, sweets and left me with nothing. I could see colours and I could taste all right, but I'd lost my sense of smell. I nearly went crazy. When Spring came, and the trees blossomed, I could see but not smell it. They removed one and a half cubic centimetres of my brain, including some kind of nerve centre connected with the sense of smell. Even now, five years later, I can't smell flowers, or tobacco smoke, or a woman's perfume. I can make out eau-de-Cologne if it's crude and strong, but only if I shove the bottle right under my nose. I suppose some other bit of my brain has taken the job on as best it can.

In hospital I got a letter from a friend of mine. He told me that our APC got blown up by an Italian land-mine. He saw a guy being blown out together with the motor – that was me.

I was discharged and then given a one-off payment of 300 roubles.* It's 150 for minor injuries and 300 for serious. After that, well, it's your look-out. Live off your parents. My father had his war without going to war. He went grey and got high blood pressure.

I didn't really grow up in Afghanistan. That came later, back home, when I saw my whole life from a different point of view.

I was sent over there in 1981. The war had been going on for two years, but the general public didn't know much about it and kept quiet about what they did know. In our family, for example, we just assumed the government wouldn't be sending forces to another country unless it was necessary. My father thought that way, so did the neighbours. I can't remember anyone thinking different. The women didn't even cry when I left because in those days the war seemed a long way away and not frightening. It was war and yet not war, and, in any case, something remote, without bodies or prisoners.

In those days no one had seen the zinc coffins. Later we found out that coffins *were* already arriving in the town, with the burials being carried out in secret, at night. The gravestones had 'died' rather than 'killed in action' engraved on them, but no one asked why all these eighteen-year-olds were dying all of a sudden. From too much vodka, was it, or flu? Too many oranges, perhaps? Their loved ones wept and the rest just carried on until they were affected by it themselves. The newspapers talked about how our soldiers were building bridges and planting trees to make 'Friendship Alleys', as they called them, and about how our doctors were looking after Afghan women and children.

At our training-camp in Vitebsk everyone knew we were being prepared for Afghanistan. One guy admitted he was scared we'd

* About one month's pay for a medium-grade civil servant.

15

all be killed. I despised him. Just before embarkation another guy refused to go. First he said he'd lost his Komsomol card! Then, when they found it, he said his girl was about to have a baby. I thought he was mad. We were going to create a revolution, weren't we? That's what we were told and we believed it. It was kind of romantic.

When a bullet hits a person you hear it. It's an unmistakable sound you never forget, like a kind of wet slap. Your mate next to you falls face down in the sand, sand that tastes as bitter as ash. You turn him over on his back. The cigarette you just gave him is stuck between his teeth, and it's still alight. The first time it happens you react like in a dream. You run, you drag him, and you shoot, and afterwards you can't remember a thing about it and can't tell anyone anyway. It's like a nightmare you watch happening behind a sheet of glass. You wake up scared, and don't know why. The fact is, in order to experience the horror you have to remember it and get used to it. Within two or three weeks there's nothing left of the old you except your name. You've become someone else. This someone else isn't frightened of a corpse, but calmly (and a bit pissed off, too) wonders how he's going to drag it down the rocks and carry it for several kilometres in that heat.

This new person doesn't have to imagine: he *knows* the smell of a man's guts hanging out; the smell of human excrement mixed with blood. He's *seen* the scorched skulls grinning out of a puddle of molten metal, as though they'd been laughing, not screaming, as they died only a few hours before. He knows the incredible excitement of seeing a dead body and thinking, that's not me! It's a total transformation, it happens very quickly, and to practically everyone.

There's no mystery about death for people caught up in war. Killing simply means squeezing the trigger. We were taught that 'he who fires first stays alive'. That's the law of war. '*You* need to do two things – run fast and shoot straight. I'll do all the thinking round here,' our CO told us. We pointed our guns where we were told, and then fired them, exactly as we'd been trained, and I didn't care, not even if I killed a child. Everyone was part of it over there: men and women, young and old, kids. One time, our column was going through a *kishlak* when the leading vehicle broke down. The driver got out and lifted the bonnet – and a boy, about ten years old, rushed out and stabbed him in the back, just where the heart is. The soldier fell over the motor. We turned that boy into a sieve. If we'd been ordered to, we'd have turned the whole village to dust.

All any of us wanted was to survive. There was no time to think. We were eighteen or twenty years old. I got used to other people's deaths but I was frightened of dying myself. I saw how a man could become nothing, literally nothing, as though he'd never been. When that happened they put empty full-dress uniforms in the coffin, and threw in a few spadefuls of Afghan earth to make up the weight . . .

I wanted to live.

Never, before or since, have I wanted to live as much as I did there. After a battle we'd just sit and laugh. I never laughed like I did then. We loved jokes, the older the better. For example: 'This currency smuggler or *fartsovshik* comes to the war zone. The first thing he does is find out how much a POW would fetch in *cheki* [hard currency vouchers, used to buy otherwise unobtainable goods in special shops.] Answer: eight *cheki*. Two days later there's this great cloud of dust in the garrison – it's the *fartsovshik* with about 200 prisoners in chains behind him. His friend says: 'Sell me one, I'll give you seven *cheki* for him.' 'Not likely,' says the *fartsovshik*, 'I paid nine myself.'

We could hear that daft joke a hundred times and still laugh. We'd laugh at any damn stupid thing till it hurt.

There's this *dukh*, a sniper, lying there calculating his 'tariff'. He gets three little stars in his sights – 1st lieutenant, that's worth 50,000 afoshki. Bang! One big star – a major, 200,000 afoshki. Bang! Two little stars – 2nd lieutenant. Bang! That evening the *dukh* boss pays him for the 1st lieutenant, the major and the – 'What. You shot the 2nd lieutenant? Our provider! Who's going to sell us our condensed milk and blankets. Hang this man!'

We talked a lot about money – more than about death. I didn't bring back a thing except the bit of shell they took from my brain. Some of the guys brought in porcelain, precious stones, jewellery, carpets. They picked them up in battle when they went into the villages, or bought them. Or else they bartered. For example, the magazine of a Kalashnikov bought you a make-up set for your girlfriend, including mascara, eye-shadow and powder. Of course the cartridges were 'cooked', because a cooked bullet can't fly, it just kind of spits out of the barrel and can't kill. We'd fill a bucket or a bowl with water, throw in the cartridges, boil them for a couple of hours and sell them the same evening. Everyone traded, officers as well as the rest of us, heroes as well as cowards. Knives, bowls, spoons, forks, mugs, stools, hammers, they all got nicked from the canteen and the barracks. Bayonets disappeared from their automatics, mirrors from cars, spare parts, medals . . . You could sell anything, even the rubbish collected from the garrison, full of cans, old newspapers, rusty nails, bits of plywood, and plastic bags. They sold it by the truckload, with the price depending on the amount of scrap metal. That's war for you.

We vets are called Afgantsi. I hate the name. It's like being branded – it marks us out as different from everyone else. But different in what way? Am I a hero, or some kind of an idiot to be stared at? Or even a criminal? People are already saying the whole thing was a political mistake; they may be whispering at the moment but soon they'll be shouting it from the rooftops. I left my blood over there, and the blood of my friends too. We were given medals we don't wear and will probably return, medals honestly earned in a dishonest war. We're invited to speak in schools, but what can we tell them? Not what war is really like, that's for sure. Should I tell them that I'm still scared of the dark and that when something falls down with a bang I jump out of my skin? How the prisoners we took somehow never got as far as regimental HQ? I saw them literally stamped and ground into the earth. In a year and a half I didn't see a single live *dukh* in captivity, only dead ones. I can't very well tell the schoolkids about the collections of dried ears and other trophies of war, can I? Or the villages that looked like ploughed fields after we'd finished bombarding them?

No, the schools need heroes, but all I can remember is what we destroyed and how we killed. And yet, we *did* build things for the locals, and give them presents. It was all mixed up together and I still can't separate the good from the bad. I'm scared of such memories, I run away from them.

I don't know anyone who's come back from Afghanistan who doesn't smoke and drink. Weak cigarettes don't help either – I buy the *Okhotnichy* brand we smoked over there if I can find them. We called them 'Death in the Swamp'.

Whatever you do, don't write about the so-called spirit of brotherhood among us Afgantsi. I never saw it and I don't believe in it. The only thing we had in common was fear. We were all lied to in the same way, we all wanted to survive and we all wanted to get home. And what we've got in common now that we're back home is that we haven't got a thing to call our own. We all have the same problems – lousy pensions, the difficulty of getting a flat and a bit of furniture together, no decent medicines or prostheses . . . If ever all that gets sorted out our veterans' clubs will fall apart. Once I get what I need, and perhaps a fridge and washing machine and a Japanese video – however much I have to push and scratch and claw to get it – that'll be it! I won't need the club any more.

The young people ignore us. There's absolutely no mutual understanding. Officially we have the same status as the World War II vets. The only difference is, they were defenders of the Fatherland, whereas we're seen as the Germans – one young lad actually said that to me! We hate the younger generation. They spent their time listening to music, dancing with girls and reading books, while we were eating uncooked rice and getting blown up by mines. If you weren't there, if you haven't seen and lived through what I've seen and lived through, then you don't mean a thing to me.

You know, in ten years' time, when our hepatitis, shell-shock, malaria and the rest of it starts getting really bad, they'll just get rid of us – at work and at home. They'll stop putting us on their committees. We'll have become a burden . . .

What's the point of this book of yours? What good will it do? It won't appeal to us vets. You'll never be able to tell it like it really was over there. The dead camels and dead humans lying in the same pool of blood. And who else needs it? We're strangers to everyone else. All I've got left is my home, my wife and our baby on the way, and a few friends from over there. I don't trust anyone else.

Private, Motorised Infantry Unit

The local newspapers calmly announced that our regiment had completed its training and firing practice. We were pretty bitter when we read that, because our 'training' was escorting trucks you could pierce with a screwdriver – the perfect target for snipers. We were shot at every day and lost a lot of men. The lad next to me was killed. He was the first man I actually saw die although we hardly knew each other. He was killed by a mortar and had a lot of shrapnel in him. He died slowly and although he recognised us, he shouted out the names of people we didn't know.

The night before we left for Kabul I almost had a fight with one guy, but his friend dragged him away from me: 'What's the point of fighting? He's flying to Afghan tomorrow.'

They were so short of things over there we didn't even have a bowl or spoon each. There was one big bowl and eight of us would attack it.

Afghan was no adventure story. My image of it is a dead peasant, all skinny with big hands . . .

During action you pray (I don't know who to, God probably): please let the earth, or this rock, open up and swallow me. At night the mine-detecting dogs whined pathetically in their sleep. They got killed and wounded too. You'd see them lying there next to the men, dead and with their legs blown off. You couldn't tell their blood apart, in the snow.

We'd throw captured weapons in a great pile: American, Pakistani, Soviet, English, all intended to be used to kill us. Fear is more human than bravery, you're scared and you're sorry, at least for yourself, but you force your fear back into your subconscious. And you try not to think that you may end up lying here, small and insignificant, thousands of kilometres from home. There are men flying around in space but down here we go on killing each other as we have done for a thousand years, with bullets, knives and stones. In the villages they killed our soldiers with pitchforks . . .

I came home in 1981. The atmosphere was one big hurrah. We'd done our 'international duty', hadn't we? I got to Moscow very early one morning, by train. I couldn't wait to get home so I didn't use my army travel warrant for the evening train. I got to Mozhaisk by local train, from there to Gagarin by long-distance bus, hitch-hiked to Smolensk, then got a truck-ride to Vitebsk. Six hundred kilometres altogether and no one asked me to pay a kopeck when they realised I was back from Afghan. I walked the last two kilometres.

Home was the smell of poplars, the tram-driver sounding his bell, a little girl eating ice-cream. God, the smell of those poplars! There's so much green there. In Afghanistan green spells danger from snipers. I was longing to see our birch-trees and tom-tits. Still now, when I approach a corner my insides tighten – who's round it?

For a whole year I was frightened to go out – no flak-jacket or helmet, no gun, I felt naked. I have nightmares. There's a gun pressed against my brow, big enough to blow my brains out. I used to scream at night, throw myself at the walls. When the phone crackles sweat breaks out on my brow, it sounds like gunfire . . .

The newspapers went on announcing that helicopter-pilot X had completed his training etc, etc, had been awarded the Red Star etc, etc. That's what really opened my eyes. Afghan cured me of the illusion that everything's OK here, and that the press and television tell the truth. 'What should I do?' I wondered. I wanted to do something specific – go somewhere, speak out, tell the truth, but my mother stopped me. 'We've lived like this all our lives,' she said.

Nurse

'You're a fool, an utter fool to have come here,' I told myself every day, or rather, every night: in the daytime I was just too busy working.

I was so shocked by the injuries, by the bullets, by the realisation that such weapons had actually been invented. The entry wound would be small but the intestines, liver and spleen a terrible twisted mess. Apparently it wasn't enough to kill or wound, there had to be torture, too. 'Mum!' they screamed, 'Mum!' when they were frightened and in pain. Always, always for their mothers.

I'd just wanted to get away from Leningrad for a year or two, I didn't care where. My child had died, and then my husband. There was nothing to keep me there – on the contrary everything just reminded me horribly of the past. It was where we'd met, had our first kiss, had the baby . . .

'Do you want to go to Afghanistan?' the consultant asked me.

'OK,' I said. To be honest, I wanted to see people worse off than I was. I certainly did that.

We were told that this was a just war, that we were helping the Afghan people to put an end to feudalism and build a wonderful socialist society. There was a conspiracy of silence about our casualties; it was somehow implied that there were an awful lot of infectious diseases over there – malaria, typhus, hepatitis, etc.

We flew to Kabul in early 1980. The hospital was the former English stables. There was no equipment: one syringe for all the patients, and the officers drank the surgical spirit so we had to use petrol to clean the wounds. They healed badly for lack of oxygen, but the hot sun helped to kill microbes. I saw my first wounded patients in their underwear and boots. For a long time there were no pyjamas, or slippers, or even blankets.

That first March a pile grew up behind the hospital – a pile of amputated arms, legs and other bits of our men. Dead bodies with gouged-out eyes, and stars carved into the skin of their backs and stomachs by the mujahedin.

Gradually we began to ask ourselves what we were all here for. Such questions were unpopular with the authorities, of course. There were no slippers or pyjamas, but plenty of banners and posters with political slogans, all brought from back home. Behind the slogans were our boys' skinny, miserable faces. I'll never forget them . . .

Twice a week we attended a political 'seminar', where we were continually told that we were doing our sacred duty to help make the border totally secure. The nastiest thing about army life was the informing: our boss actually ordered us to inform. Every detail, about every sick and wounded patient, had to be reported . . . It was called 'knowing the mood'. The army must keep healthy and we must banish pity from our minds. But we didn't, it was only pity which kept the whole show going.

We went to save lives, to help, to show our love, but after a while I realised that it was hatred I was feeling. Hate for that soft, light sand which burnt like fire, hate for the village huts from which we might be fired on at any moment. I hated the locals, walking with their baskets of melons or just standing by their doors. What had they been doing the night before? They killed one young officer I knew from hospital, carved up two tents full of soldiers and poisoned the water supply. One guy picked up a smart cigarette-lighter and it exploded in his hands.

These were our boys they were killing, do you realise, our own boys. You've never seen someone badly burnt, have you? Face gone, eyes gone, body gone, just a kind of wrinkled something covered with the yellow crust of the lymphatic liquid, and a growling coming from under the crust . . .

We probably survived by hating, but I felt full of guilt when I got back home and looked back on it all. Sometimes we massacred a whole village in revenge for one of our boys. Over there it seemed right, here it horrifies me. I remember one little girl lying in the dust like a broken doll with no arms or legs . . .

And yet we went on being surprised that they didn't love us. They'd come to our hospitals. We'd give a woman some medicine but she wouldn't look at us, and certainly never give us a smile. Over there, that hurt, but now I'm home I understand exactly what she was feeling.

My profession is a good one, it means saving others but it saved me too, and made sense of my life. We were needed over there. But we didn't save everyone we could have. That was the worst thing of all. We lost so many because we didn't have the right drugs, the wounded were often brought in too late because the field medics were badly trained soldiers who could just about put bandages on; the surgeon was often drunk. We weren't allowed to tell the truth in the next-of-kin letters. A boy might be blown up by a mine and there'd be nothing left except half a bucket of flesh, but we wrote that he'd died of food poisoning, or in a car accident, or he'd fallen into a ravine. It wasn't until the fatalities were in their thousands that they began to tell families the truth. I got used to the bodies, but I could never, never reconcile myself to the fact that they were ours, our kids.

Once they brought in a boy while I was on duty. He opened his eyes, said 'Thank God . . . ' and died. They'd searched the mountains for him for three days and nights. He was delirious, raving 'I want a doctor, I want a doctor.' He saw my white gown and thought he was safe. But he'd been fatally wounded . . .

I saw skulls shot to pieces. All of us who were there have a graveyard full of memories.

Even in death there was a hierarchy. For some reason dying in battle was more tragic than dying in hospital. Even though they cried and cried . . . I remember how one major died in the reanimation unit. He was a military adviser. His wife came to his bedside. He died looking at her and afterwards she started screaming horribly, like an animal. We wanted to shut the doors so no one would hear, because there were soldiers dying alone next door, boys with no one to weep for them. 'Mum! Mum!' they'd shout, and I'd lie to them, 'I'm here.' We became their mothers and sisters, and we wanted to be worthy of their trust.

Once, two soldiers brought in a wounded man, handed him over but wouldn't leave. 'We don't need anything, girls, can we just sit by you for a bit?' Here, back home, they've got their mums and sisters and wives. They don't need us now – but over there they told us things you wouldn't normally tell anybody. For example, if you stole a sweet from a friend – well that's meaningless here, but over there it was a dreadful act – something that created an intense disillusion *with yourself.*

In that kind of situation you find out what kind of a person you really are. If you're a coward, or a grass, or woman-crazy, it soon comes out. They might not admit it back home but over there I often heard men say that killing could be a pleasure. One junior lieutenant I know went back home and admitted it. 'Life's not the same now, I actually want to go on killing,' he said. They spoke about it quite coolly, some of those boys, proud of how they'd burnt down a village and kicked the inhabitants to death.

But they weren't all mad, were they? Once an officer came to visit us from Kandahar, where he was stationed. That evening, when it was time to say goodbye and leave, he locked himself into an empty room and shot himself. They said he was drunk, but I'm not so sure. It was very hard living like that, day in, day out. One young soldier shot himself at his guard-post after standing in the sun for three hours. He'd never been away from home before and he just couldn't take it. Lots of them went crazy. To begin with they were on the general wards but later they were put in secure wards. Many ran away; they just couldn't bear the bars. They preferred to be with all the rest. I remember one young chap. 'Sit down,' he said to me, 'I'll sing you a demob song.' He just sang and sang until he fell asleep, then woke up: 'I want to go home, I want to go home to Mum. I'm so hot here . . . ' He never stopped asking to go home.

There was a lot of opium and marijuana smoked, and whatever else they could get hold of. It made you feel strong and free of everything, especially of your own body, as if you were walking on tip-toe. Every cell in your body felt light, and you could sense each individual muscle. You wanted to fly and you were irrepressibly happy. You liked everything and would giggle at any old nonsense. You discovered new sights and sounds and smells. For a moment you could believe that the nation loves its heroes! In that kind of mood it was easy to kill – you were anaesthetised and had no pity. And it was easy to die, too. Fear disappeared and you felt you had a magical flak-jacket that would protect you . . .

So they'd smoke themselves into a stupor and go into action. I tried it a couple of times myself, when I was at the end of my tether but I just had to carry on. I was working in the infectious department, which was intended for thirty beds but instead held 300, mainly typhoid and malaria cases. Each patient was given a bed and blankets but we often found them lying on their army coats or even just in their underpants on the bare ground, with their heads shaven but still crawling all over with lice.

In the village nearby the Afghans were walking around in our hospital pyjamas and with our blankets over their heads instead of turbans. Yes, that's right, our boys had sold them. And I couldn't really blame them. They were dying for three roubles a month – that was a private's pay. Three roubles, meat crawling with worms, and scraps of rotten fish. We all had scurvy, I lost all my front teeth. So they sold their blankets and bought opium, or something sweet to eat, or some foreign gimmicks. The little shops there were very colourful and seductive. We'd seen nothing like it before. The boys sold their own weapons and ammunition knowing they'd be used to kill them.

After all that – well, I saw my own country with different eyes. Coming home was terribly difficult and very strange. I felt I'd had my skin ripped off. I couldn't stop crying, I could bear to be only with people who'd been there themselves. I spent my days – and nights – with them. Talking to anybody else seemed a futile waste of time. That phase lasted six months. Now I have rows in the meat queue like everybody else.

You try and live a normal life, the way you lived before. But you can't. I didn't give a damn about myself or life in general. I just felt my life was over. And this whole process was much worse for the men. A woman can forget herself in her child – the men had nothing to lose themselves in. They came home, fell in love, had kids – but none of it really helped, Afghanistan was more important than anything else. I too wish I could understand what it was all about, and what it was all for. Over there we had to force such questions back inside us, but at home they just come out and have to be answered.

We must show understanding for the kids who went through all that. I was a grown woman of thirty and it was devastating enough for me, but they were just boys, they didn't understand a thing. They were taken from their homes, had a gun stuck in their hands and were taught to kill. They were told they were on a holy mission and that their country would remember them. Now people turn away and try to forget the war, especially those who sent us there in the first place. Nowadays even we vets talk about it less and less when we meet up. No one likes this war. And yet I still cry when I hear the Afghan national anthem. I got to like all Afghan music over there. I still listen to it, it's like a drug.

Recently in a bus I met a soldier who'd been in our hospital. He'd lost his right arm. I remembered him well because he was from Leningrad like me. 'Can I help you in any way, Seryozha?' I asked him, but he was so angry: 'Just leave me alone!' he hissed at me.

I know he'll come to me and apologise. But who'll apologise to him, and to everyone else who was broken over there? And I'm not just talking about the cripples. Nowadays I don't just hate war. I can't even stand seeing a couple of boys having a scrap in the park. And please, don't tell me the war's over now. In summer, when I breathe in the hot dusty air, or see a pool of stagnant water, or smell the dry flowers in the fields, it's like a punch in the head. I'll be haunted by Afghanistan for the rest of my life . . .

Private, Driver

I've been back from the war a long time now, and it may be hard for me to convey my fury at what happened to us. Before I was called up* I'd done a two-year course at an autotransport technical college, so my first job was driving the battalion commander. That was fine, but then they began to harangue us about the 'small Soviet contingent in Afghanistan'. Not a single political instruction period went by without them telling us that 'our forces were bravely protecting the frontiers of the Fatherland and providing assistance to a friend and ally'. That was when we started worrying that we might be sent over there; which is exactly why the authorities decided to lie to us.

We were summoned to battalion HQ and asked: 'Now, lads, how would you like to work on the latest engines?' Of course we all shouted 'Yes please!' with one voice. Next question: 'First, you'll have to spend some time helping with the harvest in the *tselina*.** Any objections?' No objections.

It was only in the plane, when we happened to find out from

---

* All Soviet males are in principle liable to two years' compulsory conscription at the age of eighteen (three in the navy).
** The virgin lands of Kazakhstan and Western Siberia which have been intensively cultivated only since 1954.

the crew that the flight was to Tashkent, that I began to wonder if we really were going to the *tselina*. At Tashkent we were lined up and marched to a barbed-wire compound a little way from the airport. We sat and waited. The officers were going around whispering, all excited. At lunch-time crates of vodka suddenly arrived. We were lined up in rows and informed that in a few hours' time we would be flying to Afghanistan to do our duty as soldiers in accordance with our military oath.

It was incredible! Fear and panic turned men into animals – some of us went very quiet, others got into an absolute frenzy, or wept with anger or fell into a kind of trance, numb from this unbelievably filthy trick that had been played on us. That was what the vodka was for, of course, to calm us down. After we'd drunk it and it had gone to our heads some of us tried to escape and others started to fight with our officers, but the compound was surrounded by troops from other units and they shoved us into the plane. We were just thrown into that great metal belly like so many crates being loaded.

That's how we got to Afghanistan. Next day we saw our first dead and wounded and heard phrases like 'reconnaissance raid', 'battle', and 'operation' for the first time. I was in shock from the whole thing – I suppose it took me several months to get back on an even keel.

When my wife enquired why I was in Afghanistan she was told that I'd volunteered. All our mothers and wives were told the same. If I'd been asked to give my life for something worthwhile I'd have volunteered, but I was deceived in two ways: first, they lied to us; second, it took me eight years to find out the truth about the war itself. Many of my friends are dead and sometimes I envy them because they'll never know they were lied to about this disgusting war – and because no one can ever lie to them again.

A Mother

My husband served in East Germany for many years and later in Mongolia. I spent twenty years of my life away from my country, which I loved and longed for with incredible passion. I even wrote a letter to General Staff HQ, in which I pointed out that I'd spent twenty years of my life abroad and warned them I couldn't stand it any longer. 'Please help me to go home,' I said.

Even on the train I couldn't believe it. 'Are we really going home?' I asked my husband, over and over again. 'It's not some joke of yours, is it?' At the first stop on Soviet territory I picked up a handful of earth. I looked at it and smiled – yes, it really was our national soil. I ate it, truly I did. I ate it and rubbed it all over my face.

Yura was my eldest son. A mother shouldn't admit it, probably, but he was my favourite. I loved him more than my husband and my younger son. When he was little I slept with my hand on his little foot. I wouldn't think of going to the cinema and leaving him with some baby-sitter, so when he was three months old I'd take him (together with a few bottles of milk) with me and off we'd go. I can honestly say he was my life. I brought him up to model himself on figures like Pavka Korchagin, Oleg Koshevoi and Zoya Kosmodemyanskaya.*

In his first year at school he knew whole pages of *Hardened Steel* by Nikolai Ostrovsky by heart, rather than fairy-tales or nursery rhymes like the other children.

His teacher was delighted with him: 'What does your Mama do, Yura? You've read such a lot already!'

'My Mummy works in the library.'

He understood ideals but not real life. And, after living for so many years away from the Fatherland, I too thought that life was a matter of ideals. Well, we went back to live in our old home town, Chernovtsi, and Yura attended Army College. At two o'clock one night the door-bell rang – and there was Yura on the door step.

'Is it you, son? Do you know how late it is?' He was standing there in the rain, wet through.

'Mum, I just wanted to tell you – I'm finding life hard. All

---

* Celebrated figures in the Soviet pantheon: Pavel Korchagin is the protagonist of *Hardened Steel*, a novel about Soviet industrialisation; Oleg Koshevoi and Zoya Kosmodemyanskaya, heroes of the war-time Resistance, were murdered by the Nazis.

those high ideals you taught me, they just don't exist. Where did you get them all from? How can I carry on living?'

I sat with him all night in the kitchen. What could I tell him? I told him yet again that our Soviet life was wonderful and our people were good. I believed it. He listened to me in silence and in the morning went back to college.

I often told him: 'Yura, give up the army. Go to university. That's where you belong. I don't understand why you have to torture yourself like this.'

He wasn't happy with his choice of career, which had been a bit of an accident. He'd have made a good historian – he was a natural scholar and lived for his books. 'What a wonderful country Ancient Greece must have been', I remember him saying once. However, in his last year at school he went to Moscow for a few days in the winter holidays to stay with my brother, a retired colonel. Yura told him that he wanted to go to university to read philosophy. His uncle's reaction was this: 'You're an honest lad, Yura. It's hard to be a philosopher in Russia at this time. You'll have to lie to yourself and to others. If you try to tell the truth you'll end up behind bars or in a lunatic asylum.'

The following spring Yura decided to become a soldier. 'Mum, I've made up my mind so don't try to change it, I'm going into the army,' he said.

I'd seen the zinc coffins in the army compound, but that was when Yura was thirteen and my other son, Gena, just a little boy. I hoped the war would be over by the time they were grown up. Could it possibly drag on that long? But, as someone said at Yura's wake: 'It lasted ten years, as long as his schooldays.'

It seemed no time at all before it was the evening of the graduation ball, and my son was an officer. I still hadn't taken it in that Yura would have to go away. I couldn't imagine life without him. 'Where will you be sent?' I asked him.

'I'm putting in for Afghanistan.'

'Yura! How could you?'

'Mum, that's the way you brought me up, so don't try and rewrite history now. You were right: all these degenerates I've come across recently – they're nothing to do with me or my country. I'm going to Afghanistan to show them that there are higher things in life than a fridge full of meat.'

He wasn't the only one. Many other boys applied to go to Afghanistan, all from the best families – their fathers were heads of collective farms, teachers and so on . . .

What could I tell my own son? That the Fatherland didn't need him? That those people he was trying to 'show' assumed, and would go on assuming, that he was going to Afghanistan because he was after imported goods, foreign currency, medals and promotion? For people like that Zoya Kosmodemyanskaya was a fanatic rather than an ideal; they couldn't conceive that a human being could be capable of such heroism.

I can't remember everything I said and did. I admitted what I'd been afraid to admit to myself; I don't know whether to think of it as abject surrender or the beginning of wisdom.

'Listen, Yurochka, life isn't the way I've always told you it is. If you tell me you're going to Afghanistan I'll go to the middle of Red Square, pour petrol over myself and set myself on fire. You'll die, not for your country but for God knows what. Can our Fatherland really send our finest sons to death for nothing? What kind of Fatherland is that?'

Yura lied to me. He told me he'd been sent to Mongolia, but I knew: he was my son and he'd be in Afghanistan.

While all this was going on my younger son, Gena, was called up. I didn't worry about him – he'd grown up quite different from Yura. They quarrelled all the time. 'Hey, Gena, you don't read much. You never have a book in your hands, just that guitar of yours,' Yura would say. 'I don't want to be like you. I want to be like everyone else,' Gena would reply.

They both left home and I moved into their bedroom. I lost interest in everything except their things, their books and their letters. Yura wrote about Mongolia but he muddled up his geography and I knew where he really was. Day after day, night after night, I brooded over the past, and cut myself into little pieces with the knowledge that I myself had sent him there. No words, no music can convey that agony to you.

Then, one day, strangers came to the door and I knew from their faces that they were bringing bad news. I stepped back into the flat. There was one last, terrible, hope: 'Is it Gena?' They wouldn't look at me but I was still prepared to give them one son to save the other. 'Is it Gena?'

'No, it's Yura', one of them said, very quietly. I can't carry on any longer, I just can't. I've been dying for two years now. I'm not ill, but I'm dying. My whole body is dead. I didn't burn myself on Red Square and my husband didn't tear up his party card and throw the bits in their faces. I suppose we're already dead but nobody knows. Even we don't know . . .

A Military Adviser

'I'll forget it all . . . in time.' That's what I told myself. It's a taboo subject in our family. My wife went grey at forty. My daughter used to have long hair but wears it short now. She used to be such a good sleeper we had to pull her pigtails to wake her up during the night bombardments in Kabul but not any more.

Now, four years later, I'm desperate to talk. Yesterday evening, for example, some friends of ours dropped in, and I couldn't stop talking. I got out the photo album and showed a few slides. Helicopters hovering over a village, a wounded man being laid on a stretcher, with his leg next to him, still in its trainer, POWs sentenced to death gazing innocently into the camera lens – they were dead ten minutes later . . . *Allah Akbar* – Allah is great!

I looked round and realised the men were having a smoke on the balcony, the women had retreated to the kitchen, and only their children were sitting listening to me. Teenagers. They were interested. I don't know what's the matter with me. I just want to talk. Why now, suddenly? So that I'll never forget . . .

I can't describe how things were over there or what I felt about them at the time. Come back in another four years, perhaps I'll be able to then. And ten years from now everything may look completely different, the picture may have shattered into a thousand tiny pieces.

I remember a kind of anger. Resentment. Why should *I* have to go? Why is this happening to me? Still, I coped with the pressure, I didn't break, and that was satisfying in itself. I remember getting ready to go, worrying about tiny details like what knife to take, which razor . . . Then I was impatient to be off, to meet the unknown while I was still on a high. I was shaking and sweating. Everybody feels that way, ask anyone who's been through it. As the plane landed I was hit by a sense of relief and excitement at the same time: this was the real thing, we'd see and touch and live it.

I recall three Afghans, chatting about something or other, laughing. A dirty little boy running through the market and diving into thick bundles of cloth on a barrow. A parrot fixing me with his green, unblinking eye. I look round and don't understand what's going on. They're still chatting, then the one with his back to me turns round and I see the barrel of a pistol. It rises . . . rises, until I'm face to face with the muzzle and at the same instant I hear a sharp crack and I'm nothing. I hover between consciousness and oblivion, but I'm standing, not lying. I want to talk to them but I can't.

The world takes shape slowly, like a negative being developed . . . A window . . . a high window . . . Something white, and something else, big and heavy, framed by it. Spectacles obscure a face from which sweat drips, painfully, on to my own face. I raise my impossibly heavy eyelids and hear a sigh of relief.

'Well, colonel, so you're back from your travels!' But if I try and lift my head, or even turn it, I feel my brain will fall out . . . Again the little boy dives into the thick bales of cloth on the barrow, the parrot's unblinking green eye is fixed on me, and the three Afghans are standing there. The one with his back to me turns and I stare into the barrel of his pistol. I see the muzzle . . . But this time I don't wait for the familiar bang, instead I scream 'I've got to kill you, I've got to kill you!'

What colour is a scream? What does it taste like? What is the colour of blood? Red in hospital, grey on dry sand and bright blue on stone, in the evening when it's all dried out. Blood spills as quickly from a seriously injured person as liquid from a broken jar . . . his life flickers out, only the eyes shine bright and stare past you, stubbornly, until the very end.

Everything's been paid for. By us. And in full.

You know how if you look up at mountains from below they

seem endless and unattainable, but from the air they look like upturned sphinxes lying there? Do you have a clue what I'm on about? *Time*, that's what. The distance between events. At the time even we who were part of it didn't know what kind of war this was. Don't confuse the man I am today with the man I was in 1979. Then I believed in it. But in 1983 I went to Moscow, where life seemed to be going on as usual, as though we didn't exist. There was no war in Moscow. I walked along the Arbat, stopped people and asked them: 'How long's the war in Afghanistan been going on?'

'I don't know.'

'How long's the war . . . ?'

'I don't know. Why d'you ask?' Or, 'Two years, I think.' Or even, 'Is there a war there? Really?'

What were we thinking about all that time? Well? Nothing to say? Nor have I. There's an old Chinese proverb which goes something like this: 'The hunter who boasts of his prowess when the lion at his feet has died of old age is worthy of the greatest contempt: but the hunter who has vanquished the lion at his feet is worthy of the highest praise.' Some may say the whole thing was a terrible mistake, but not I. Sometimes I'm asked: 'Why did you keep silent at the time? You were no youngster, you were nearly fifty.'

Well, I admit it. I had the greatest respect for the Afghan people, even while I was shooting and killing them. I still do. You could even say I love them. I like their songs and prayers, as peaceful and timeless as their mountains. But the fact is that I, personally, truly believed that their nomadic tents, their *yurts*, were inferior to our five-storey blocks of flats, and that there was no true culture without a flush toilet. We flooded them with our flush toilets and built concrete homes to put them in, brought in desks for their offices, carafes for their water and pretty tablecloths for their official meetings, together with countless portraits of Marx, Engels and Lenin. You'd see them on every office wall, just above the boss's head. We imported thousands of shiny black Volgas, and tractors, and our finest breeding-bulls. The peasants, *dekhkani* they were called, wouldn't accept the land we gave them because it belonged to Allah. The broken skulls of the mosques looked down on us as if from outer space . . .

We have no idea how the world appears to an ant. Look that up in Engels. As Speserov, a famous orientalist said: 'You cannot buy Afghanistan new, only secondhand.' One morning I lit up a cigarette and there was a lizard, no bigger than a mayfly, sitting on the ashtray. I came back a few days later and the lizard was still sitting there in exactly the same position. He hadn't even moved his little head. It suddenly occurred to me, that's the essence of the Orient! I could disappear and reappear a dozen times, break things up and change things round as often as I wanted, and he'd *still* be in no great hurry to turn his tiny little head. It's the time-scale, you see. It's 1365 according to their calendar.

Now I sit at home in my armchair in front of the TV. Could I kill a man? I couldn't swat a fly! If we buy a live chicken from the market, it's my wife who has to slaughter it. Those first few days I was there, with the bullets slicing off the mulberry branches, there was a sense of unreality. The psychology of war is so different from anything else. You run and aim at the same time, moving in front of you, to the side. I never did body-counts, I just ran; took aim, here, there . . . I was a target too, a living target. No, you don't come back a hero from a war like that . . .

We've paid our debt. In full.

We have this image of the soldier returning home in 1945, loved and respected by all. Naïve, a bit simple-minded, with his heavy army belt, asking nothing except victory and to go home. But these soldiers back from Afghanistan are something else – they want American jeans and Japanese cassette-recorders. You know that saying: Let sleeping dogs lie? It's a mistake to ask more of human beings than they can humanly be expected to give.

I couldn't bear to read my beloved Dostoevsky over there. He was too grim. I took science fiction with me everywhere. Ray Bradbury I liked. Who wants to live for ever? No one.

I remember once seeing a mujahedin leader in prison. He was lying on his metal bed reading a book with a familiar cover. Lenin's *The State and Revolution.* 'What a pity I shan't have time to finish this,' he said, 'but perhaps my children will.'

Once a school got burnt down and just one wall was left standing. Every morning the kids came to school and wrote on that wall with bits of charcoal from the fire. After school the wall was whitewashed as clean as a blank sheet of paper, ready for the next day's lessons.

A lieutenant was brought back from the bush with no arms or legs. They'd cut off his manhood too. You know what his first words were, when he came out of shock? 'How are my men?'

The debt has been paid and we've paid more than anybody – more than you, that's for sure.

We don't need anything. Just listen to us and try to understand. Society is good at *doing* things, 'giving' medical help, pensions, flats. But all this so-called giving has been paid for in very expensive currency. Our blood. We come to you, now, to make our confession. We want to confess, and don't forget the secrecy of the confessional.

Private, Artillery Regiment

No, it's not a bad thing it ended the way it did, in defeat. It opened our eyes.

It's impossible to give you a complete picture of life out there. I saw only a small part of it and I can describe only a tiny part of what I saw. What's the point anyway? It won't help Alyoshka, who died in my arms with eight bits of shrapnel in his belly. We got him down from the mountains at six in the evening, he'd been alive an hour earlier. You think all this might be a memorial to Alyoshka? That would mean something only to people who believe in God and an after-life. Most of us feel no pain, no fear and no guilt about what we did. So why rake over the past? Do you expect us to talk about our 'socialist ideals' like all those interviews in the official media? I don't need to tell you it's hard to have ideals when you're fighting a useless war in a foreign country. We were all in the same boat there but that didn't mean we all thought the same way. What we had in common was that we were trained to kill, and kill we did. We are all individuals but we've been made into sheep, first here at home and then over there.

I remember when I was twelve or thirteen our Russian literature teacher called me to the blackboard and asked: 'Who is your favourite hero, Chapayev or Pavel Korchagin*?'

'Huckleberry Finn,' I answered.

'Why Huck Finn?'

'Because when he had to decide whether to turn in Jim the runaway slave or burn in hell, he said, "I don't give a damn, I'll burn," and didn't turn him in.'

'What if Jim had been a White Russian, a counter-revolutionary in the Civil War, and you'd been in the Red Army?' asked my friend Alyoshka after class. It's been like that all our lives, red or white, 'he who is not with us is against us'.

I remember once in Afghanistan, near Bagram it was, we came to a village and asked for something to eat. According to their law it is forbidden to refuse warm food to a person who comes to the door hungry. The women sat us down and fed us. After we left the other villagers beat them and their children to death with sticks and stones. They knew they'd be killed but they didn't send us away. We tried to force our laws on to them, we entered their mosques with our army caps on . . .

Why force me to remember all this? It's terribly private – the first man I shot dead, my own blood on the sand, the camel swaying high over me just before I lost consciousness. And yet I was there, no different from all the others.

Only once in my life did I refuse to be like all the rest. At primary school. They made us hold hands and march in twos, but I wanted to walk on my own. The young teachers tolerated this little quirk of mine but then one of them got married and left and we got a new one we called Old Mother Klava. 'Hold Seryozha's hand!' said Old Mother Klava.

'Don't want to!'

'Why not?'

'I want to walk on my own!'

'Do what all the good little boys and girls do!' said Old Mother Klava.

* Korchagin: see p. 29 above. Vassily Chapayev was a hero of the civil war who died in action.

'No.'

After our walk Old Mother Klava undressed me, she even took my pants and vest away, and left me in a dark empty room for three hours. Next day I took Seryozha's hand and behaved like all the rest.

At school and university it was the class or the course which dictated everything: at work the collective was in charge. It was always *other* people making decisions for *me*. We had it drummed into us that one person on his own could achieve nothing. In some book or other I came across the phrase 'the murder of courage'. When I was sent over there I didn't want to kill anybody but when they said: 'Volunteers, two paces forward, march!', forward I stepped.

In Shindanda I saw two of our soldiers who'd gone crazy. They kept talking to the mujahedin, trying to explain socialism to them the way we'd learnt it in our last year at school. They reminded me of that fable of Krylov's*, where the pagan priests climb inside the hollow idol to harangue the credulous populace.

When I was about eleven we had a visit and lecture at school from a woman called Old Mother Sniper, whose claim to fame was that she'd killed 78 Germans in the war. When I got home that day I started stammering and my temperature shot up. My parents thought I'd caught the flu. I stayed at home for a week and read my favourite book, *The Gadfly*, by Voinovich.**

Why force me to remember all this? After I got back I couldn't bear to wear my 'pre-war' jeans and shirts. They belonged to some stranger, although they still smelt of me, as my mother assured me. That stranger no longer exists. His place had been taken by someone else with the same surname – which I'd rather you didn't mention. I rather liked that other person.

'Father,' the gadfly asks his former mentor, Montanelli, 'is your God satisfied now?' I'd like to throw these words like a grenade – but at who?

* Ivan Krylov: early nineteenth-century writer, the 'Russian Aesop'.
** A popular novel on the school syllabus.

38

Civilian Employee

How did I end up here? I simply believed what I read in the papers. 'There was a time when young people were really capable of achieving something and sacrificing themselves for a great cause,' I thought, 'but now we're good for nothing and I'm no better than the rest. There's a war on, and I sit here sewing dresses and thinking up new hair-dos.' Mum wept. 'I'll die,' she said. 'I beg you. I didn't give birth to you just so as to bury your arms and legs separately from the rest of you.'

My first impressions? Kabul Airport was all barbed wire, soldiers with machine-guns and barking dogs. Officers turned up to pick out the prettiest and youngest of us girls. Quite openly. A major came up to me. 'I'll give you a lift to your battalion if you don't mind my truck'.

'What truck's that?'

'It's a 200.'

I already knew that '200' meant dead bodies and coffins. 'Any coffins?' I asked.

'They're being unloaded right now,' he told me.

It was an ordinary KamaZ truck with a tarpaulin. They were throwing the coffins out like so many crates of ammunition. I was horrified and the soldiers realised I was a new arrival.

I got to my unit. The temperature was 60 degrees Celsius and there were enough flies in the toilet to lift you from the ground with their wings. No showers. I was the only woman.

Two weeks later I was summoned by the battalion commander. 'You're going to live with me, sweetheart!' he informed me. I had to fight him off for two months. Once I almost threw a grenade at him: another time I grabbed a knife and threatened him with it. 'You're just after bigger fish. You know which side your bread's buttered!' was his usual comment. I got as tough as old boots there. Then one day he just said, 'Fuck off!' and that was the end of it.

I started swearing too. In fact, I got really coarse. I was transferred to Kabul as a hotel-receptionist. To begin with I reacted to men like a wild animal. Everyone could tell there was something wrong with me. 'Are you crazy? We won't bite you!' they'd say.

I just couldn't get out of the habit of self-defence. If someone asked me for a cup of tea I'd yell at them: 'Yeah, and what else – a quickie?' Then one day I found . . . love? That's not a word much used over there. He used to introduce me to his friends as his 'wife', and I'd whisper in his ear, 'Your *Afghan* wife, you mean.'

Once, when we were driving together in an armoured car, we were shot at. I threw myself over him but luckily the bullet went into the hatch. He'd been sitting with his back to the sniper and hadn't seen him. When we got back he wrote to his wife about me. He didn't get any letters from home for two months after that.

I love shooting. I enjoy emptying a whole magazine at a single burst – it makes me feel good. Once I killed a muj. We'd gone into the hills to get some fresh air and make love. I heard a noise from behind a rock. I was so scared it was like an electric shock. I fired a burst, then went to look and saw this strong, good-looking bloke lying there. 'You can come with us on recce patrol!' the lads said. That was the highest compliment they knew and I was as pleased as Punch. They also liked the fact that I didn't loot the body, except for the gun. On the way back, though, they kept an eye on me, because I started retching and vomiting. But I felt OK. When I got home I went to the fridge and ate as much as I'd normally get through in a week. Then I broke down. They gave me a bottle of vodka – which I drank down without getting drunk – and realised with horror that if I hadn't shot straight my mother would have been sent a '200'.

I wanted to be in a war, but not like this one. Heroic World War II, that's what I wanted.

Where did all the hatred come from? There's a simple answer to that. They killed your mate. You'd shared a bowl of chow, and there he was, lying next to you, burnt to a cinder. So you shot back like crazy. We stopped thinking about the big questions, like who started it all and who was to blame? That reminds me of our favourite joke on the subject. Question to Radio Armenia:* 'What is the definition of politics?' Radio Armenia replies: 'Have you heard a mosquito piss? That's the definition, except politics is even thinner.'

The government's busy with politics while here you see blood all around you and you go crazy. You see burnt skin roll up like a laddered nylon stocking. It's especially horrible when they kill the animals. Once they ambushed a weapons caravan. The humans and mules were shot separately. Both lots kept quiet and waited for death – except one wounded mule, which screeched like metal scratching metal . . .

This place has changed the way I look and speak. The other day some of us girls were talking about a bloke we knew and one of us said: 'Silly idiot! He had a row with his sergeant and deserted. He should have shot him and they'd have put it down as killed in action.' That just shows how life here coarsens us all, even the women.

The fact is many officers assumed it was the same here as back home, that they could hit and insult their men as much as they liked. Quite a few who thought that way have been found dead in battle, with a bullet in the back. The perfect murder!

Some of the boys in the mountain outposts don't see anybody for months at a time, except a helicopter three times a week. I went to visit one once. A captain came up to me. 'Miss, would you take off your cap? I haven't seen a woman for a whole year.' All the men came out of the trenches, just to have a look at my long hair. Later, during a bombardment, one of them protected me with his own body. I'll remember him as long as I live. He didn't know me, but he risked his life simply because I was a woman. How could you ever forget something like that? In ordinary life you'd never find out if a man was prepared to give his life for yours.

In these conditions good men get better and the bad get even worse. During that same bombardment one soldier shouted some obscenity at me and a few minutes later he was dead, his brain

---

* 'Radio Armenia', a fictional station, is the source of hundreds of such bitter, absurd or paradoxical social and political jokes.

blown to bits before my eyes. I started shaking like in an attack of malaria. Even though I'd seen plenty of body-bags, and bodies wrapped in foil like big toys, I never shook as much as I did at that moment. In fact, I couldn't calm down all the time I was up there.

I never saw any of us girls wearing military medals, even when we'd won them honestly. Once someone wore the one 'for Military Merit' but everyone laughed and said, 'For sexual merit', because they knew you could win a medal for a night with the battalion CO.

Why are there so many women here? Do you think they could do without them? Certain officers I can think of would simply go mad. Why are women so desperate to get here? The short answer's money. You can buy cassette-recorders, things like that, and sell them when you get home. You can earn more here in two years than in half a lifetime at home.

Look, we're talking honestly, woman to woman, right? They sell themselves to the local traders right in those little shops of theirs, in the small store-rooms at the back, and they are *small*, I can tell you! You go to the shops and the kids follow you, shouting 'Khanum [woman], jig-jig . . . ' and point you to the store-room. Our officers pay for women with foreign currency cheques, in fact they're called *chekists*.*

Want to hear a joke? Zmei Gorynych, Kashei Bessmertny and Baba Yaga** meet at a transportation centre here. They're all off to defend the revolution. Two years later they meet again on the way home. Zmei Gorynych has only one head left (the others have been shot off), Kashei Bessmertny is alive only because she's immortal, but Baba Yaga is looking marvellous in the latest French fashions. She's in a wonderful mood and says she's signing on for another year. 'You must be mad, Baba Yaga!' say the others, but she replies: 'Back home I'm Baba Yaga, but over here I'm Vasilis Prekrasnaya.'***

* A pun: the Chekists were Lenin's forerunners of the KGB, who are also popularly called by this name.
** Three characters from Russian folklore: Zmei, a dragon, has many heads, Kashei is immortal (*Bessmertny*) and Baba Yaga is an old and ugly witch.
*** Another figure from folklore: a beautiful young girl.

Yes, people leave here morally broken, expecially the ordinary soldiers, the eighteen- and nineteen-year-olds. They see how everything is for sale here, how a woman will sell herself for a crate, no, for a couple of tins of corned beef. Then they go home, these boys, and look at their wives and sweethearts in the same way. It's not surprising they don't behave themselves too well. They're used to deciding things with the barrel of a gun.

Once I saw a local selling melons at 100 Afganis each. Some of our boys reckoned that was too much, but he refused to go down – so one of them shot up the whole pile of melons with his machine-gun. When that boy gets back home just you try to tread on his foot in the bus or not let him push in front of you in the queue . . .

I used to dream that I'd go home, take the little camp-bed into the garden and lie under the apple-trees, but these days the thought frightens me. You hear that a lot, especially now we're being withdrawn in large numbers. 'I'm scared to go home' people say. Why? Simple! We'll get home and everything will have changed in those two years, different fashions, music, different streets even. And a different view of the war. We'll stick out like a sore thumb.

Sergeant-Major, Medical Instructor in a Reconnaissance Unit

I accepted the official line so completely that even now, after all I've read and heard, I still have a minute hope that our lives weren't entirely wasted. It's the self-preservation instinct at work. Before I was called up I graduated from an institute of physical culture. I did my final practical and diploma at Artek*, where I was a group-leader. I was always intoning high-sounding phrases about the Pioneer spirit, the Pioneer sense of duty, and when I was called up I naturally volunteered for Afghanistan. The political officer gave this lecture about the international situation: he told

* *The* model Pioneer camp for gilded Soviet youth. The Pioneer movement is roughly equivalent to the Scouts and Guides, but far more politically inspired.

us that Soviet forces had forestalled the American Green Berets airborne invasion of Afghanistan by just one hour. It was so incessantly drummed into us that this was a sacred 'international duty' that eventually we believed it.

I can't bear to think of the whole process now. 'Take off your rose-tinted spectacles!' I tell myself. And don't forget, I didn't go out there in 1980 or 1981, but in 1986, the year after Gorbachev came to power. They were still lying then. In 1987 I was posted to Khost. We took a ridge but lost seven of our boys in the process. A group of journalists arrived from Moscow and were told that the Afghan National Army (the Greens, as they were known) had taken the ridge. The Greens were posing for victory photographs while our soldiers lay in the morgue.

Only the cream were selected. No one wanted to be posted to dreary provincial Russian towns like Tula, or Pskov, or Kirovabad. We begged to go to Afghanistan. Our Major Zdobin tried to convince me and my friend Sasha Krivtsov to withdraw our applications. 'Let Sinytsin get killed instead of either of you,' he advised us. 'The State's invested too much in your education.' Sinytsin was a simple peasant lad, a tractor-driver, but I had my degree and Sasha was studying at the faculty of German and Romance Philology at Keremovo University. (He was a good singer, played the piano, violin, flute and guitar, composed his own music and had a talent for drawing. We were like brothers.) At our political instruction seminar the talk was all of heroic deeds, and how the Afghanistan war was like the Spanish civil war – and then, lo and behold! 'Let Sinytsin get killed instead of either of you.'

War was interesting from a psychological point of view. First of all, it was a test of oneself, and that attracted me. I used to ask lads who'd been out there what it was really like. One, I realise now, completely pulled the wool over our eyes. He had a patch on his chest, like a burn in the shape of a 'p', and he deliberately wore his shirt open so that everyone could see it. He claimed that they'd landed in the mountains from 'copters' at night. I can hear him now, telling us that paras were angels for three seconds (until the parachutes opened), eagles for three minutes (the descent) and cart-horses the rest of the time. We swallowed it hook, line and sinker. I'd like to meet that little Homer now! If he ever had any brains they must have been shell-shocked out of him.

Another lad I spoke to tried to talk us out of going. 'Don't bother,' he'd say. 'It's dirty and it ain't romantic!' I didn't like that. 'You've had a go, now it's my turn,' I told him. Still, he taught us the ten commandments for staying alive: 'The moment you've fired, roll a couple of metres away from your firing position. Hide your gun-barrel behind a wall or rock so the enemy can't see the flame when you fire. When you're fighting, don't drink, or you're finished. On sentry-duty, never fall asleep – scratch your face or bite your arm to keep awake. A para runs as fast as he can, then as fast as he has to, to keep alive.' And so on.

My father's an academic and my mother's an engineer. They always brought me up to think for myself. That kind of individualism got me expelled from my *Oktyabryata* group [an approximate Soviet equivalent of the Cubs and Brownies] and I wasn't accepted into the Pioneers for ages. When eventually I was allowed to wear that bright red Pioneer scarf I refused to take it off, even to go to bed. Our literature teacher once stopped me while I was saying something in class. 'Don't give us your own ideas – tell us what's in the book!' she said.

'Have I made a mistake?' I asked.

'It's not what's in the book.'

You remember that fairy-tale where the King hated every colour but grey? Everything in our kingdom-state was dull grey, too. 'Teach yourselves to think so that you won't be made fools of like we were, and come home in zinc coffins!' That's what I tell my own pupils now.

Before I went into the army it was Dostoevsky and Tolstoy who taught me how I ought to live my life. In the army it was sergeants. Sergeants have unlimited power. There are three to a platoon.

'Now hear this! Repeat after me! What is a para? Answer: a bloody-minded brute with an iron fist and no conscience!

'Repeat after me: conscience is a luxury we can't afford! Conscience is a luxury we can't afford!

'You are a medical unit! The medical unit is the cream of the airborne forces! Repeat!'

Extract from a soldier's letter: 'Mum, buy me a puppy and call it Sergeant so I can kill it when I get home.'

Army life itself kills the mind and saps your resistance to the point that they can do what they want with you. Six a.m. – reveille. Three times or more, in succession, until we've got it right: reveille – lights out! Get up – lie down! You've got three seconds to fall in for take-off on a strip of white lino – white so that it needs to be washed and scrubbed every day; 180 men have to jump out of bed and fall in in three seconds; 45 seconds to get into number three fatigues, which is full uniform but without belt and cap. Once someone didn't manage to get their foot bindings on in time. 'Fall out and repeat.' He still didn't manage in time. 'Fall out and repeat!'

Physical training was hand-to-hand combat, a combination of karate, boxing, self-defence against knives, sticks, field-shovels, pistols and machine-guns. You have the machine-gun, your partner just his bare hands: or he has the shovel and you have your bare hands. Hundred metre hurdles. Breaking ten bricks with your bare fist. We were taken to a building-site and told we'd stay there till we'd learnt it. The hardest part is overcoming your own fear and of not being scared of the smash.

'Fall in! Fall out! Fall in! Fall out!'

Morning inspection involved checking buckles – they've got to be as shiny as a cat's arse – and white collars. You have two needles and thread in your cap to sow into your collar a clean white cotton strip each day. One pace forward – march! Pre-sent arms! One pace forward – march! Just half an hour free per day – after lunch. Letter-writing.

'Private Kravtsov, why aren't you writing?'

'I'm thinking, sarge.'

'I can't hear you – speak up!'

'I'm thinking, sarge.'

'You're meant to yell, you know that! Hole training for you, my lad!'

'Hole training' meant yelling into a lavatory bowl to practise military responses, with the sergeant behind you checking the echo.

There was constant hunger. Paradise was the army store, where you could buy buns, sweets and chocolate. A bull's-eye at target practice earned you a pass to the shop. If you didn't have enough money, you sold a few bricks. This is how it works. A couple of us big tough soldiers find ourselves a brick and go up to a new boy who's still got some money.

'Buy a brick!'

'What do I need a brick for?'

We edge a bit closer. 'Just buy a brick!'

'How much?'

'Three roubles.'

He hands over the three roubles, goes off and throws the brick away, while we stuff ourselves silly. One rouble buys you ten buns. 'Conscience is a luxury the para can't afford! The medical unit is the cream of the airborne forces!'

I must be a pretty good actor. I soon learnt to play the part. The worst thing that can happen is to be called a *chados*, from the word *chado*, which means a weakling or baby.

After three months I got leave. It was a different world. It was only twelve weeks since I'd been kissing a girl, sitting in cafés and going dancing, but it seemed like twelve years.

My first evening back at camp and it was: 'Fall in, you apes! What's the first thing for a para to remember? Not to fly past the earth!'

We went on a twelve-day patrol. We spent most of our time running away from a guerrilla gang and only survived on dope. On the fifth day one soldier shot himself. He lagged behind the rest of us and then put his gun to his throat. We had to drag his body along, including his backpack, flak-jacket and helmet. We weren't too sorry for him – he knew we'd have to take him with us – but I did think of him when we got our demob papers.

Dum-dum wounds from exploding bullets were the worst. My first casualty had one leg blown off at the knee (with the bone left sticking out), his other ankle ripped away, his penis gone, his eyes blown out and one ear torn off. I started shaking and retching uncontrollably. 'If you don't do it now you'll never make it as a medic,' I told myself. I applied tourniquets, staunched the blood, gave him a pain-killer and something to make him sleep. Next was a soldier with a dum-dum in the stomach. His guts were

47

hanging out. I bandaged him, staunched the blood, and gave him a pain-killer, something to make him sleep. I held him for four hours, then he died.

There was a general shortage of medication. Even the iodine ran out. Either the supply system failed, or else we'd used up our allowance – another triumph of our planned economy. We used equipment captured from the enemy. In my bag I always had twenty Japanese disposable syringes. They were sealed in a light polyethylene packing which could be removed quickly, ready for use. Our Soviet 'Rekord' brand, wrapped in paper which always got torn, were frequently not sterile. Half of them didn't work, anyhow – the plungers got stuck. They were crap. Our home-produced plasma was supplied in half-litre *glass* bottles. A seriously wounded casualty needs two litres – i.e. four bottles. How are you meant to hold them up, arm-high, for nearly an hour in battlefield conditions? It's practically impossible. And how many bottles can you carry? We captured Italian-made polyethylene packages containing one litre each, so strong you could jump on them with your army boots and they wouldn't burst. Our ordinary Soviet-made sterile dressings were also bad. The packaging was as heavy as oak and weighed more than the dressing itself. Foreign equivalents, from Thailand or Australia, for example, were lighter, even whiter somehow . . . We had absolutely no elastic dressings, except what we captured – French and German products. And as for our splints! They were more like skis than medical equipment! How many can you carry with you? I carried English splints of different lengths for specific limbs, upper arm, calf, thigh, etc. They were inflatable, with zips. You inserted the arm or whatever, zipped up and the bone was protected from movement or jarring during transportation to hospital.

In the last nine years our country has made no progress and produced nothing new in this field – and that goes for dressings and splints. The Soviet soldier is the cheapest in the world – and the most patient. It was like that in 1941, but why fifty years later? Why?

It's terrible being shot at when you can't fire back. I never sat in the first or last armoured carrier in a convoy. I never had my legs dangling in the hatch; I preferred to sit over the side so there'd be less chance of them being blown off by a mine. I had German tablets with me for suppressing fear, but I never took them.

We'd come back from battle looking very unlike Soviet soldiers. We looted enemy boots, clothes and food. Our flak-jackets were so heavy you could hardly lift them. The American ones were preferred – they didn't have a single metal part. They were made from some kind of bullet-proof material which a Makarov pistol couldn't penetrate at point-blank range, and a tommy-gun only from a hundred metres at most. American sleeping-bags we captured were 1949 models, but as light as a feather. Our padded jackets weigh at least seven kilograms. When we found mercenaries dead we took their jackets, their wide-peaked forage caps and their Chinese trousers with inner linings which didn't wear out. We took everything, including their underwear (yes, there was a shortage of underwear too!), their socks and trainers. I picked up a little torch and a stiletto knife once.

We used to shoot wild sheep (they were 'wild' if they were standing five metres away from the rest of the herd), or barter for them. Two kilos of tea – captured tea, of course – bought you a sheep. We'd find money on raids as well, but the officers always made us hand it over and then shared it out among themselves before our eyes! So you'd put a few notes in a cartridge case and cover them over with gunpowder. Hey presto! A little nest-egg.

Some men got drunk, others put all their energies into surviving. Others, like me, wanted to win medals. You go back home and what do they say? 'So, what've you got? Sergeant-Major, eh? What, in the Pay Corps?'

It hurts me to think how gullible I was. The political education officers managed to convince us of things they didn't believe themselves. They'd known the truth for a long while. There was this slogan: 'Afghanistan makes brothers of us all.' Crap! There are three classes of soldier in the Soviet army: new recruits, 'grandads' or veterans, and *dembels*, conscripts nearing the end of their two-year service.

When I got to Afghanistan my uniform was smartly pressed and neatly tailored to my own measurements. Everything fitted perfectly, buttons glistening, tapered jacket, the lot. The problem was, new recruits aren't allowed to have tailored uniforms. Anyway, one of these *dembels* came up to me. 'How long've you been here?' he asked me.

'Just arrived'.

'New recruit? Why're you dressed up like that?'

'Don't let's fight about it.'

'Listen, boy, don't get me angry. You've been warned!' He was used to people being frightened of him.

That evening the recruits were washing the barracks floor while the *dembels* sat around smoking.

'Move the bed!' ordered the *dembel*.

'It's not my bed!' I said.

'You still haven't cottoned on, have you?'

That night they beat me up, eight of them, and gave me a good kicking with their army boots. My kidneys were crushed and I pissed blood for two days. They didn't touch me during the day. I tried not to antagonise them but they still beat me up. I changed tactics: when they came for me at night I was ready for them and hit out first. Then they beat me very carefully, so as not to leave a mark, with towel-covered fists in the stomach every night for a week.

After my first tour of active duty they never touched me again. They found some fresh recruits and the order went out: 'Leave the medic alone!'

After six months recruits graduated to veteran status. A feast was laid on (paid for by the recruits). The *dembels* stuffed themselves with pilaff and kebabs and began on the ritual: applying the buckle and the side of the belt as hard as they could to the backside. Twelve for the 'graduation', another six on account of being a para, another three for being in a reconnaissance unit, and a few more for cheek and bloody-mindedness. In my case it was twenty-nine strokes. You have to take it without a squeak or else they do it again right from the beginning. If you *can* take it – join the club! Shake hands! You're one of us!

The *dembel's* departure was a story in itself. To begin with there was a compulsory whip-round to buy him a brief-case, a towel, a scarf for his mother and a present for his girlfriend. Then his dress uniform had to be prepared. The belt had to be brilliant white – you're not a para without your white belt – and his aiguillettes had to be braided (we nicked parachute shroudlines for that). Shining the belt-buckle was a work of art. First you used medium, then fine, wire-wool, then a needle, then felt, and finally 'Goya' brand polish. The uniform was steeped for a week in engine-oil to restore its dark-green colour, then cleaned with petrol, and finally hung up to air for one month. All ready! The *dembels* go home and the next lot of vets take their place.

The farewell address from the political education officer to the departing *dembels* was a list of what we could and could not talk about back home. No mention to be made of fatalities, nor of any 'unofficial activities', because we are a 'great, powerful and *morally healthy*' army. All photographs and films to be destroyed. We did not shoot, bombard, use poisons or lay mines here. We are a great, powerful and morally healthy army.

Customs stole all the gifts we had with us, even the perfumes, scarves and watches with built-in calculators. 'Sorry, boys, not allowed!' they said, but we never got a receipt for anything. Our presents were their perks.

Still, the smell of the green spring leaves, and the girls walking around in short dresses, made up for all that. I've just remembered a girl called Svetka Afoshka. We never knew her real surname, but apparently when she arrived in Kabul she'd sleep with a soldier for 100 Afganis – or afoshki as we called them – until she realised she was selling herself cheap. Within a couple of weeks she'd upped her price to 3,000 afoshki, which an ordinary soldier couldn't afford.

A friend of mine called Andrei Korchagin* (we called him Pashka, of course, because of his surname) had a girlfriend back home, but one day she sent him a photo of her wedding. We kept an eye on him for nights after that, in case he did something stupid. One morning he stuck the photo to a rock and riddled it with his Kalashnikov. Long after that we still heard him crying at night. Hey, Pashka! Look at all these girls, now! Take your pick!

In the train home I dreamt we're getting ready for battle. 'Why

* See p. 29 above.

have you got 350 rounds instead of 400?' my friend Sasha Krivtsov asks me.

'Because I'm carrying medication.'

A little later he asks: 'Could you kill that Afghan girl?'

'What girl?'

'The one who led us into that ambush. You know, the one where we lost four of our lads.'

'I don't know. Probably not. At school I was called "lover-boy" because I always defended the girls. Would you?'

'I'm ashamed . . . ' he starts to say, but I woke up and never discovered what it was he was ashamed of. When I got home I found a telegram from Sasha's mother waiting for me: 'Please come. Sasha killed.'

'Sasha,' I say to him at the cemetery, 'I'm ashamed that in my finals I got an "A" in Scientific Communism* for my critique of bourgeois pluralism. I'm ashamed that after the Congress of People's Deputies pronounced this war a disgrace we were given 'Internationalist Fighters' badges and a Certificate from the Supreme Soviet of the USSR.

'Sasha, you're there and I'm here . . . '

A Mother

He was always small. He was as small as a girl when he was born, just a couple of kilos, and he grew up small. I'd cuddle him and call him my little sunshine.

The only thing he was afraid of was spiders. Once he went out to play. We'd bought him a new coat and when he returned I hung it up in the cupboard and went into the kitchen. A few minutes later I heard this strange noise, shlep-shlep, shlep-shlep. The entrance-hall was full of frogs. They were jumping out of his pockets. He picked them all up. 'Don't be frightened, Mum,' he said, stuffing them back in the pockets, 'they're nice little creatures.' My little sunshine . . .

* Until recently a compulsory subject at Soviet universities and indispensable for the acquisition of a degree.

He loved toys to do with war, tanks, machine-guns, pistols. He'd strap guns round himself and march round the house. 'I'm a soldier, I'm a soldier.'

When he went to school we couldn't find a uniform to fit him and he was lost in the smallest one they had. My little sunshine . . .

Then they took him off to the army. I prayed he wouldn't be killed. I prayed he wouldn't be beaten up and humiliated by the bigger, senior ones – he was so small. He told us how they could force you to clean out the toilets with a toothbrush and wash out other people's underpants. That's what I was afraid of. He wrote and told us he was being posted and to send him photos of his mum and dad and sister . . .*

He didn't write where he was being sent. Two months later we had a letter from Afghanistan. 'Don't cry, Mum, our flak-jackets are very good,' he wrote. 'Our flak-jackets are good . . . ' My little sunshine . . .

I was already expecting him home, he had only a month more to go in the army. I managed to buy him some shirts, and a scarf, and shoes. They're still in the cupboard.

The first thing I knew about it was when a captain from head-quarters arrived.

'Try to be strong, mother . . . ' That's what he called me.

'Where is my son?'

'Here in Minsk. They're bringing him now.'

I fell to the floor. 'My little sunshine. My little sunshine.' I got up and threw myself at the captain. 'Why are you alive and my son dead? You're big and strong and he's so small. You're a man and he's just a boy. Why are you alive?'

They brought in the coffin. I collapsed over it. I wanted to lay him out but they wouldn't allow us to open the coffin to see him, touch him . . . Did they find a uniform to fit him? 'My little sunshine, my little sunshine.' Now I just want to be in the coffin with him. I go to the cemetery, throw myself on the gravestone and cuddle him. My little sunshine . . .

---

* As part of the regime of military secrecy conscripts are generally sent to their units straight from training-camp.

I put a little lump of earth from our village in my pocket and had such strange feelings in the train . . .

Of course, some of us were cowards. One lad failed his medical on account of his eyes and ran out crowing about his good luck. The very next guy was failed too, but he was almost in tears. 'How can I go back to my unit? The send-off they gave me lasted two weeks. If I had an ulcer, at least, but not for tooth-ache!' He ran, still in his underpants, straight to the general, begging to have the teeth pulled out so he could go.

I got an 'A' in geography at school, so I shut my eyes and imagined mountains, monkeys, getting a sun-tan and eating bananas. The reality was being stuck in a tank in our greatcoats, with machine-guns poking out left and right. I was in the rear vehicle with a machine-gun pointing backwards, of course, and all automatics cocked. We were like a great iron hedgehog. Then we'd come across the paras in their special T-shirts and panama hats, sitting on their APCs and laughing at us. I saw a dead mercenary and got a shock. He had an athlete's physique and there was I, who didn't even know how to climb a rock.

I lugged the field-telephone up ten metres of sheer rock. The first time a mine went off I shut my mouth when you're meant to open it – to avoid your eardrums bursting. We were issued with gas-masks but threw them away the same day because the mujahedin didn't have chemical weapons. We sold our helmets. They were just one more thing to carry and they get as hot as frying-pans. My big problem was how to steal extra magazines. We were issued with four, so on my first payday I bought a fifth from a friend of mine and I was given a sixth. In battle you take out the last round from your last magazine and hold it between your teeth. To use on yourself if necessary.

We went to Afghanistan to build socialism but found ourselves penned in by barbed wire. 'Don't leave the compound, lads! No need to spread the message, we've got specialists for that.' Pity they didn't trust us.

I talked to a shopkeeper once. 'You've been living you·

lives the wrong way. Now we'll teach you how to build socialism.'

He smiled. 'I did business before the revolution and I do business now. Go home. These mountains belong to us. Let us sort out our problems in our own way.'

When we drove through Kabul the women threw sticks and stones at our tanks, kids swore at us in perfect Russian: 'Russky, go home!'

What were we doing there?

We got hit by mortar-fire. The shell was going straight for my chest but I managed to turn the machine-gun round in its path, which saved my life. One hand was shattered and the other was full of shrapnel. I remember having a nice warm feeling, no pain, and someone shouting above me: 'Fire! Fire!' I tried to squeeze the trigger but the machine-gun wouldn't fire. Then I saw my arm hanging down, and my palm all scorched. I thought I was squeezing the trigger but my fingers had gone.

I didn't lose consciousness, but crawled out of the vehicle with the others. Someone applied a tourniquet. Then I tried to walk but after a couple of paces I collapsed. I lost about a litre and a half of blood. 'They're surrounding us!' I heard someone shouting, and another voice: 'We'll have to dump him or we'll all be killed.'

'Shoot me!' I begged.

One lad just ran away, the other loaded his gun, but very slowly. When you do it slowly the cartridge can go in crooked. Which it did. He threw the gun at me: 'I can't! Do it yourself!' I dragged it towards me, but you can't do anything with one hand.

I was lucky: I found a small gully and lay in it behind some rocks. Some mujahedin walked right past without seeing me. I kept thinking, if they notice me I must kill myself somehow. I tugged at a big stone, dragged it towards me and tried to lift it.

Next morning I was found by the two boys who'd scarpered the night before. They made a stretcher out of my greatcoat and carried me on it to the dressing-station. I realised they were worried I'd report what had happened, but I kept quiet. In the hospital I was taken straight to theatre. I heard the surgeon ordering amputation. When I woke up I sensed my arm was gone.

Everyone on the ward was missing an arm or a leg, or both, or all. They used to cry quietly. Some lost themselves in drink. I started learning how to hold a pencil in my left hand.

I went home to my grandfather's house – I haven't got any parents. My grandma was in tears for her grandson with only one arm. 'You don't understand Party policy!' Grandpa shouted at her. I met some old friends. 'Did you bring back a sheepskin? A Japanese cassette-player? What, nothing? Are you sure you were in Afghanistan?' I only wish I'd brought my gun back with me!

I started looking other vets up. We spoke the same language, and it was a language only we could share. The dean of the university called me in to see him. 'Look,' he said, 'we gave you a place even though your grades weren't really good enough. We gave you a grant. Now don't go spending your time with that lot. Why do you keep going to the cemetery? It doesn't go down too well here, you know.'

The powers-that-be stopped us meeting. They were frightened of us, because they knew that if we organised we'd fight for our rights and they'd have to give us flats and so on. We made them give some help to the mothers of those boys in the cemetery here and we're going to insist on memorials and railings for the graves. The authorities don't give a damn. 'Now, lads,' they tried to persuade us, 'don't talk too much about what you did and saw over there.' A State Secret, with 100,000 soldiers in a foreign country! Even the temperature in Kabul was classified information.

War can't make a man better. Worse, yes, but not better, that's for sure. I'll never be the way I was before I went to war. How can I be better, after some of the things I've seen?

For a few foreign currency vouchers the medics would sell you a couple of glasses of urine from a hepatitis patient. You drank it, fell ill and then got yourself discharged from the army. Some of the lads shot their fingers off or mutilated themselves. Then I remember seeing planes taking off for home with a cargo of zinc coffins, plus suitcases full of leather jackets, jeans, women's underwear, China tea . . .

My lips used to tremble when I said the word 'Motherland'. I don't believe in anything now, let alone in fighting for something.

What's there to fight for? And who against? We fought. Fair enough. Perhaps it *was* justified, after all. If the newspapers start saying it was right, it'll be right again. Now they're starting to say we're murderers. Who to believe? I don't know. I don't believe anything. Newspapers? I don't read them or buy them. They write one thing today and the opposite tomorrow. I don't know where the truth is. I have two or three friends I trust. I can rely on them. I've been home six years now, and I've seen it all.

I have an invalid card – it's meant to give you a few privileges. So, at the cinema, for instance, I go to the window for war veterans. I hear someone say, 'Hey, you! Boy! you're in the wrong queue!' I clench my teeth and say nothing. Behind my back a voice says, 'I defended the Motherland but . . . what's *he* done?'

If a stranger asks me how I lost my arm I tell him I was drunk and fell under a train and he's full of understanding and sympathy.

Recently I read a novel by Valentin Pikul about an officer in the Imperial Russian Army. 'Nowadays,' (this was in the dreadful aftermath of the Russo-Japanese War of 1905) 'many officers are resigning because, wherever they go they are treated with ridicule and contempt. It has reached the point where an officer is ashamed to wear his uniform and prefers to go about in civilian dress. Even severely wounded cripples arouse no sympathy. A legless beggar will earn more if he tells people that he lost his leg under a tram in Nevsky Prospect than if he mentions Mukden or Lyagolyan.'*

They'll soon be writing the same thing about us. I think I could find another 'Motherland' now, or at any rate get out of this one.

Private, Gunner

I volunteered to go to Afghanistan. I longed to go. I thought it would be interesting. I used to go to bed and imagine what it was like out there. I wanted to know what it was like to have one apple and two friends, you're hungry and they're hungry, so you give

* Battles of the Russo-Japanese War. The war was subsequently seen as a cynical adventure initiated by the Tsar for his own political ends.

them the apple. I thought it would be one big happy family. That's the reason I went.

I got off the plane, stared at the mountains and a *dembel* going home on the same plane gave me a shove.

'Give me your belt!'

'Why should I?' It was my own belt, foreign-made.

'You idiot, they'll take it anyhow.'

Sure enough, I lost it the very first day. So much for the big happy family! What a fool I was. The new recruit is an object. He can be got out of bed at night and beaten up with chairs, sticks, fists and feet. In the daytime, he's beaten up in the toilet, and his backpack, personal possessions, his cans of meat and biscuits from home (if any) are stolen. There's no television or radio or newspapers, so entertainment goes according to the law of the jungle. 'Wash my socks, sweetie-pie!' That's nothing compared to 'Now, lick my socks, sweetie-pie, lick them good so that everyone can see you!'

The temperature's 70 degrees Celsius. It's so hot you just stagger about and they can do what they like with you. On the other hand, when it came to fighting the *dembels* went up front and protected us, I admit. They saved our lives, in fact. But back to barracks and it's 'Now, sweetie-pie, lick my socks . . . ' all over again. It's more frightening than your first taste of action.

First 'op', well, that *is* interesting. It's like being in the cinema. Hundreds of times I've seen them walk into attack – well that's sheer rubbish. You don't walk, you run, and I'm not talking about an elegant jog, you run as fast as you can, like crazy. You zigzag like a mad rabbit.

I used to love those parades on Red Square, all that weaponry going by. Now I realise that there's nothing particularly admirable about it. Those tanks and armoured carriers would be better off kept under their wraps. Better still, they should parade all the Afghan *protesniki*, the veterans with artificial limbs, including me, through Red Square.

Both my legs were amputated above the knee. If only they'd been taken off *below* the knee – that would've been fine! I'd be a happy man! I envy men who kept their knees. In hospital, after my dressings were changed I used to have a fit of shaking for a good hour and a half. I felt so tiny without my prostheses. I'd lie there in my underpants and para T-shirt, which was as long as I was. At first I refused to see anybody, or even speak. Both legs gone. If only I could have kept one . . . The hardest thing of all is to forget that I once had two legs.

I gave my mother an ultimatum: 'Don't come if you're going to cry.' That was what I was most afraid of over there – that I'd be killed, brought home in a coffin, and my mother would cry. After a battle we'd be sorry for the wounded – but not for the dead, only for their mothers.

When I left hospital I wanted to say thank you to the nurse, but I couldn't, I'd actually forgotten the word.

Would I go back to Afghanistan? Yes. Because there you know who are your friends and who are your enemies. Here I'm tortured by one question which won't go away: 'What did my best mate die *for*?' For these fat speculators and black marketeers you see everywhere? It's all wrong here, and I feel like a stranger in my own country.

I started learning to walk, with various people hovering behind me. I fell over. 'Take it easy!' I said to myself. Step number one: turn over and lift yourself up by your arms. Step number two: stand up and walk. For the first few months I could only crawl – so I crawled.

My most vivid memory of Afghanistan now is a black boy with a round Russian face. There are plenty of them out there.

Yes, I'd go again, definitely! If I hadn't had both legs amputated above the knee, if only they'd been below the knee . . .

Army Doctor

I used to wonder why I'd volunteered. There were a hundred different reasons but the main one was this bit of verse. I can't remember who it's by:

> 'Women and wine
> Are all very fine
> But a real man needs more:
> The sweet taste of war!'

I envied my colleagues who'd been to Afghanistan for their tremendous professional experience, which couldn't really be got in peacetime conditions. I had ten years' experience as a surgeon in a big city hospital, but the first time a transport vehicle arrived with wounded men I almost went crazy. Arms and legs missing, just breathing torsos. It was far worse than anything you could see in the most brutal film. We did operations you could only dream about back home. The young nurses couldn't take it. Some of them just laughed or else cried hysterically. One simply stood there and did nothing except smile. They often had to be sent home.

A man doesn't die the way it happens in the cinema, where you get shot in the head, throw up your hands and fall down dead. What actually happens if you get shot in the head is that your brains fly out and you run after them, up to half a kilometre, trying to catch them. You go to the very limit, until physiological death overtakes you.

It would be easier to shoot men than watch and hear them sobbing, begging for death and release – the ones who've got enough strength to do it. Others lie there with fear creeping over them, their hearts faltering, shouting, calling. You take their pulse – it's normal so you aren't too worried. But the brain is waiting for that moment when a person is most relaxed: you've hardly left the boy's bedside and he's dead.

You don't forget things like that so soon. And as these boy-soldiers who survive get older they'll relive it over and over again. They'll see things very differently. My father was a World War II pilot but he never talked about it. He didn't think it was anything very special; that was something I could never understand. Now just one word, just the slightest reference, brings it all back to me.

Yesterday I read in the paper about some soldier who'd fought until his last bullet and then shot himself. What does that really mean – to shoot oneself? In battle it comes down to a simple question of survival: you or him? Obviously – you. But you're alone, covering your comrades' retreat, either because you were ordered to or else because you volunteered (knowing it meant your almost certain death). In that moment, I'm sure, it's psychologically not difficult to shoot yourself. In such a situation suicide can be seen as the normal reaction of many men. Afterwards they are called heroes. In everyday life suicides are considered abnormal, in the old days they weren't even allowed to be buried in the cemetery . . . Two lines in the newspaper and I can't sleep all night, the whole thing comes up and swamps me all over again.

No one who was over there wants to fight another war. We won't be fooled again. All of us, whether we were naïve or cruel, good or rotten, fathers, husbands and sons, we were all killers. I understood what I was really doing – I was part of an invading army, let's face it – but I don't regret a thing. Nowadays there's a lot of talk about guilt-feelings, but I personally don't feel guilty. Those who sent us there are the guilty ones. I enjoy wearing my army uniform, I feel a real man, and women go crazy over it. But once I went to a restaurant in my field-uniform, and the manager-ess stared at me in a very hostile way, and I just longed for her to make trouble. I would have told her: 'You don't like the way I'm dressed? Too bad! Make way for a hero!'

Just let someone even hint they don't like my field-uniform! For some reason I'm looking for that someone – I'm spoiling for a fight.

A Mother

My first was a girl. Before she was born my husband used to say, girl or boy, he didn't mind, but a girl would be better because she'd be able to do up her little brother's shoelaces! And that's the way it turned out.

Second time round, my husband rang the hospital.

'It's a girl.'

'Good. That's two we've got.'

Then they told him the truth: 'You have a son, a little boy!'

'Oh, thank you, thank you, thank you!' That showed his true feelings.

The first two days the nurses brought the babies to their

mothers, all except mine. No one said a thing. I started crying and ran a temperature. The doctor came. 'Now, Mum,' she comforted me. 'Nothing to worry about. You've got a little giant there. He's still asleep and he won't wake up till he's hungry.' But I didn't calm down until they brought him to me, unwrapped him and let me see him asleep.

What name to choose, that was the next thing. Our three favourites were Sasha, Alyosha and Misha. So my husband and daughter came to the hospital and Tanechka decided to draw 'lotths' – she couldn't say 'lots'. The bit of paper with 'Sasha' written on it came out of the hat twice, so that was that. He was born big, four and a half kilos and sixty centimetres long. I remember he could walk at ten months and speak at a year and a half, but until he was three he couldn't say his 'r's and 's's. 'I'll do it myshelf' he used to say, and he called his friend Sergei 'Tiglei'. His nursery-school teacher, Kira Nikolayevna, was 'Kila Kalavna'. The first time he saw the sea he shouted: 'I wasn't born, a wave threw me up on to the shore!'

I gave him his first photo-album when he was five. He had four altogether, one from his nursery-school days, one from his big school, one for his military academy days and the last for the photos he sent us from Afghanistan. I gave my daughter her own albums too. I loved my home and my children. I wrote them poems:

> 'Through the frosty springtime snows
> A little snowdrop poked his nose
> When the sun shone bright each morn
> My little baby boy was born . . .'

At the school where I taught my pupils loved me, I was always cheerful and happy . . .

Sasha loved playing cops-and-robbers and always wanted to be the goodie. When he was five and Tanechka nine we went on holiday to the Volga. We got off the boat to walk the half-kilometre to their grandma's house. Sasha refused to budge. 'I'm not walking. Carry me!'

'Carry a big boy like you?'

'I'm not walking and that's that!' And he didn't. We used to tease him about that.

At nursery school he loved dancing. He had lovely red trousers – we've got a photo of him in them. He collected stamps until he was fourteen, we've still got his album; then it was badges, there's a big basket full of them somewhere. He liked music, we've kept his cassettes with all his favourite songs . . .

When he was a child he wanted to be a musician, but as he grew up he was surrounded by army life. His father was a soldier and we'd lived in army compounds all our lives. He ate with soldiers, cleaned cars with them, so there was no one to say 'no' when he applied for the military academy. On the contrary, all he heard was: 'You will be a true defender of the Motherland, my son'. He was a good student and joined in everything. He passed out well and the Commandant wrote us a personal letter about him.

1985. Sasha was in Afghanistan. We were proud of him, of the fact that he was at the front. I'd tell my pupils and his friends about him, and longed for him to come home on leave.

Living in garrison towns we never locked our front door. So one fine day he came in without ringing the bell, shouting, 'Was it you that wanted the television repairman?' From Kabul he and his friends had flown to Tashkent and then as far as Donetsk. Then on to Vilnius, where he had to wait three hours for his train, which was frustrating because home was only a couple of hundred kilometres away. In the end they took a taxi.

He was tanned and thin, but his teeth were lovely and white.

'You're skin and bones, my love!' I cried.

'I'm alive, Mama, I'm alive!' He swung me round the room. 'Do you realise, I'm alive, alive, alive!'

Two days later it was New Year's Eve. He'd hidden presents under the Christmas Tree. Mine was a big scarf. A big black scarf.

'Why did you choose black, my love?' I asked.

'There were various colours there, Mama, but by the time I got to the front of the queue there was only black left. Anyhow, it suits you.'

I buried him in that scarf, and wore it for two years afterwards.

He always loved giving presents. 'My little surprises,' he used to call them. Once, when the children were still small, I came home with their father and we couldn't find them. I went to the neighbours, on to the street – they were nowhere to be found and nobody had seen them. I started crying and carrying on. Suddenly, out they crawled from the big box our new television had been packed in. We hadn't got round to throwing it away! They'd laid the table, made the tea, and while they were waiting for us Sasha had an idea for one of his surprises – hiding in the box. They'd got in the box and then fallen asleep!

He was unusually affectionate for a boy. He loved kissing and cuddling me, and after he went to Afghanistan he became even more loving. He loved his home, but there were times when he'd just sit there, saying and seeing nothing. At night he'd jump out of bed and pace up and down his room. Once he woke me up with his shouting. 'Explosions! Explosions! Mama, they're firing!' Another time I was woken up by crying. Who could it be? There were no small children in the house. I opened his door. He was holding his head in his hands and sobbing.

'Why are you crying, my love?'

'It's horrible, Mama, horrible.' He wouldn't say another word, to me or his father.

His leave came to an end and off he went. I baked him a suitcaseful of his favourite nutty biscuits, enough for him and all his friends. They missed home cooking over there.

He spent the following New Year with us too. We originally expected him for the summer. 'Mama, make lots of preserves and jam. I'll eat the lot!' he wrote. He postponed his August leave until September because he wanted to walk in the woods and pick the chanterelles, but still hadn't arrived by November. Then he wrote to say he'd like to come for New Year, for the Christmas Tree, for his father's birthday in December and mine in January.

I spent the whole day at home on 30 December, reading his latest letter. 'Mama, bake lots of your special blueberry dumplings, cherry dumplings and cream cheese dumplings.' When my husband got home from work he waited while I rushed to the shop to buy a guitar we'd ordered and which had just come in. Sasha had asked for one. 'Nothing too professional,' he'd said.

By the time I got back he'd arrived.

'Oh, and I wanted to be here to welcome you'.

'What a beautiful guitar!' he said when he saw it. He danced round the room. 'I'm home. How lovely it is! I could smell that special smell downstairs in the street.'

He said we lived in the most beautiful town, and the most beautiful street, with the most beautiful acacias in our courtyard. He loved this flat. It's hard to stay in now – everything reminds us of Sasha. And it's hard to go out – he loved it all so much.

He had changed, though. We all noticed it, his family as well as his friends. 'How lucky you are!' he told them. 'You don't know how lucky you are. Every day's a holiday here.'

I went to the hairdresser and came home with a new hair-do. He liked it. 'Have your hair done like that all the time, Mama. You're beautiful!'

'It's expensive, dear.'

'I've brought money. Take it all. I don't need it.'

A friend of his had a baby son. I remember the way Sasha looked when he asked to hold him. Towards the end of his leave he got toothache, but he'd been scared of the dentist ever since he was a child, so I had to drag him by the hand to the clinic and wait with him until it was his turn. He was literally sweating with fear.

If a TV programme about Afghanistan came on he'd leave the room. A week before he was due to go back his eyes became full of real anguish, that's the only word for it. Can it be that I'm imagining it now? But I was a happy woman then. My son was a major at thirty and this time he'd come home with a Red Star, awarded for valour. At the airport I looked at him and couldn't believe that this handsome young officer was really my son. I was proud of him.

A month later we had a letter wishing his father all the best on Soviet Army Day and praising me for my mushroom pies. But after that letter something happened inside me. I couldn't sleep. I'd lie in bed, wide awake, until five o'clock.

On 4 March I had a dream. There was a great field with explosions of white everywhere, and flashes and long ribbons of white stretching into the distance. Sasha was running, running in

65

zigzags, with nowhere to hide. Still there were flashes everywhere. I raced behind him, trying to overtake him, to get in front of him. Once in the country I had thrown myself over him during a thunderstorm, and I had heard him scratching under me like a little mouse, whimpering, 'Save me, Mama, save me . . .' But in the dream I can't catch up with him, he's so tall and his strides are so long. I run until I drop, but I can't reach him . . .

The door slammed and my husband came in. I was sitting with my daughter on the sofa. He walked across the room towards us in his boots, overcoat and cap, a thing he'd never done before – he's a tidy, orderly man who's spent his whole life in the army. He knelt in front of us: 'My little ones, I have tragic news . . .'

Then I noticed people in the hall, a nurse, the CO, a teacher from my school, friends of my husband . . .

That was three years ago, and we still can't bring ourselves to open the suitcase full of his things that they brought with the coffin. They seem to have his smell about them, even now.

He died almost immediately from fifty shrapnel wounds. His last words were, 'It hurts, Mama.'

What did he die for? Why him? He was so affectionate, so kind. These thoughts are slowly killing me. I know that I'm dying – there's no sense in going on. I force myself to be with people, I take Sasha with me, I talk about him. Once I gave a talk at the Polytechnic and afterwards a student came up to me. 'If you'd stuffed less patriotism into him he'd be alive today,' she told me. When I heard that I felt ill and fainted.

I gave that talk for Sasha's sake. He can't be allowed to just disappear like that . . .

Now they say it was all a dreadful mistake – for us and for the Afghan people. I used to hate Sasha's killers . . . now I hate the State which sent him there. Don't mention my son's name. He belongs to us now. I won't give him, even his name, to anyone.

Helicopter Pilot, Captain

A flash, a fountain of light, then night. Darkness. I open one eye and crawl along a wall. Where am I? In hospital. I check – are

66

my arms there? Yes. Further down I touch myself. I'm too short. I realise I've lost both legs . . . Hysteria. Desperate thoughts: death would be a better hiding-place than this ward. Death straightaway and then nothing. I wouldn't have to look at myself, or the rest of the world. Then I black out. I forgot all my previous life. Acute amnesia. I opened my passport and read my surname, place of birth and age: thirty. I read that I was married, with two boys. I try to remember their faces, but can't.

Mother was my first visitor. 'I'm your Mama . . . ' she said. She told me about my childhood and schooldays, details like the overcoat she bought me when I was fourteen, the marks I got in class, how I loved her pea-soup. I listened to her and seemed to see myself from a distance, like an objective observer.

One day in the canteen the nurse called me. 'Into your wheel-chair! Your wife's come to see you!' I noticed a beautiful woman standing by the ward, but where's my wife? She *is* my wife.

She told me about our love for each other, how we met, how I kissed her the first time, our wedding, the birth of the boys. I listened and couldn't remember, but then it began to come back, faintly. When I tried to recall things I got terrible headaches . . .

I tried to remember the boys from photographs, but when they came they were so different, mine yet not mine. The fair one had got darker, the toddler was quite grown up. I looked at myself in the mirror and saw they were like me.

I've completely forgotten the war, all two years of it. The only thing is, I hate winter now. Mother tells me that when I was a boy I loved wintertime and snow more than anything else . . .

The lads talk about the war, and I watch films. 'What was I doing there?' I wonder. They sent young kids out there, but I was an officer, a professional, I volunteered.

The doctors say that my memory may come back. When that happens I'll have two lives – the one they've told me about, and the one I know myself.

The Second Day

'But another dies with a broken heart'

Author: He phoned again today. From now on I'm going to call him my leading character.

Leading character: I wasn't going to call you again, but I got on a bus and heard two women talking. 'Fine heroes they were! Murdering women and children over there. They're sick. And just think, they get invited to speak at schools! They even get special privileges . . . ' I jumped off at the next stop and stood there crying. We were soldiers obeying orders. In wartime you can be shot for disobedience, and we *were* at war. Obviously it wasn't the generals themselves who killed women and children, but they gave the orders – and now they're blaming us. Now we're told that to obey a criminal command is itself a crime. But I trusted the people giving the orders. As far back as I can remember I've been taught to have faith in authority. No one ever told me to judge for myself whether or not to trust the authorities, whether or not to shoot. The message was hammered into us over and over again: have faith, trust us.

Author: It was the same for all of us.

Leading character: Yes, I was a killer and I'm covered in blood . . . But I saw him lying there, my friend who was like a brother to me, with his head cut off, and his arms, and his legs, and his flayed skin . . . I volunteered for the very next raid. I watched a funeral procession in a village, there were a lot of people there. The body was wrapped in white. I could see everything quite clearly through my field-glasses and I gave the order: 'At the funeral – FIRE!'

Yes, I killed because I wanted to go on living and get home again. Why do you want to drag all this up again? I've only just begun to stop thinking about death night after night. For three years I spent my nights choosing between a bullet in the mouth and a noose made from my tie. Now I can smell that horrible stink of thornbush again, it'll drive me mad eventually . . .

Author: Why is it that, as he slams down the receiver again, I have the feeling that I've known him for a long, long time?

Sergeant, Infantry Platoon Leader

It's like in a dream, as if I've already seen this before in some film, and the feeling now is that I've never killed anyone . . .

I volunteered. I wanted to find out what I was capable of. I'm very ambitious. I went to university, but you can't show – or know what you're made of in a place like that. I dropped out in my second year. I wanted to be a hero and looked for a chance to be one. They say it was a man's war but the truth is, it was a boy's war. It was kids not long out of school who did the fighting. It was like a game for us. Self-esteem and pride were terribly important: can I do it or can't I? *He* can – can I? That's what we were worried about, not politics. I'd been preparing myself for a challenge of some kind since I was a young boy. My favourite author was Jack London. A real man had to be strong – and war makes you strong. My girlfriend tried to talk me out of it. 'Do you really think writers like Bunin or Mandelstam thought that way?' she asked me. None of my friends understood me either. Some got married, others got involved in Zen or yoga and such-like. I was the only one who went to the war.

The mountains above you, scorched by the sun, down below, a little girl calling her goat, and a woman hanging out her washing. Just like at home in the Caucasus . . . To tell the truth, I was a bit disappointed, until one night they shot at our camp-fire. I picked up the tea kettle and there was a bullet under it.

On route-marches the thirst was sheer torture and utterly humiliating. Your whole mouth dried up, it seemed to be full of dust and you couldn't work up enough saliva to swallow. We licked up the dew and even our own sweat. I was determined to get through it. I caught a tortoise, slit its throat with a sharp stone, and drank its blood. No one else could face it. I was the only one. I realised I was capable of killing. I had a gun in my hand. The first time we went into battle I noticed how some of the lads were in a state of shock. They fainted, or started vomiting when they realised they'd killed people or saw human brains or eyes being blown out. I could take it though. One of the lads was a hunter who bragged that before he joined the army he'd killed hares and wild boar, but he vomited with the rest of them. It's one thing to shoot animals, quite another to kill human beings. In battle you go as stiff as wood, cold reason takes over, you calculate . . . This is my gun and my life. The gun becomes part of your body, like a third arm . . .

It was a partisan war, and set-piece battles were rare. It was you against him. You grew as sharp as a lynx. You fire a burst – he stays still. You wait what next? You feel the bullet whistle past you even before you hear the bang. You crawl from stone to stone, you hide, you race behind him like a hunter. Your body's like a coiled spring and you don't breathe until you pounce. If it comes to it you kill him with your gun-butt. You kill him and you sense you're alive! 'I'M ALIVE!' But there's no joy in killing a man. You kill so you can get home safe.

No two dead bodies look the same. Water, for instance, does something to the human face that gives it a kind of smile. After rain they all look clean. Death in the dust, without water, is more honest, somehow. The uniform may be brand-new but there's a dry red leaf where the head should be, squashed flat like a lizard. You find bodies propped against the wall of a house: I saw one by a pile of nut-shells he must've just cracked, his eyes were open because there'd been no one to close them. You've only got 10–15 minutes to close the eyes after death – then it's too late . . . BUT I'M ALIVE! I saw another, curled up, with his flies undone, he was relieving himself. They lie there the way they were at the last moment of their lives . . . BUT I'M ALIVE! I need to touch myself to make sure . . .

Birds aren't scared of death, they sit and watch. Nor are

children, – they sit there too, and look on calmly, like the birds. They're curious.

Back in the canteen you eat your soup, look at your neighbour and imagine him dead. There was a time when I couldn't bear to look at photos of my family. When I got back from action I wouldn't look women and children in the face. Eventually you get used to it, go and work out next morning as ususal – I was into weight-training. I was keen on fitness and wanted to be in good shape to go home. I admit I couldn't sleep, but that was because of the lice, especially in winter. We sprayed the mattresses with some kind of dust, but it didn't make much difference . . .

I only started to be afraid of dying when I was back home and my son was born. Then I was scared that if I died he'd grow up without me. I was hit seven times, I could easily have kicked the bucket, but I didn't. Sometimes I even have the feeling I didn't play the game to the end, or fight to the finish, rather . . .

I don't feel guilty and I don't get nightmares. I always chose honest combat – him against me. If I saw a couple of our lads beating up a POW with his hands tied behind his back, lying on the ground like a bundle of rags, I'd chase them away. I despised people like that. One chap started shooting eagles with his automatic and I socked his ugly mug for him. The birds hadn't done anything wrong, after all.

When my family asked what it was like over there I'd just say, 'Look, I'm sorry, I'll tell you some other time.'

I graduated and now I'm an engineer. I just want to be an engineer, not a 'veteran of the Afghan war'. I want to forget all that, although I don't know what will become of us, the generation that went through it.

This is the first time I've talked about it, talking like we're strangers in a train and getting off at different stops. Look, my hands are shaking, I'm upset for some reason. I thought I'd come out of it relatively unscathed. If you write about me don't mention my surname. I'm not afraid of anything, I just don't want to be involved again . . .

Civilian Employee

I was due to be married that December, but in November I went to Afghanistan. My fiancé laughed when I told him. 'Doing your "solemn duty to defend the southern borders of our Socialist Motherland", I suppose?' You know what he said when he realised I wasn't joking? 'Aren't there enough boys for you to sleep with here?'

I thought, I missed out on the *BAM* and *tselina* projects [the Baikal–Amor Railway and the Siberian Virgin Lands], but I'm in luck – I've got Afghanistan! I believed the songs the boys brought back, and sang them all day long:

> So many of our Russian sons
> Lie among the rocks and stones
> Of Afghan soil . . .

I was an ordinary, rather bookish, Moscow girl. I thought I'd find real life only somewhere far away, where the men were strong and the women beautiful. I wanted adventure and escape from everyday life . . .

The three nights I was en route for Kabul I didn't sleep a wink. At the customs they thought I was a drug addict. I remember I had tears in my eyes trying to convince them:

'I'm not a junkie. I just need some sleep!'

I was lugging a heavy suitcase full of Mum's home-made jam and biscuits and not a single man offered to help. And these weren't just any old men, but healthy, strong, young officers! In Moscow I had all the boys running after me – they adored me. So I was utterly amazed. When I asked, 'Can someone give me a hand?' they looked at me as if to say, 'We know what kind of girl you are!'

I had to hang about at the clearing-centre for another three days. On the first day a junior lieutenant came up to me. 'If you want to stay in Kabul, spend the night with me,' he said. He was fat and soft – later on a girl told me his nickname was Balloon!

I was taken on as a typist. We used World War II army machines. The first few weeks my fingers bled and I had to type all bandaged up – my nails were dropping off.

One night, a couple of weeks later, a soldier came to my room. 'The CO wants to see you,' he said.

'I'm not going.'

He looked at me. 'Why make life hard for yourself? You knew what you were getting into when you came here.'

Next morning the CO threatened to post me to Kandahar, which was generally recognised as the dirtiest and most dangerous dump in the country. For a few days I was really scared of being 'accidentally' hit by a car, or shot in the back. Two girls shared the room next to mine in the hostel. One had a job in electricity supply, so everyone called her 'Elektrichka'; the other worked in water purification so she was 'Chlorka'! Whenever I complained about things they just shrugged their shoulders: 'Well, that's life . . . '

Just at that time there was an article in *Pravda* called 'Afghan Madonnas'. As a result we got admiring letters from girls from back home, and some of them were so impressed they went down to their local recruiting offices and asked to be sent to Afghanistan. The reality was rather different: we couldn't walk past a group of soldiers without sneering comments like 'Well, Bochkarevka! How's our little heroine today? Doing our international duty in bed, are we?' The name 'Bochkarevka' comes from the little houses (they look a bit like railway carriages) known as 'bochki' reserved for senior officers – majors and above, so the girls who, well, 'serviced' them were known as 'Bochkarevki'. You'll often hear soldiers who've served here say things like this: 'If I hear that a certain girl's been in Afghanistan she just doesn't exist for me.' We got the same diseases as they did, all the girls got hepatitis and malaria, we were shot at too, but if I meet a boy back home he won't let me give him a friendly hug. For them we're all either whores or crazy. 'Don't sleep with a woman like that, don't soil yourself . . . ' 'Me? Sleep with that? I sleep with my gun', etc, etc. It's hard even to smile at a man after you've heard that kind of thing.

'My daughter's in Afghanistan,' my mother told all her friends proudly. Poor naïve Mum! I wanted to write and tell her, 'Keep quiet, Mum, unless you want someone to tell you your daughter's a tart.' Perhaps I'll calm down and get over it gradually once I'm home. But here I feel broken to bits inside. You asked me what I've learnt in Afghanistan? Well, I'll tell you what you can't learn here: about goodness, kindness or happiness.

Little boys run after me shouting: 'Khanum! [woman] Show us your . . . ' They even offer me money, so presumably some of the girls take it.

I used to think I'd never make it home. I'm over that now. I have two dreams, over and over again. In the first, we go to a gorgeous shop, with carpets on the walls and jewellery everywhere . . . And I'm being sold by some of our boys. Sacks of money are brought out, they count the notes while two mujahedin twist my hair round their fingers . . . The alarm clock wakes me up and I'm screaming with fear, so I never find out how it ends.

In the other dream we're flying in an Ilyushin-65 troop transport plane from Tashkent to Kabul. We can see the mountains through the portholes: then it gets dark. We begin to sink into some kind of abyss. there's a layer of heavy Afghan soil over us. I dig like a mole but I can't reach the light. I'm suffocating. I go on digging and digging . . .

If I don't stop now I'll go on talking for ever. There isn't a day that passes without something terribly upsetting happening here. Yesterday a boy I know got a letter from his girlfriend back home: 'I don't want to be friends with you any more, your hands are dripping with blood.' He ran to me and I held him tight.

We all think of home but don't talk about it much. We're superstitious. I'm longing to go home, but where *is* home? We don't talk much about that, either.

We tell jokes instead:

Teacher: 'Children, what do your Daddies do for a living?'

Hands go up. 'My Daddy's a doctor.'

'My Daddy's a plumber.'

'My Daddy's in the circus . . .

Little Vova stays quiet. 'Vova, don't you know what your Daddy does?'

'He used to be a pilot, but now he's got a job as a fascist in Afghanistan.'

At home I used to love books about war, but here I carry

Dumas around with me. When you're at war you don't want to see it around you; although some of the girls did go and see some dead bodies. 'They were lying there in their socks,' they told me. There are so many men hopping about the streets on crutches here. Not everyone can take it. I can't, really. I wanted to be a journalist, but now I'm not so sure, I find it hard to believe in anything.

Once I'm back home in Moscow I'm never going south again. Whenever I see mountains now I get the feeling I'm going to get bombed. Once, during a bombardment, I saw a girl just kneeling and crying and praying. I wonder who she was praying *to*. We're all a bit secretive here, no one's really honest about themselves. Everyone's harbouring some disappointment or other.

I spend most of my time crying and praying for that bookish Moscow girl who doesn't exist any more.

Private, Grenadier Regiment

I went to Afghanistan thinking I'd come home with my head held high. Now I realise the person I was before this war has gone for ever.

Our company was combing through a village. I was patrolling with another lad. He pushed open a hut door with his leg and was shot point-blank with a machine-gun. Nine rounds. In that situation hatred takes over. We shot everything, right down to the domestic animals. In fact, shooting animals is the worst. I was sorry for them. I wouldn't let the donkeys be shot – they'd done nothing wrong, had they? They had amulets hanging from their necks, exactly the same as the children. It really upset me, setting fire to that wheat-field – I'm a country boy myself.

When I was over there I only remembered the good things about life back home, especially my childhood, like the way I used to lie on the grass among the bluebells and marguerites, how we roasted ears of wheat over a log-fire and ate them . . .

The heat from the fire was so terrific that it melted the iron on the roofs of the little shops. The field was swallowed up by the flames in an instant. It smelt of bread and that reminded me of when I was a boy, too.

In Afghanistan night falls like a curtain. One moment it's light, the next – night. A bit like me – I was a boy but I became a man all at one go. That's war for you.

Sometimes when it rains there you look up and see the rain falling, but it never hits the ground. We watched TV programmes by satellite showing life at home going on as normal, but it was irrelevant to us somehow . . . I can talk about all this to you but I feel terribly frustrated, because I can't get over to you what it was really all about.

Sometimes I want to write down everything I saw. Like, in hospital, the lad who'd lost his arms, his legs and his mate. I remember sitting on his bed writing a letter for him to his mother. Or the little Afghan girl who pinched a sweet from a Soviet soldier and had both her hands hacked off *by her own people*. I'd like to write it all down exactly as it was and without any comments. If it rained I'd say it rained, just that, without a lot of talk about whether it was a good or bad thing that it was raining.

When it was our time to go home we expected a warm welcome and open arms – then we discovered that people couldn't care less whether we'd survived or not. In the courtyard of our block of flats I met up with the kids I'd known before. 'Oh, you're back – that's good,' they said, and went off to school. My teachers didn't ask about anything either. This was the sum total of our conversation:

I, solemnly: 'We should perpetuate the memory of our school fellows who died doing their international duty.'

They: 'They were dunces and hooligans. How can we put up a memorial plaque to them in the school?'

People back home had their own view of the war. 'So you think you were heroes, were you? You lost a war, and anyhow, who needed it, apart from Brezhnev and a few warmongering generals?'

Apparently my friends died for nothing, and I might have died for nothing too.

Well, at least my Mum was looking out of the window, the day I got home, and saw me coming, and ran out on to the road shouting for joy. Whatever anyone says, and however much history gets rewritten, I *know* that those boys who died there *were* heroes. I had a talk with an old lecturer at college. 'You were a victim of a political mistake,' he said. 'You were forced to become accomplices to a crime.'

'I was eighteen then,' I told him. 'How old were you? You kept quiet when we were being roasted alive. You kept quiet when we were being brought home in body-bags and military bands played in the cemeteries. You kept quiet over here while we were doing the killing over there. Now all of a sudden you go on about victims and mistakes . . . '

Anyhow, I don't want to be a victim of a political mistake. And I'll fight for the right not to be! Whatever anyone says, those boys were heroes!

Artillery Captain

I was lucky. I've come home alive, with my arms, legs and eyes. I wasn't burnt and I didn't go mad. We soon realised this wasn't the war we'd expected to fight, but we just decided to get it over with, stay alive and go home. There'd be plenty of time to analyse it later.

Mine was the first relief contingent to go to Afghanistan. We had orders, not ideals. You don't discuss orders – if you did you wouldn't have an army for long. You know what Engels said? 'A soldier must be like a bullet, constantly ready to be fired.' I learnt that by heart. You go to war in order to kill. Killing is my profession – that's what I was trained to do.

Was I afraid for myself? I just assumed that other people might get killed, but not me. You can't really comprehend the possibility of your own annihilation. And don't forget – I wasn't a boy when I went out there, I was thirty years old.

That's where I learnt what life was about. I tell you straight – they were the best years of my life. Life here is rather grey and petty: work – home, home – work. There we had to work everything out for ourselves and test our mettle as men.

So much of it was exotic, too: the way the morning mist swirled in the ravines like a smokescreen, even those *burubukhaiki*, the high-sided, brightly decorated Afghan trucks, and the red buses with sheep and cows and people all crammed together inside, and the yellow taxis . . . There are places there which remind you of the moon with their fantastic, cosmic landscapes. You get the feeling that there's nothing alive in those unchanging mountains, that it's nothing but rocks – until the rocks start shooting at you! You sense that even nature is your enemy.

We existed between life and death – and we held other men's life and death in our hands too. Is there any feeling more powerful than that? We'll never walk, or make love, or be loved, the way we walked and loved and were loved over there. Everything was heightened by the closeness of death: death hovered everywhere and all the time. Life was full of adventure: I learnt the smell of danger – I've got a sixth sense for it now. We're homesick for it, some of us; it's called the 'Afghan syndrome'.

We never bothered ourselves with questions about whether we were doing the right thing or not. We carried out our orders the way we were trained to. Now, of course, with the benefit of hindsight and a lot of information which we didn't have at the time, the whole business is being reconsidered and re-evaluated. After less than ten years! At the time we had the clear image of an enemy, an enemy very familiar to us from books and school and all those films about the *basmach* [members of the anti-Soviet independence movement in Central Asia, particularly in the late 1920s]. *The White Desert Sun*, for instance. I must have seen that film five times at least. Just when we were complaining that we'd been born too late for World War II – eureka! A ready-made enemy appeared on the horizon. We were brought up to find inspiration in war and revolution – and nothing else.

As I said, we were the first relief contingent to be sent out. We were quite happy digging foundations for barracks, canteens and army clubs. We were issued with TT-44 pistols dating from World War II, the ones you see political commissars swaggering about with in old films. They were no use at all except to shoot yourself with, or sell in the bazaar. We walked around like partisans, in whatever we could find, usually sweatpants and trainers. I was like the Good Soldier Schweik. When it was 50° Celsius our superiors still expected us to wear ties and full uniform as per Army Regulations from the North Pole to the Equator!

In the morgue I saw body-bags with human flesh hacked to pieces. That was a nasty shock. But within a few months we'd be watching a film in the open air and if tracer shells flashed past the screen we'd just carry on watching . . . Or we'd be playing volley-ball and a bombardment would begin, so we'd check where the shells were coming from and go back to the game. The films they sent out were either about war, or Lenin, or wives cheating on their husbands. I'd gladly have machine-gunned all those women sleeping with other men while their husbands were away! We all wanted comedies but they never sent a single one. The screen was two or three sheets sewn together and strung between a couple of trees, with the audience sitting on the sand.

Once a week we had bath and drinks night. A bottle of vodka cost 30 *cheki*, so we brought it with us from home. Customs regulations permitted two bottles of vodka, four of wine but unlimited beer, so we'd pour out the beer and fill the bottles with vodka. Or else you might open a bottle of mineral water and find it was 40° proof! People drank used aeroplane kerosene and antifreeze. We'd warn new recruits not to touch antifreeze, whatever else they drank, but within a few days they'd be in hospital with their insides corroded.

We smoked hash. One friend of mine got so high in battle he was sure every bullet had his name on it, wherever it was really headed. Another smoked at night and hallucinated that his family was with him, started kissing his wife. Some had all-colour visions such as in a film. At first the traders in the bazaar sold us the stuff but later they gave it us for free. 'Go on, Russky, have a smoke!' they would say. The kids would run after us, pushing it into our hands.

A lot of my friends were killed. One touched the tripwire of a mine with his heel, heard the detonator click and, as always happens, looked at the noise in surprise instead of hurling himself to the ground. He died of dozens of shrapnel wounds. Then there was a tank which exploded so violently that the base opened up like a can of jam and the caterpillars blew off their rollers. The driver tried to escape through the hatch, we saw one arm emerge and that was all – he was burnt in his tank. Back in barracks no one wanted to sleep in his bed. One day a new recruit arrived so we told him to take the bed. 'It doesn't matter to you, you never knew him anyhow . . . '

We were most upset by the ones with children, children who'd grow up without a Dad. On the other hand, what about those who left no one behind, who died as if they'd never been?

We were incredibly badly paid for fighting that war: we got twice basic pay (basic pay being worth 270 foreign currency vouchers), less all kinds of stoppages, compulsory membership-fees, subscriptions and tax. At that time an ordinary volunteer worker in the far north was getting 1,500. 'Military advisers' earned five to ten times more than us. The difference was particularly obvious going through customs at the border: we'd have a tape-recorder and a couple of pairs of jeans, they'd have half a dozen trunks, so heavy the squaddies could hardly carry them.

When we got back in the Soviet Union, in Tashkent, it was no easier.

'Back from Afghan? Want a girl? I've got one for you as soft as a peach, dear . . . '

'No thanks, I'm trying to get home on leave. To my wife. I need a ticket.'

'Tickets cost money . . . D'you want to sell your Italian sunglasses?'

'It's a deal.'

To get on the plane to Sverdlovsk cost me 100 roubles, those Italian sun-glasses, a Japanese lurex scarf and a French make-up set. In the ticket-queue I learnt the way things worked: 'Why stand here for days? Forty vouchers slipped into your service passport and you'll be home next day.'

I get to the ticket-window. 'Ticket for Sverdlovsk.'

'No tickets. Open your eyes and look at the board!'

I slip the forty vouchers in and try again. 'Ticket to Sverdlovsk please, miss.'

'I'll just go and check. Oh, lucky you came by, we've just had a cancellation.'

You get home and land in a completely different world – the world of the family. The first few days you don't hear a thing they say. You just watch them, touch them. I can't explain what it means to stroke your child's head after everything that's happened. The morning smell of coffee and pancakes, your wife calling you to breakfast . . .

In one month you have to leave again. Why and where – you don't know. You don't think about it – you simply *mustn't* think about it. You just know you'll go because you must. At night, lying beside your wife, you still taste the Afghan sand, soft as flour, between your teeth. A few days ago you were lying in that red dust next to the APC . . . You wake up, jump out of bed – no, you're still home, it's tomorrow you're going back.

Today my father asked me to help him slaughter a piglet. In the past I'd refuse and run out of the house with my hands over my ears so as not to hear the screaming.

'Hold it a moment,' says my father.

'No, not like that, straight to the heart, like this,' I say, and take the knife and kill it myself.

In the morgue I saw body-bags with human limbs hacked off. Yes, that was a nasty shock. You should never be the first to spill blood – it's a process that's hard to stop. Once I saw some soldiers sitting around while an old man and a little donkey passed by on the street below. Suddenly they lobbed a mortar and killed the old man and his donkey.

'Hey, lads! Have you gone mad? It was just an old man and a donkey. What did they do to you?'

'An old man and a donkey came by here yesterday, too. By the time they'd gone past our mate was lying here dead.'

'But it might have been a different old man and a different donkey?'

Never be the first to spill blood, or you'll forever be shooting yesterday's old man and yesterday's donkey.

We fought the war, stayed alive and got home. Now's the time to try and make sense of it all . . .

A Mother

I sat by the coffin. 'Who's in there? Is it you, my little one?' I repeated over and over again. 'Who's in there? Is it you, my boy?' Everyone thought I'd gone insane.

Time passed, and I wanted to find out how my son was killed. I went to the local recruitment HQ. 'Tell me how and where my son was killed,' I begged. 'I don't believe he's dead. I'm sure I've buried a metal box and my son is alive somewhere.'

The officer in charge got angry and even started shouting at me. 'This is classified information! You can't go around telling everyone your son has been killed! Don't you know that's not allowed?'

He had a long and painful birth, but when I realised I had a son I knew the agony had all been worthwhile. I worried about him from the day he was born – he was all I had in this world. We lived in a little one-room hut with just enough space for a bed, pram and two chairs. I worked on the railways, switching points, for 60 roubles a month. The day I left hospital I went straight on nightshift. I took him to work with me in the pram, I had my little hot-plate with me and fed him and put him to sleep at the same time I was meeting the trains. When he was a bit older I left him at home alone; I had to tie his ankle to the pram and leave him alone all day long. Still, he grew up a fine boy.

He got into building college in Petrozavodsk, up in Karelia, near the Finnish border. I went to visit him there once. He gave me a kiss and then ran off somewhere. I was quite hurt – until he came back, smiling.

'The girls are coming,' he said.

'What girls?'

He'd gone off to tell these girls I'd arrived and they were coming to inspect this mother of his they'd heard so much about.

No one had ever given me a present. He came home for Mother's Day and I met him at the station.

'Let me help you with that bag,' I said.

'It's heavy, Mum. You take my portfolio-case, but be careful with it!'

83

I carried it carefully and he made sure I did. Must be important drawings, I thought. When we got home he went to change and I rushed to the kitchen to check on my pies. I looked up and there he was with three red tulips in his hand. How on earth had he managed to get hold of tulips up there in March? He'd wrapped them in cloth and put them in his case so they didn't freeze. It was the first time anyone had ever given me flowers.

That summer he worked on one of those special intensive building projects. He came home just before my birthday. 'I'm sorry I couldn't get here earlier, but I've brought you a little something,' he said, handing me a money order. I looked at it. '12 roubles 50 kopecks,' I read out.

'Hey, Mum, you've forgotten the noughts! That's for *1250* roubles!'

'Well, I've never had a crazy sum like that in my hands! How would I know how it's written?'

He was very good-hearted. 'You're going to retire and I'm going to earn a lot of money for both of us. Do you remember when I was a boy, I promised I'd carry you in my arms when I grew up?'

And so he did. He was 6 foot 5 inches tall and he carried me around like a little girl. We loved each other so much because we had no one else, probably. I don't know how I'd have let a wife have him. I don't suppose I would have.

He got his conscription papers and decided he wanted to be a paratrooper. 'They're enlisting for the paras, Mum, but they won't take me because I'm so big. They say I'll break the parachute shroud-lines! And I just love those berets.'

All the same, he got into the Vitebsk Parachute Division. I went to the swearing-in ceremony, when they have to take the oath. I noticed he'd straightened up – he wasn't ashamed of his height any more.

'Why are you so tiny, Mum?' he asked.

'I've stopped growing because I miss you so much,' I tried to joke.

'We're being sent to Afghanistan, but I'm not going because I'm an only child. Why didn't you have a little girl after you had me?'

Lots of the parents came to the oath-taking ceremony. All of a sudden I heard someone on the platform asking, 'Where is Mama Zhuraleva? Mama Zhuraleva, come up and congratulate your son!' I went up to give him a kiss, but I couldn't reach the 6 foot 5 inch bean-pole. 'Private Zhuralev! Bend down so that your mother can give you a kiss!' ordered the commandant. As he bent down and kissed me someone took a photograph of us. It's the only photo I've got of him in uniform.

After the ceremony they were given a few hours off and we went to a nearby park. We sat on the grass. When he took off his boots I saw that his feet were covered in blood. He told me they'd done a 30-mile route-march, but there were no size 11 boots so he had to wear 9½s. But he didn't complain – on the contrary. 'We had to run with our backpacks full of sand, and I didn't pour half mine out like some of the lads.'

I wanted to do something special for him. 'Shall we go to a restaurant, dear? We've never been to a restaurant together.' 'I tell you what, Mum – buy me a couple of pounds of sweets. That's what I'd really like!'

Then it was time for him to go back to barracks. He waved me goodbye with his bag of sweets.

They put us relatives up for the night on mattresses in the sports hall, but we hardly slept a wink – we couldn't help walking round and round the barracks where our boys were fast asleep. When reveille sounded I rushed outside, hoping to see him one more time as they marched off to the gym, even if it was only from a distance. I saw them running, but they all looked the same in their striped vests so I couldn't make him out. They had to keep in groups all the time, even going to the canteen or the toilet – they weren't allowed to go anywhere on their own because before, when the lads realised they were going to Afghanistan, some had hanged themselves in the toilets or slashed their wrists.

In the bus I was the only one who cried. I just sensed I'd never see him again. Soon I had a letter from him: 'I saw your bus, Mum, and ran after it so that I could see you one last time.' When we were sitting in the park they'd played that lovely old song over the loudspeakers, 'When my mother said goodbye to me'. I hear it in my head all the time now.

His next letter began, 'Hello from Kabul . . . ' I started screaming, so loud that the neighbours rushed in. 'It's against the law and civil rights!' I shouted, banging my head on the table. 'He's my only child – even under the Tsar they didn't take an only child into the army. And now he's been sent to fight a war.' It was the first time since Sasha was born that I was sorry I hadn't got married. Now I had no one to protect me.

Sasha used to tease me: 'Why don't you get married, Mum?' he'd ask.

'Because you'd be jealous!' I told him. He'd laugh and say no more about it. We thought we'd be living together for a long, long time.

He wrote a few more letters and then there was such a long gap that I wrote to his commanding officer. Soon afterwards I got a letter from Sasha. 'Mum, don't write to the CO any more, your last letter got me into trouble. The reason I didn't write is, I was stung on the hand by a wasp. I didn't ask anyone else to write a letter for me because a stranger's handwriting on the envelope would have given you a shock.' He was sorry for me and made up stories – as if I didn't watch TV every day and couldn't guess he'd been wounded. After that, if I didn't get a letter every day I could hardly get up in the morning. He tried to explain. 'How can you expect them to send off our letters every day when we only get fresh drinking-water delivered every ten days?'

One letter was happy: 'Hurrah! Hurrah! We escorted a convoy to the Soviet border, and even though we weren't allowed to cross, we saw the Motherland in the distance. It's the best country in the world!'

In his last letter he wrote: 'If I can get through the summer I'll be home.' On the 29th of August I decided summer was over and went to buy him a suit and some shoes. They're still in the cupboard . . .

On the 30th I took off my ear-rings and ring before I went to work. For some reason I just couldn't bear to wear them.

That was the day he was killed.

I only went on living after his death thanks to my brother. For a whole week he slept by my bed like a dog, watching over me, because all I wanted to do was run to the balcony and throw myself out of our seventh-floor window. When the coffin was brought into the sitting-room I lay on it, measuring it with my arms over and over again. Three foot, six foot, six and a half, because that's how tall he was. Was it long enough for him? I talked to the coffin like a madwoman: 'Who's there? Is it you, my love? Who's there? Is it you, my love? Who's there? Is it you, my love?' The coffin was already sealed when they brought it so I couldn't kiss him goodbye, or stroke him one last time. I don't even know what he's wearing.

I told them I'd choose a place for him in the cemetery myself. They gave me a couple of injections and I went with my brother. There were already some 'Afghan' graves in the central alley.

'That's where I want my son to be – he'll be happier with his friends.'

The man who was with us, some boss or other, shook his head. 'It's forbidden for them to be buried together. They have to be spread about the rest of the cemetery.'

That was when I exploded! 'Don't get so angry, Konya, don't get so angry,' my brother tried to calm me down. But how can I not be angry?

When I saw their Kabul on TV I wanted to get a machine-gun and shoot the lot of them. I'd sit there 'shooting' until, one day, it showed one of their old women, an Afghan mother, I suppose. 'She's probably lost a son, too,' I thought. After that I stopped 'shooting'.

I'm thinking of adopting a boy from the children's home, a little blond chap like Sasha. No, I'd be frightened for a boy, he'd only get killed, a girl would be better. The two of us'll wait for Sasha together . . . I'm not mad, but I am waiting for him. I've heard of cases where they've sent the mother the coffin and she's buried it, and a year later he's home, alive, wounded but alive. The mother had a heart attack. I'm still waiting. I never saw him dead so I'm still waiting . . . '

I won't begin at the beginning. I'll begin from when everything started to collapse.

We were on the road to Jalalabad. A little girl, about seven, was standing by the side of the road. She had a broken arm hanging down, like the arm of an old rag doll dangling by a bit of thread. Her olive eyes stared and stared at me. I jumped out of the car to pick her up and take her to our hospital but she was in a state of sheer terror, like a little wild animal. She leapt away from me screaming, with her little arm still dangling, looking as though it would drop off at any moment. I ran after her, I was shouting too. I caught up with her and clutched her to me, stroked her. She started biting and scratching, then shaking, as though some other wild animal had caught her. I suddenly realised she thought I was going to kill her.

A stretcher went past with an old Afghan woman lying on it, smiling.

'Where's she been wounded?' someone asked.

'In the heart,' the nurse answered.

I went to Afghanistan full of enthusiasm. I thought I could do something useful out there. I expected to be needed by the people. Now all I remember is how the little girl ran away from me, trembling, how frightened she was of me. It's something I'll never forget.

I never dreamt about the war while I was there. Now I'm scared to go to sleep at night. I keep chasing that little girl with her olive eyes and her dangling arm . . .

'Do you think I ought to see the shrink?' I asked some of the lads.

'What for?'

'About being afraid to go to sleep.'

'We're all afraid to go to sleep.'

I don't want you to think we were supermen, with cigarettes clenched between our teeth, opening cans of bully beef over the bodies of the enemy and carelessly eating water-melons after battle. That image is utter rubbish. We were ordinary boys and any other boys could have taken our place. When I hear people accusing us of 'killing people over there' I could smash their faces in. If you weren't there and didn't live through it you can't know what it was like and you have no right to judge us. The only exception was Sakharov. I would have listened to him.

No one can understand that war. We were left to sort the whole thing out on our own. Now we're expected to feel guilty and justify ourselves. To whom? may I ask. We were sent by our leaders and we trusted in them. *Don't confuse those who sent us with those who were sent.* A friend of mine, Major Sasha Krivets, was killed. Go and tell his mother, or his wife, or his children, that he's guilty. 'You're in good condition,' the doctor told me. How can we be in good condition after what we've been through?

The idea of the Motherland seemed completely different over there. We didn't even use the term, we called it the 'Union' instead. 'Say hello to the Union,' we'd tell the boys going home.

We assumed there was something big and strong behind us which would always be there to defend us. Once, I remember, we'd returned to barracks after a battle, with many dead and wounded, and in the evening we switched on TV, just to relax and find out what was going on back home. A huge new factory was being built in Siberia; the Queen of Britain had given a luncheon for some VIP; a gang of teenagers had raped two school-girls in Voronezh, out of boredom. Some prince had been killed in Africa . . . We realised we weren't important and that life at home was going on as usual. Suddenly Sasha Kuchinski exploded. 'Turn it off!' he shouted. 'Or I'll blow the thing to bits!'

After battle you make a report by walkie-talkie: '6 three zero zeroes and and 4 zero twenty-ones,' or whatever. 'Three zero zero' is the code for 'wounded'; 'zero twenty-one' means 'fatality'. You look at a dead soldier and think of his mother. I know her son's dead, you think, and she doesn't – yet. Could she sense it? It was even worse if someone fell into the river or a ravine and the body wasn't found. The mother would be told he was 'missing'.

This was the mothers' war, they were the ones who did the fighting. The Soviet people in general didn't suffer much. They were told we were fighting 'bandits'. But why couldn't a regular army, 100,000 strong, with all the latest equipment, defeat a few disorganised bandits after nine long years? You can't imagine the power and accuracy of our 'Grad' and 'Hurricane' jet-propelled rocket-launchers: they make telegraph poles fly about like match-sticks and all you want to do is crawl into the ground like a worm. All the so-called bandits had were those Maxim machine-guns, the sort you see only in old films. Later, I admit, they got Stinger missiles and Jap non-recoil automatics, but still . . .

We'd bring in POWs, skinny exhausted men with big peasant hands. They weren't bandits, just ordinary people.

It didn't take us long to understand they didn't want us there, so what was the point of our being there? You'd go past abandoned villages with smoke still curling over the log-fires, you could smell food cooking . . . Once I saw a camel dragging its insides after it, as though its humps were uncoiling. I should have finished it off, I know, but I couldn't, I have a natural dislike of violence. Some-one else might well have shot a perfectly *healthy* camel, just for the hell of it. In the Soviet Union that kind of behaviour means gaol, but over there you'd be a hero for 'punishing bandits'. Why is it that seventeen- and eighteen-year-olds find it easier to kill than thirty-year-olds, for example? Because they have no pity, that's why. When the war was over I noticed how violent fairy-tales were. People are always killing each other, Baba Yaga even roasts them in her oven, but the children are never frightened. They hardly ever even cry!

We wanted to stay normal. I remember a singer who came to entertain us troops. She was a beautiful woman and her songs were very moving. We missed women so much – I was as excited to see her as if she were a member of my family. Eventually she came on stage. 'When I was on my way here,' she announced, 'I was allowed to use a machine-gun. I can't tell you how I enjoyed firing that thing.' She started singing, and when it came to the refrain she urged us to clap in time: 'Come on boys, let's hear you now!' No one clapped. No one made a sound. She walked off stage and the show was abandoned. She thought she was some kind of supergirl come to visit superboys. But the fact was that there were ten or fifteen empty bunks in those boys' barracks every month, with the occupants lying in the morgue. The other lads arranged letters from their mothers or girlfriends diagonally across the sheet – it was a kind of tradition.

The most important thing in that war was to survive – to avoid getting blown up by a mine, roasted in a tank or shot by a sniper. For some, the next most important thing was to take something back home, a TV or a sheepskin coat, for example. There was a joke that people back home got to know about the war through the commission shops, where things like that fetched a good price. In winter you see all the girls in their Afghan sheepskins – they're very trendy just now.

All us soldiers had amulets round our necks, charms our mothers had given us. When I got home my mother confessed, 'I didn't tell you, Kolya, but I had a spell cast over you, that's why you've come home safe and sound.' She'd actually taken a lump of earth from our garden to the local witch!

When we went on a raid we'd pin a note to the upper part of our body and another to the lower part, so that if we were blown up by a mine one or the other would be found. Or else we wore bracelets with our name, number and blood group engraved on them. We never said 'I'm going . . . ' always 'I've been sent . . . ' And we never said the word 'last':

'Let's go and have a last drink.'

'Are you crazy? There's no such word! Final, ultimate, fourth, fifth, anything, but not that word!'

Superstition was rife. For example, if you shaved, or had your photo taken before going on an operation, you wouldn't come back alive. War has a strange logic of its own. The blue-eyed boys, determined to be heroes, were always the first to die. 'I'm going to be a hero!' you'd hear someone say, and he'd be killed next time out. In action we relieved ourselves where we lay. There's a soldier's saying that goes, 'It's better to roll in your own shit than to be blown into shit by a mine.' (Excuse my language.) Most fatalities occurred during the first or last month of a tour of duty. The early ones were due to curiosity, the late ones to a kind of blunting of the self-preservation instinct.

Joke: An officer in Afghanistan goes back home on army business. He goes to the hairdresser.

'How are things in Afghanistan?' she asks him.

'Getting better,' he replies.

A few minutes later she asks him again: 'How are things in Afghanistan?'

'Getting better.'

A little while later: 'How are things in Afghanistan?'

'Getting better.'

Eventually he pays and goes. 'Why did you keep asking him the same question?' her colleagues ask her.

'Whenever I mentioned Afghanistan his hair stood on end and it was easier to cut.'

I've been home three years and I still yearn to go back. Not to the war, or the place, but to the men I lived and worked with. When you're there you can't wait to get home, but when the day comes you're sorry and go around collecting your friends' addresses.

Valeri Shirokov, for example. He was a slim, delicate chap, but with a soul of iron. He never said an unnecessary word. At one time we had a real miser with us, who did nothing but hoard, buy, sell, and barter. One day Valeri went up to him, took 200 foreign currency vouchers out of his wallet, tore them up into little pieces before his very eyes, and then left the room without saying a word.

Or Sasha Rudik. I saw the New Year in with him on a raid. We made a Christmas tree out of guns stacked in a pyramid and hung grenades on them instead of presents. We wrote 'Happy New Year!!!' in toothpaste on the rocket-launcher, with three exclamation marks for some reason. He was a good painter. I've still got a landscape of his, with a dog, a girl and maple trees, painted on a sheet. He never did mountains – they soon lost their charm for us. If you asked men there what they missed most they'd answer: 'I'd like to walk in the woods, swim in the river, drink a whole jug of milk.'

Or Sashik Lashuk. He was a decent lad who wrote home often. 'My parents are old,' he'd say. 'They don't know I'm here. I've told them I was posted to Mongolia.' He arrived with his guitar and left with it, too.

No two of us were alike, so don't think we were all the same over there. To begin with the media kept quiet about us, then we were all heroes for a time, and now we're being knocked off our pedestals again so we can be forgotten about. One chap might throw himself on a mine to save the lives of men he didn't even know, while another would come to you and say: 'Look, I'll do your laundry for you if you want, but don't send me into action.'

Our KamaZ trucks would drive around with the names of cities written on them – 'Odessa', 'Smolensk', 'Leningrad'. Others might say 'I want to go home to Alma-Ata', etc. When an Odessan or Leningrader met someone from his home town they'd hug each other like brothers. And here, back home, we're like brothers too. After all, if you see a young man hopping down the road on crutches, wearing a nice shiny medal, he's obviously one of us. We might sit down on a bench and have a smoke, and chat all evening. We're all suffering from a wasting disease, you know. Over there it showed itself as a mismatch between our weight and our height, but here, back home, it's a mismatch between our feelings and our ability to express them in what we say and do.

When we landed back in the Soviet Union we were taken by bus from the airport to a hotel. We were all silent, overwhelmed by the first few hours in our own country. All of a sudden, though, our collective nerve broke. 'Drive in the ruts!' we shouted at the driver. 'Keep to the ruts!' Then we burst into hysterical laughter – we were home and didn't need to worry about mines. We could drive on the side of the road, in the ruts or out of them, wherever we wanted – we were drunk with happiness.

A few days later we noticed we were all walking about round-shouldered. We'd lost the habit of walking upright. I used to tie myself to the bed at night to train myself to straighten up.

I gave a talk at the officers' club. 'Tell us about the romantic side of service life in Afghanistan,' I was asked. 'Did you personally kill anyone?' Young girls were especially keen on bloodthirsty questions. Ordinary life is a bit dull, I grant you, but can you imagine anyone asking about the romantic side of World War II? Three generations fought side by side against the Germans – grandfathers, fathers and sons. This war was fought by naïve boys looking for adventure. I saw how keen they were to try everything. They wanted to know what it felt like to kill, to be scared, to take hashish. Some got high on it, others got into the state we called

93

shubnyak, where a bush turned into a tree, or a rock became a hill, so that when they marched they had to lift their feet twice as high as the rest of us. That made the world even more frightening for them.

Another question I got asked was this: 'Could you have refused to go to Afghanistan?' Me personally? Only one of our group of professional army officers, Major Bondarenko, a battery commander, refused. The first thing that happened was, he had to face a 'court of honour', which convicted him of cowardice. Can you imagine what that does to a man's self-esteem? Suicide might be the easiest way out. Then he was demoted to captain and posted to a building battalion as punishment. Then he was expelled from the party and eventually discharged with dishonour. How many men could go through all that? And he was a military man to the bone – he'd spent thirty years in the army.

When I went through customs they wiped my Rosenbaum [a mildly 'dissident' singer] tape. 'Hey, lads, what are you doing?' I asked.

'We've got this list of what's allowed and what isn't.'

When I got home to Smolensk I heard Rosenbaum blaring out of all the student hostel windows!

Nowadays, if the police need to frighten the local mafia they come to us Afgantsi. 'Come on boys!' they say, 'give us a hand!' Or if they want to harass or break up some unofficial political group, 'Call the Afgantsi in!' they say. An Afganets, in other words, is a killing-machine, with big fists, a weak head and no conscience. No wonder we're feared and disliked by everyone.

But if you've got a bad arm you don't amputate it, do you? You nurse it until it's better.

Shall I tell you why we go on meeting, we veterans? To save ourselves by staying together. All the same, once you're home you're on your own.

1st Lieutenant i/c Mortar Platoon

I have the same dream every night. It's like watching a film over and over again. Everyone's running and firing, including me. I

94

fall down and wake up and I'm on a hospital bed. I start to get
up to go and have a smoke in the corridor. Then I realise my legs
have gone and I'm back in the real world . . .

I don't want to hear any talk about a 'political mistake', OK?
Give me my legs back if it was really a mistake.

Have you taken unfinished letters from soldiers' pockets . . .
'Dear Mama . . . ', 'My Darling . . . '? Have you seen soldiers shot
to pieces by old blunderbusses and modern Chinese machine-
guns at the same time?

We were sent to Afghanistan to obey orders. In the army you
obey orders first and then, if you like, discuss their merits – when
it's all over. 'Go!' means exactly that. If you refuse you get thrown
out of the party. You took the military oath, didn't you? And back
home, when you ask the local party committee for something you
need, they tell you, 'It wasn't us that sent you!' Well, who did
send us?

I had a friend out there. When I went into action he always
said goodbye to me and hugged me when I came back alive. I'll
never find a friend like that here at home.

I hardly ever go out now. I'm ashamed . . .

Have you ever tried our Soviet-manufactured prostheses? I've
heard that abroad people with artificial limbs go skiing, play tennis
and dance. Why don't the authorities use foreign currency to buy
decent arms and legs instead of wasting it on French cosmetics,
subsidised Cuban sugar or Moroccan oranges?

I'm twenty-two, with my whole life in front of me. I need to
find a wife. I had a girlfriend. 'I hate you,' I told her, to make
her leave me. She pitied me, when what I wanted was her love.

> 'I dreamt of home, of nights I lay
> Listening to the rowans sigh.
> "Cuckoo, cuckoo, tell me pray
> How many years before I die . . . ?" '

That was my favourite song. I used to go into the forest, and ask
the cuckoo, and count his calls, but now – sometimes I don't want
to go on living one day longer.

I still long to see that landscape again, that biblical desert. We all have that yearning, it's like standing at the edge of a precipice, or high over water, and looking down until your head spins.

Now the war's over they're trying to forget all about us, or else hide us out of sight. They treated the veterans of the war with Finland the same way*. Thousands of books have been published about World War II but not one about the Finnish war. Our people are too easy on their rulers – and I'll have accepted it myself in ten years or so.

Did I kill anybody in Afghanistan? Yes. You didn't send us over there to be angels – so how can you expect us to come back as angels?

It took me six days by train to get to Moscow from Khabarovsk. We crossed the whole of Russia via the Siberian rivers and Lake Baikal. The railway attendant in charge of the tea-urn ran out of tea on the very first day; the water-boiler broke down the day after that. My family met me in Moscow, there were tears all round, but duty came first.

I got off the plane and saw the kind of blue sky that in our country you find only over rivers. There was a lot of noise and shouting – but all of it from our own people. There were new recruits being met, old friends seen off, and packages from home picked up. Everyone looked tanned and cheerful. Hard to believe that somewhere out there it was 30° Celsius below freezing and armour-plating was cracking from cold. I saw my first Afghan through the barbed wire of the clearing-compound. I remember having no particular feelings (apart from a mild curiosity) towards this 'foreigner'.

I was posted to Bagram to take command of the road-engineers' platoon in a sapper battalion.

We lived a regular routine of getting up early and reporting for work. We had a mine-sweeper tank, a sniper unit, a mine-detecting dog, and two APCs to provide protection. We covered the first few miles in the armoured vehicles, just as long as the tracks of previous vehicles were clearly visible on the road. Dust covered everything like a fine powdery snow. If a bird landed on it you

* The 'Winter War' of 1939–40, about which the Soviet public was, until very recently, permitted to know almost nothing.

96

could see the traces. If a tank had passed that way the day before, though, special care was needed, because the caterpillar tracks could be concealing a mine. After planting the device the mujahedin would recreate the tracks with their fingers and clear their own footprints using a bag or an unrolled turban.

The road wound past two abandoned villages of smouldering mud huts – perfect cover for enemy snipers, so we needed to be extra-vigilant. Once we were past the villages we'd get out of the vehicles. This was the procedure: the dog ran zigzagging in front of us, followed by the sappers with their probing rods poking the soil as they went. All you had going for you was God, your sixth sense, experience and flair. You might notice a broken branch, or a bit of rusty iron, or a rock, which hadn't been there the day before. The muj would leave little markers like that to avoid getting blown up themselves.

That bit of iron, now, was it there by chance or was there a battery under the sand, connected to a bomb or a crate of TNT? A man's weight won't trigger an anti tank mine – it needs a 250–300 kilo load to set it off.

After my first explosion I was the only man left sitting on our tank. All the others got blown off. My place was by the barrel so I was protected from the full force of the blast by the gun turret. I quickly checked my arms, legs and head were all where they should be. We picked ourselves up and carried on.

We set off another blast a little further on. The lightly armed trailer-tractor was blown up and split in two by a powerful *fougasse*, or landmine, which left a crater three metres long and as deep as a tall man. The tractor was transporting mines, about 200 mortars – they were thrown into the branches and on to the side of the road like a giant fan. We lost all five soldiers and the lieutenant on the tractor. I'd spent the past few evenings with them, talking and smoking and now they were literally blown to pieces. We went and collected them up, including a dust-covered head, so completely squashed it looked as though there wasn't any bone.

We filled five crates and divided them so that there would be something of each man to be sent home.

The dogs were a tremendous asset. They're just like people, some gifted with intuition, others not. A sentry might doze, but a dog – never. I was very fond of one called Toby. He'd snuggle up to us but bark at our Afghan National Army allies! Admittedly, their khaki was a bit greener, and ours rather yellowish, but still, how could he tell the difference? He could sense a mine at several paces. He'd stop dead with his tail sticking up straight, as if to say: KEEP OFF!

No two mine-traps are the same, but the worst are the home-made devices which never repeat themselves exactly. They might be hidden in a rusty tea-kettle, or a tape-recorder, watch, or can. Units who went out without sappers were known as 'suicide squads'. Mines were everywhere, on mountain paths, on the roads and in houses. It was always the sappers who went in first.

We were checking out a trench one day. There'd already been one explosion and we'd spent two days raking it through. I jumped down into it and – BANG!

I didn't pass out – I looked up at the sky, which seemed to be on fire. A sapper's first reaction after a blast is to look upwards to check that his eyes are intact. I kept a tourniquet on my gun-butt which they used to bandage me above the knees. But I knew that limbs are always amputated three to five centimetres above the wound.

'Where are you tying it?' I shouted at the medic.

'You've lost them both up to the knee, sir.'

The field hospital was fifteen kilometres away and it took them 1½ hours to get me there. There my wounds were sterilised and I was given novocaine to kill the pain. My legs were amputated the same day; I lost consciousness only when I heard the saw, it sounded like a circular saw. The following day they operated on my eyes. The flame from the blast had seared my face – the surgeons practically darned my eyes and gave me twenty-two stitches. Only two or three a day could be removed – otherwise the eyeball would have fallen to bits. They'd shine a torch into my eyes, left and right, to find out whether I reacted to light and whether the retina was intact.

I'll never forget the red beam of that torch.

I'd like to write a book about the way an officer can be reduced to a housebound wreck, earning his bread assembling lamp-sock-ets and wall-plugs, about a hundred a day, or putting the metal bits on the ends of shoelaces. What colour shoelaces? Red, black, or white, he never knows, because he can't see; he's been officially declared totally blind. He ties string-bags, and glues little boxes – the sort of work he used to think only lunatics did. Thirty bags a day and I've reached my daily target, my 'norm'.

Sappers were the least likely of all to come back intact, or even alive, particularly the specialised mine-clearing units. They were all either dead or wounded. Out of habit, we never shook hands before going into action. The day of that last explosion our new CO shook my hand, out of sheer friendliness – no one had warned him. And I got blown up . . . Was it just superstition? Who knows? There was another belief: if you'd volunteered for Afghanistan you'd end up dead, but if you were just posted there you might get home alive.

That was five years ago. I still have this dream. I'm in a long mine-field. I've drawn up a plan, based on the number of mines and the number of rows, and markers to find them by. But I've lost the plan. (In fact we often did lose them, or else the marker was a tree which had been destroyed, or a pile of stones which had been blown up. Nobody wanted to go and check, and risk getting blown up by our own mines.) In my dream I see children running near the mine-field, they don't know there are mines there. I want to shout: 'Stop! Mines!' I want to warn the children. I want to warn the children . . . I'm running . . . I have both my legs back, and I can see, my eyes can see again . . . But that's only at night, only in my dream. Then I wake up.

Doctor, Bacteriologist

Perhaps it sounds ridiculous, especially in the context of this particular war, but I'm a romantic. I hate the pettiness and materialism of everyday life. The very day I arrived the medical director called me in. 'What makes a woman like you come here?' he asked me, and I was obliged to tell the story of my life to a complete stranger, a military man at that, someone I might just have met in the street. For me, that was the most unpleasant and humiliating aspect of life in Afghanistan: the complete absence of privacy and intimacy. Everything took place on a public stage. Do you know a film called *Off Limits*, about convict life in the camps? We lived life by exactly the same rules, right down to the little barbed-wire compounds we were restricted to.

The girls I lived with were young waitresses and cooks, whose sole subject of conversation seemed to be roubles, foreign currency vouchers, and how to steal meat, smoked sausage or Bulgarian biscuits from the hospital kitchens. Before I arrived I imagined an elevating and inspiring atmosphere of self-sacrifice, with the womenfolk fulfilling their role of protecting and caring for our boys. If men were spilling their blood for the cause I would give my blood too! I realised just how wrong I was even before I left the clearing-centre in Tashkent. I sat in the plane and burst into tears. Life here was exactly the same as everything I was running away from at home. Vodka flowed like water at the centre. You know that song:

'We dream of the grass at the cosmodrome
The green green grass that means we're home!'

Well, I felt as though I were flying into outer space. Back home everyone at least has their own home they can make into their little fortress, but we slept four to a room. The girl who worked as a hospital cook used to bring meat she'd stolen from the canteen and hide it under the bed.

'Wash the floor!' she orders me.

'I washed it yesterday, it's your turn today.'

'I'll give you a hundred roubles to wash that floor.' I say nothing.

'I'll give you some meat.'

I say nothing. Then she takes a bucket of water and empties it over my bed. They all burst into laughter.

Another girl was a waitress. Her speech consisted entirely of foul language but she loved the poet Marina Tsvetayeva [1892–1941, one of the three or four greatest Russian poets of the century]. When she came back from her shift she'd sit down and play patience: 'Will I, won't I, will I, won't I?'

'Will I won't I what?'

'Fall in love, of course.'

There were real weddings out there, and love too, though not much of it. Love usually stopped at Tashkent – after that it was 'him to the left, her to the right'.

Tanya the Tank, as we called her on account of her build, liked to sit and talk into the early hours. She drank only pure alcohol. 'How can you take it?' I asked her.

'Vodka's just too weak, love! It doesn't do a thing for me.' When she went home she took five or six hundred postcards of movie stars she'd bought in the bazaars, where they were expensive. 'Money spent on art is never wasted,' she told us proudly.

I remember another girl, Verochka Kharkov, sitting in front of the mirror with her tongue stuck out. She was worried about typhoid and somebody had told her that one of the symptoms was toothmarks on the tongue!

They hardly even acknowledged my existence. For them I was some idiot who carried test-tubes full of germs about. I was the chief bacteriologist at the infectious diseases hospital, and all I ever talked about was typhoid, paratyphoid, hepatitis and the like. Casualties didn't arrive at hospital straightaway – they might have been lying for up to ten hours, or even a day or two, in the mountain sand before they were located, with the result that open wounds became breeding-grounds for every kind of infection. I'd examine a patient in reanimation, for example, and find he had typhoid on top of everything else.

They died quietly. Only once did I see an officer crying. He was a Moldavian and the surgeon, who was also Moldavian, talked to him in their own language.

'What's the problem, my friend? Where's the pain?'

That was when he began to weep. 'Save me!' he begged. 'I must live. I have a sweet wife and lovely daughter. I must get back to them . . .' He would have died quietly too, if he hadn't heard his mother tongue.

I hated going to the morgue, where human flesh still mixed with earth was regularly brought in. I'd think of that meat hidden under the girls' beds . . . They'd put the frying-pan on the table shouting '*Ruba, Ruba!*' which means 'Let's go!' in Afghan. It was so hot their sweat dripped into the pan.

I was seeing wounded soldiers and their microbes all day long – and you can't sell microbes, can you? At the army store you could buy toffees, which I adored, for foreign currency vouchers. Once, I remember, someone gave me two raw eggs from the hospital kitchen, because we doctors went around half-starved (we survived on reconstituted potato and frozen meat which was tough, tasteless and colourless). I grabbed the eggs and wrapped them in a handkerchief to take them back to my room to make an onion omelette. I looked forward to that omelette all day. Then I saw a young lad on a stretcher in a corridor, waiting to be evacuated to Tashkent. I couldn't see what there was under the blanket, only his handsome face on the pillow. He looked up at me. 'I'm starving,' he said. It was just before lunch and I realised he'd be taken away before they brought the big tubs of food up from the kitchens. 'OK,' I said, and gave him the two eggs. I turned and left, not thinking to find out if he still had his arms and legs. I'd put the eggs on his pillow without breaking them or feeding him. What if he had no arms?

Once I was in a van for two hours with four corpses beside me, lying there in track-suits . . .

When I got back home to the USSR I couldn't bear to listen to music or chat with people in the street and the bus queue. I'd have liked to shut myself into my room with just the TV for company. The day before I left, the medical director of our hospital, Yuri Yefimovich Zhibkov, shot himself. In Afghanistan some officer showed me this passage from the French writer, Fourrier, and I copied it down: 'The foreigner who happens to find himself in Afghanistan may consider himself blessed by God if he leaves that country healthy, unharmed and with his head still on his shoulders . . . '

I keep away from other Afgantsi – I'm always nervous they'll put me down. I have a very gentle character but I sometimes think that even I have turned into a cruel and aggressive person. We had to prepare young soldiers for their discharge back into the army. They'd hide in the hospital attics and cellars and we'd have to catch them and drag them out.

At the clearing centre the girls told me to whom you had to give a bottle of vodka in order to get a comfortable job. Those seventeen- and eighteen-year-olds taught me all sorts of things like that – and I'm forty-five.

At the customs I was made to strip stark naked. 'What's your job?'

'I'm a doctor – a bacteriologist.'

'Your papers!' Then: 'Open your cases. Let's have a poke around . . . ' All I was taking home with me was the same old overcoat, blanket, bed-cover, a few hair-pins and forks I'd come out with. They piled it all up on the table, looked at it and sneered, 'She must be mad – or a poet of some kind.'

I can't stand it back home either. It's worse than over there. There, when anyone got or brought something from home we'd all sit round the table and share it. The third toast was always drunk in silence, to 'absent friends'. We'd sit there with the mice playing round our feet and in our shoes. At four in the morning we'd hear a howling noise. The first time I heard it I jumped up and shouted, 'Wolves! Wolves!'

'It's only the mullahs saying their prayers,' the girls laughed, but for ages after that I always woke up at four in the morning. Do I want to move on again. I've applied to go to Nicaragua. Someplace where there's a war going on. I can't settle down to this life any more. War's better than this. It gives you a justification – or an excuse – for anything you do, good or bad. It's incredible, I know, but that's the way I catch myself feeling sometimes.

A Widow

The moment I saw him I knew he was the one for me. He was a tall, good-looking boy. 'He's mine, girls!' I asked him to dance the ladies' waltz, the one when the girls invite the gentlemen, and my fate was sealed.

I very much wanted a son. We agreed that if it was a girl I'd choose the name – I liked Olechka – and if it was a boy he'd choose between Artem and Denis. So Olechka it was.

'Will we have a boy?'

'Of course, just let Olechka grow up a bit.' I wish I'd given him a son too.

'Lyudochka!' he told me, 'don't get upset now, or your milk will dry up (I was breast-feeding) but I'm being posted to Afghanistan.'

'Why you? You've got a baby daughter.'

'If I don't go, someone else will have to take my place. "The party's wish is the Komsomol's command," as they say.'

He was a perfect army type. 'You don't discuss orders!' he used to say. His mother is a very dominant character and he got used to being obedient and submissive when he was young. Army life was easy for him.

We threw a goodbye party. The men smoked, his mother sat silent and I cried. The baby slept in her cot.

I met a madwoman in the street, a kind of witch, really – she was always wandering round the compound or the market. People said she'd been raped as a young girl, gone crazy and couldn't even recognise her own mother afterwards. She stopped by me.

'They'll send you your husband back in a zinky,' she said. Then she laughed and ran away.

After that, I knew something would happen. I didn't know what. I waited for him like the girl in that poem of Simonov's:

'If you await me, I'll return . . . '

Sometimes I wrote and posted him three or four letters a day. I felt that I was protecting him by thinking about him and longing for him. He wrote back that army life in Afghanistan was the same as everywhere else. Trust in fate, he told me, don't worry and keep waiting.

When I went to visit his parents Afghanistan was never mentioned. Not a word about it from either his mother or his father. It was an unwritten rule. We were all too scared to say the word.

Then, one day, I was getting Olechka ready for nursery school. I'd just given her a kiss when I opened the door to two soldiers, one of them carrying my husband's small brown suitcase – I'd packed it myself. I had an urgent feeling that if I let them in they would bring something terrible into our home, but if I could keep them out everything would be as it had been before. They were pulling the door open and I was pushing it shut.

'Is he wounded?' It was just a faint hope.

The military commissar came in: 'Ludmilla Iosifovna, with the deepest sorrow we must inform you that your husband . . . '

I didn't cry – I screamed. I caught sight of my husband's friend,

Tolya, and threw myself at him. 'Tolik, if you tell me it's true I'll believe it.'

He brought over the young cadet who was accompanying the coffin. 'Tell her . . . ' But the boy was shaking so much he couldn't open his mouth.

Women came to kiss me. 'Try to be calm. Give us your family's phone numbers.' I sat down and babbled out all the addresses and phone numbers, lots of them, all I could remember. Later, when they came across my address book, they found I'd got them all right.

We have a small, one-room flat, so the coffin was placed in the clubhouse. I threw myself over it. 'Why? Why? What harm did you ever do anyone?' I cried and passed out. When I came to again I looked at that box and remembered the crazy woman's words: 'They'll send him back in a zinky . . . ' I started shouting again. 'I don't believe this is my husband. Prove it's him. There isn't even a little window for me to see him through. Who have you brought me? What have you brought me?'

His friend was fetched again. 'Tolik,' I said, 'swear that this is my husband.'

'I swear on my daughter's life that this is your husband. He died immediately and without suffering. That's all I can say.'

I remembered something my husband had said: 'If I have to die I hope I don't suffer.' It's us who are left who will suffer.

There's a big photograph of him hanging on the wall. 'Take Daddy down for me,' my little girl asks, 'I want to play with Daddy.' She puts her toys round his picture and talks to him. When I put her to bed at night she asks, 'Who shot Daddy? Why did they just choose Daddy?' I take her to nursery school and when it's time to take her home she's in tears. 'I'm not leaving school until Daddy comes to fetch me. Where's my Daddy?'

What can I tell her? How can I explain? I'm only twenty-one myself. This summer I took her to my mother in the country, hoping she'd forget him.

I'm not strong enough to go on crying day after day . . . I watch a man with his wife and child, three of them going somewhere together and my soul begins to scream . . . 'If only you could get up for one single minute to see what a lovely daughter you've got.

This incomprehensible war is over for you, but not for me, and for our daughter it will never be over for she'll go on living after us. Our children are the unhappiest generation of all – they'll have to take responsibility for everything . . . Can you hear me?'

Who am I crying to . . . ?

A Mother

I always wanted a son. That way, I thought, I'll have a man of my own to love and be loved by. My husband and I got divorced – he left me for a young girl. I probably only fell in love with him in the first place because there was no one else.

My son grew up with my mother and me – we were two women and a little boy. I was always checking up to see who he was playing with. 'I'm grown up now, Mum,' he'd complain when he came home, 'and you're still treating me like a baby.'

He was as small as a girl, though, and skinny with it. He was a month premature and I couldn't breast-feed him. How could our generation be expected to produce healthy children? We grew up with air-raids, bombardments and starvation . . . He liked playing with girls – they accepted him the way he was and he didn't tease them. He liked cats, too, and used to tie ribbons to them.

'Can I have a hamster, Mum? I love the feel of their soft damp fur,' he said one day.

I bought him a hamster, and an aquarium with lots of little fish. When we went to the market he started again, 'Can we buy a day-old chick, Mum?'

I remember all that and wonder: did he really shoot people out there, that little boy we loved and pampered?

I went to visit him at training-camp in Ashkhabad. 'Andryusha,' I told him, 'I'm going to have a word with the Commandant. You're my only child and . . .'

'Don't you dare, Mum! They'll all laugh at me and say I'm a mummy's boy.'

'How do you like it here?'

'The lieutenant's great, he's just one of the lads, but the cap-

106

tain's quite likely to give us a punch in the face if he feels like it.'

'What? Grandma and I never once even gave you a smack on your behind!'

'It's a man's life here, Mum. Things go on here that you and grandma . . . Well, it's best you don't know about them.'

He was only truly mine when he was tiny. He'd jump in and out of puddles like a little devil, and I'd scrub him clean, wrap him up in a towel and cuddle him. I thought nothing could ever take him away from me and I wouldn't let anyone else look after him. But they got him in the end . . .

When he was about fourteen I persuaded him to go to technical college, to learn the building trade. I thought he'd have an easier time of it when he was called up – he might even avoid conscription and go on to higher education. His ambition was to be a forester. He was always happy in the forest, he could recognise birds from their song and knew just where to find which wild flowers. In that way he was just like his father, who's from Siberia. He was so fond of nature he even stopped them cutting the grass in the yard in front of the flats. 'Everything's got a right to grow!' Andryusha fancied the forester's uniform and cap: 'It's like an army uniform, Mum,' he'd say.

Did he really shoot human beings out there?

He often wrote to us from Ashkhabad. I've read one of his letters a thousand times. I know it off by heart:

'Dearest Mum and Grandma. I've been in the army over three months now and I'm doing fine. I can cope with all the things we have to do here and haven't had any complaints from above. Recently our company went to a field-training camp in the mountains 80 kilometres from Ashkhabad. They spent two weeks on a special course preparing for mountain warfare, including tactics and firearms practice. Three other lads and I didn't go with them. We stayed at the base because we've been working in a furniture factory nearby, building a new extension. In return our company is getting new tables from the factory. We've been doing bricklaying and plastering, both of which I'm good at.

'You asked whether I got your letter. Yes, I did, and the parcel and the ten roubles inside! We spent the money on quite a few meals in the canteen and bought sweets as well . . . '

I tried to cheer myself up with the hope that he might go on being used for building work. I didn't mind if they made him put up their own private dachas and garages*, just so long as he wasn't sent away.

This was in 1981. There were all sorts of rumours of wholesale slaughter going on in Afghanistan, but how could we believe that kind of thing? We knew very few people; on television we saw pictures of Soviet and Afghan troops fraternising, tanks strewn with flowers, peasants kissing the ground they'd been allotted by the Socialist government . . .

The next time I went to visit him at Ashkhabad the hotel was full. 'Fine, I'll sleep on the floor!' I said. 'I've come a long way to visit my son and I'm not budging from here!'

'OK, you can share a four-bed room. There's another mother in there who's come to see her son.'

This woman told me (and this was the first I'd heard of it) that they were selecting a new group of conscripts to go to Afghanistan. She told me she'd come with a large amount of money, ready to pay off someone who'd make sure her son wasn't among them. She went home a happy woman, and her last words to me were: 'Don't be a naïve idiot!'

My mother burst into tears when I told her the story. 'You should have gone on your knees and begged them! You could have offered them your earrings.' Those earrings, worth a few kopecks, were the most expensive things in our lives. To my mother, who'd lived more than modestly all her life, they were riches. My God, what have we been reduced to? If he hadn't gone some other boy would have had to take his place, some other boy with a mother . . .

Andryusha himself never understood how he came to be chosen for the paratroop battalion and Afghanistan. He was terribly chuffed about it, though, and didn't try to hide his feelings.

---

* An allusion to the widespread practice of officers using their men for private gain. His work at the furniture factory may well have been on the same basis, despite the reference to 'our company getting new tables'.

I know nothing about military matters, so perhaps there's something I don't understand here. But I wish someone would explain to me why my son was kept busy bricklaying and plastering when he should have been training for war. The authorities knew what they were sending those boys into. Even the papers published photographs of the mujahedin, strong men thirty or forty years old, on their own land and with their wives and children beside them... How did he come to join the paratroop battalion *one week* before flying off to Afghanistan? Even I know that they choose the toughest boys for the paras, and then put them through specially gruelling training. Afterwards the Commandant of the training-camp wrote to me. 'Your son was outstanding in both his military and political training,' he said. *When* did he become outstanding? And *where?* At his furniture factory? I gave my son to them and they didn't even bother to make a soldier of him.

We had only a single letter from Afghanistan. 'Don't worry, everything's lovely and peaceful here,' it said, 'It's beautiful and there's no fighting.' He was just reassuring us so that we wouldn't start writing letters to have him transferred. They were just raw boys, almost children, who were thrown into the fire and accepted it as a matter of honour. Well, that's the way we brought them up.

He was killed within a month of arriving in Afghanistan. My boy, my skinny little thing. How did he die? I'll never know.

They brought him back to me ten days after his death. Although I hadn't been informed, of course, my dreams during those ten days were full of my losing and not being able to find things. There were so many signs... The kettle whistled strangely on the stove. And I love house-plants, I always had lots on the window-sill, the cupboards and the bookshelves, but every morning, during those ten days, I dropped the pots when I watered them. They just seemed to jump out of my hands and break, so there was a perpetual smell of damp earth in the flat...

I saw the cars stopping outside our block – two jeeps and an ambulance. I knew straightaway they were coming to us. I opened the door: 'Don't speak! Don't say a word! I hate you! Just give me my son's body. I'll bury him my own way, alone. We don't need your military honours.'

Only a madman will tell you the whole truth about what went on there, that's for sure. There's a lot you'll never know. When the truth is too terrible it doesn't get told. Nobody wants to be the first to come out with it – it's just too risky.

Did you know that drugs and fur coats were smuggled in in coffins? Yes, right in there with the bodies! Have you ever seen necklaces of dried ears? Yes, trophies of war, rolled up into little leaves and kept in matchboxes! Impossible? You can't believe such things of our glorious Soviet boys? Well, they could and did happen, and you won't be able to cover them up with a coat of that cheap silver paint they use to paint the railings round our graves and war memorials ...

I didn't go over there with a desire to kill people. I'm a normal man. We were told over and over again that we were there to fight bandits, that we'd be heroes and that everyone would be grateful to us. I remember the posters: 'Soldiers, Let Us Strengthen Our Southern Borders!' 'Uphold The Honour Of Your Unit!' 'Flourish, Lenin's Motherland!' 'Glory To The Communist Party!' When I got home I caught sight of myself in a big mirror – over there I'd only had a small one – and didn't recognise the person staring back at me, with his different eyes in a different face. I can't define how I'd changed, but I had, outside and inside.

I was serving in Czechoslovakia when I heard about my transfer to Afghanistan.

'Why me?' I asked.

'Because you're not married.'

I made my preparations as if I were going away on ordinary army business. What should I pack? No one knew, because we didn't have any Afgantsi with us. Someone recommended rubber boots, which I didn't use once in my two years there and left in Kabul. We flew from Tashkent sitting on crates of ammunition and landed in Shindanta. The first thing I saw was the Tsarandoi, or Afghan police, armed with Soviet tommy-guns of World War II vintage. Soviet and Afghan soldiers were equally dirty and shabby and looked as though they'd just crawled out of the trenches – a sharp contrast to what I'd been used to in Czechoslovakia. Casualties were being loaded on to the plane. One, I remember, had shrapnel wounds in the stomach: 'This one won't survive, he'll die on the way,' I heard one of the helicopter crew, ferrying the wounded from the front line, comment casually. I was shocked how calmly they talked of death.

I think that was the most incomprehensible thing of all over there – the attitude to death. As I said before, the whole truth you'd never . . . What's unthinkable here was everyday reality over there. It's frightening and unpleasant to have to kill, you think, but you soon realise that what you really find objectionable is shooting someone point-blank. Killing *en masse*, in a group, is exciting, even – and I've seen this myself – fun. In peacetime our guns are stacked in a pyramid, with each pyramid under separate lock and key and protected by alarms. Over there you had your gun with you all the time – it was a part of you. In the evening you'd shoot out the light bulb with your pistol if you were feeling lazy – it was easier than getting up and switching it off. Or, half-crazy with the heat, you'd empty your submachine-gun into the air – or worse . . . Once we surrounded a caravan, which resisted and tried to fight us off with machine-guns, so we were ordered to destroy it, which we did. Wounded camels were lying on the ground, howling . . . Is this what we were awarded medals from 'the grateful Afghan people' for?

War is war and that means killing. We weren't given real guns to play cops and robbers with. We weren't sent to mend tractors and build houses. We killed the enemy wherever and whenever we could, and vice versa. But this wasn't the kind of war we knew about from books and films, with a front line, a no man's land, a vanguard and rear echelons, etc. You know the word *kiriz*? It's the word the Afghans use for the culverts, originally built for irrigation purposes. This was a 'kiriz war'. People would come up out of them like ghosts, day and night, with a Chinese sub-machine-gun in their hands, or the knife they'd just slaughtered a sheep with, or just a big stone. Quite possibly you'd been haggling with that same 'ghost' in the market a few hours before. Suddenly, he wasn't a human being for you, because he'd killed your best friend, who was now just a lump of dead flesh lying on the ground. *My* friend's last words to me were: 'Don't write to my mother, I beg you, I don't want her to know anything about this . . . ' And to them you're just a Russky, not a human being. Our artillery wipes his village off the face of the earth so thoroughly that when he goes back he literally can't find a trace of his mother, wife or children. Modern weaponry makes our crime even greater. I can kill one man with a knife, two with a mine . . . dozens with a missile. But I'm a soldier and killing's my profession. I'm like the slave of Aladdin's magic lamp, or rather the slave of the Defence Ministry. I'll shoot wherever I'm told to. When I hear the order 'Fire!' I don't think, I fire, that's my job.

Still, I didn't go there to kill people. Why couldn't the Afghan people see us as we saw ourselves? I remember their kids standing in the snow and ice, barefoot except for their little rubber slip-overs, and us giving them our rations. Once I saw a little boy run up to our truck, not to beg, as they usually did, but just to look at us. I had twenty Afganis in my pocket, which I gave him. He just knelt there in the sand, and didn't move until we'd got back in the APC and driven away.

On the other hand, there were instances of our soldiers stealing a few miserable kopecks from the kids who brought us water and so on . . . No, I wouldn't go there again, not for anything. I repeat: the truth is too terrible to be told. You lot, who stayed at home, don't need to know it, and neither do we, who were over there. There were more of you, but you kept quiet. Our behaviour there was a product of our upbringing. Our children will grow up and deny their fathers ever fought in Afghanistan.

I've come across fake veterans. 'Oh, yes, I was there . . . ' they'll say.

'Where was your unit?'

'Er . . . in Kabul.'

'What unit was that?'

'Well . . . er . . . Spetsnaz' [Special Forces, somewhat equivalent to the SAS in the public mind].

Lunatics in asylums used to shout, 'I'm Stalin!'; now, normal guys stand up and claim: 'I fought in Afghanistan.' I'd put the lot of them in the madhouse.

I prefer to be on my own when I think about those days. I have a drink, sit down and listen to the songs we used to sing. Those times are pages from my life, and, although they're soiled I can't throw them away.

The young vets get together and get very angry that nobody wants to know. They find it hard to settle down and find some kind of moral values for themselves. 'I could kill someone – if I knew I'd get away with it,' one admitted to me. 'I'd do it just like that, for no particular reason. I wouldn't care.' They had Afghanistan, now it's gone and they miss it.

You can't go on repenting and praying for forgiveness all your life. I want to get married and I want a son. The sooner we shut up about all this the better it'll be for everyone. The only people who need this 'truth' are the know-nothings who want to use it as an excuse to spit in our faces. 'You bastards! You killed and robbed and now you expect special privileges?' We're expected to take all the blame, *and* to accept that everything we went through was for nothing.

Why did it all happen? Why? Why? Why?

Recently in Moscow I went to the toilet at one of the railway stations. I saw a sign saying 'Cooperative toilet' [i.e. private enterprise]. A young lad sat there, taking money. Another sign behind him read: 'Children up to 7 years, invalids, veterans of World War II and wars of liberation – free.'

I was amazed: 'Did you think that up yourself?' I asked him.

'Yes!' he said proudly. 'Just show your ID and in you go.' 'So my father went through the whole war, and I spent two years with my mouth full of Afghan sand, just so we could piss for nothing in your toilet?' I said. I hated that boy more than I hated anyone all the time I was in Afghan. *He* had decided to pay *me*.

Civilian Employee

I flew home to Russia on leave. When I went to the baths [the Russian equivalent of a sauna or Turkish bath] I heard people groaning with pleasure, but their groans reminded me of the agonised moaning of wounded soldiers.

At home I missed my friends in Afghanistan, but after a few

days back in Kabul I was homesick. I come from Simferopol in the Crimea and have a diploma in music. People who are contented with their lives don't come over here. All us women are lonely and frustrated in some way. Try and live on 120 roubles a month, as I do, especially if you want to dress decently and have an interesting holiday once a year. 'They only go over there to find themselves a husband,' people often say. Well, what's wrong with that? Why deny it? I'm thirty-two years old and I'm alone.

The worst kind of mine was the one we called the 'Italianka'. You have to collect a person's remains in a bucket after an Italianka. I learnt about it when one of the boys came up to me and just talked and talked about seeing his friend being turned into mincemeat. I thought he'd never stop. When he noticed me getting frightened he said, 'I'm sorry, I wanted . . . ' A boy I'd never met, but he'd found a woman and needed to talk. I thought he'd never stop.

We have two women's hostels here: one's called the 'Cathouse', that's for women who've been in Afghanistan for two or three years; the other's known as 'Daisy', the idea being that it's full of innocent girls plucking petals and sighing 'he loves me, he loves me not'! Soldiers go to the baths on Saturdays; Sunday is for the women, but they're not allowed in the officers' bath-house. This is because women are 'dirty', yet those same officers want us for sex. They show us photos of their wives and children stuck up on the walls above their beds . . .

When a bombardment starts and those RS rockets whistle over your head you just shake with fear. Two young soldiers went on patrol with a dog, but the dog came back without them . . .

Everyone's at war here. Some are sick, in mind or body, others are wounded, but everyone's damaged in some way, no one escapes intact. When the bombardment starts we run to the shelters while the Afghan kids dance on the roofs for joy. As I say, everyone's damaged. Those kids even dance and sing when they see our casualties being carried out. We take presents to their villages, flour, or mattresses, or cuddly toys – sweet little rabbits and mice – but none of that makes any difference. Everyone's corrupted by war.

The first two questions I get asked back home are, 'Did you

get married out there?' and 'Do you get any concessions?' The only concession for us civilian employees is that our families get 1000 roubles if we're killed. When you go to the army store out there the men always push in first. 'Who the hell are you? We've got to get presents for our wives,' they say. And at night they expect us to go to bed with them . . .

You 'fulfil your international duty' and make money on the side. Everyone does it. You buy sweets, biscuits or canned food at the army store and sell it to the local shops. There's a tariff: a tin of dried milk goes for 50 afoshki, a service cap 400; a car-mirror fetches 1000, a wheel from a KamaZ truck 20,000. You can get up to 18,000–20,000 for a Makarov pistol; 100,000 for a Kalashnikov; and the going rate for a truck-load of rubbish from the garrison is 70,000–200,000 (depending on the number of cans). The women who do best here are those who sleep with the quartermasters, who live it up while the boys up at the front go down with scurvy and have to eat rotten cabbage.

In the amputee wards the men'll talk about anything except the future, according to some girls I know. In fact no one likes to think of the future here. Perhaps it's more frightening to die if you're happy, but it's my mother I'd be sorry for.

I've seen cats creeping between bodies, looking for something to eat, but still wary, as though the boys were lying there alive.

Stop me. I could go on talking for ever. But I've never killed anyone . . .

Private, Gunlayer

Sometimes I wonder how things would have turned out if I hadn't gone to the war. I'd be happy, I think, and wouldn't have found out things about myself which I'd rather not have known. Thus spake Zarathustra: Not only have I looked into the abyss but the abyss has looked into my soul . . .

I was in my second year at the radio-technical institute here in Minsk, but my main interest was in music and art. I was vacillating between those two worlds when I got my call-up papers. I have no will-power – by which I mean I'm not the sort of person who tries to meddle with his fate. If you do try to influence it you lose anyhow. My way, whatever happens you're not responsible – or guilty. I didn't want to go into the army, of course. The first thing I learnt about army life was that you're a slave. I felt the army took my personality away from me.

They didn't say it straight out but it was obvious we were going to Afghanistan. I didn't try to influence my fate. We were lined up on the parade-ground and they read out this order that we were 'fighters in the international struggle'. We listened very quietly – well, we couldn't very well shout out, 'I'm frightened! I don't want to go!' We were off to fulfil our internationl duty – it was all cut and dried.

It really started at the Gardez clearing-centre, when the *dembels* took everything of any value off us, including our boots, paratroop vests and berets. *And* we had to pay: an old beret cost us 10 foreign currency vouchers, a set of badges 25. A para's meant to have a set of five – one to show you're a member of a guards' regiment, the others are the insignia for the airborne forces and your para battalion, your class-number and your army-sportsman badge. They also stole our parade shirts, which they traded with Afghans for drugs. A gang of *dembels* came up to me. 'Where's your kit-bag?' They poked around in it, took what they wanted and there was nothing I could do about it. All of us in our company had our uniforms taken and had to buy old ones in return. The Quartermaster's department said simply, 'You won't be needing your new togs – they will, they're going home.' I wrote a letter home describing the beautiful Mongolian sky, the good food and the sunshine. But my war had already started.

The first time we drove out to a village the battalion commander taught us how to behave towards the local populace: 'You call all Afghans, regardless of age, "*batcha*", which means "boy", roughly. Got that? I'll show you the rest later.' On the way we came across an old man. 'Halt! Watch this!' The commander jumped down from the vehicle, went up to the old man, pushed his turban off his head, poked his fingers in his beard. 'Right, on your way, *batcha*!' Not quite what we'd been expecting. In the village we threw briquettes of pearl barley to the kids, but they ran away thinking they were grenades.

My first taste of action was escorting a convoy. This is exciting and interesting – this is war! I thought. I'm holding a gun and carrying grenades, just like in the posters! As we approach the so-called 'green' zone (scrub and bush) I, as gunlayer, look carefully through the gunsight. I see some kind of turban.

'Seryozha!' I shout to the chap sitting by the barrel. 'I can see a turban! What do I do?'

'Fire!'

'What d'you mean – fire?'

'What d'you think I mean?' He shoots.

'The turban's still there. It's white. What do I do?'

'Fire!!!'

We use up half the carrier's ammunition supply firing the 30mm gun and the machine-gun.

'Where's this white turban? It's a mound of snow.' Then: 'Seryozha! Your mound of snow's moving! Your little snowman's got a gun!'

We jump down and let him have it with our automatics.

It wasn't a question of, 'do I kill him or don't I?' Never. All you wanted was to eat and sleep and get it all over and done with, so you could stop shooting and go home. We'd be driving over that burning sand, breathing it in, bullets whistling round our heads – and we'd sleep through the lot. To kill or not kill? That's a post-war question. The psychology of war itself is a lot more urgent. The Afghans weren't people to us, and vice versa. We couldn't afford to see each other as human beings. You blockade a village, wait 24 hours, then another 24, with the heat and tiredness driving you crazy. You end up even more brutal than the 'greens', as we called our allies, the Afghan National Army. At least these were their people, they were born in these villages, whereas we did what we did without thinking, to people quite unlike us, people we didn't understand. It was easier for us to fire our guns and throw our grenades.

Once we were going back to barracks with seven of our boys dead and two more shell-shocked. The villages along the way were silent, the inhabitants had either fled into the mountains or gone to ground. Suddenly an old woman hobbled up to us, crying, screaming, beating her fists on the APC. We'd killed her son and she was cursing us – but our only reaction was, what's she crying and threatening us for? We ought to shoot her, too. We didn't, but the point is, we could have done. We pushed her off the road and drove on. We were carrying seven dead – what was she crying for? What did she expect?

We didn't want to know anything about anything. We were soldiers in a war. We were completely cut off from Afghan life – the locals weren't allowed to set foot in our army compound. All we knew about them was that they wanted to kill or injure us, and we were keen to stay alive. Actually I wanted to be lightly wounded, just to have a rest or at least a good night's sleep, but I didn't want to die.

One day two of our lads went to a shop, shot the shopkeeper and his family and stole everything they could lay their hands on. There was an enquiry and of course everyone denied having anything to do with it. They examined the bullets in the bodies and eventually charged three men: an officer, an NCO and a private. But when our barracks were being searched for the stolen money, etc, I remember how humiliated and insulted we felt – why all this fuss about a few dead Afghans? There was a court martial and the NCO and the private were sentenced to the firing squad. We were all on their side – the general opinion was that they were being executed for their stupidity rather than for what they'd done. The shopkeeper's dead family didn't exist for us. We were only doing our international duty. It was all quite cut and dried. It's only now, as the stereotypes begin to collapse, that I see things differently. And to think, I used not to be able to read 'Mumu' [a sentimental story by Turgenev about the relationship between a dumb peasant and his dog] without crying my eyes out!

War affects a person in a strange way: it takes some of his – or her – humanity away. When we were growing up we were never taught 'Thou shalt not kill'. On the contrary – all these war veterans, with rows of medals pinned to their splendid uniforms, came to our schools and colleges to describe their exploits in detail. I never once heard it said that it was wrong to kill in war. I was brought up to believe that only those who killed in peace-time were condemned as murderers. In war such actions were known as 'filial duty to the Motherland', 'a man's sacred work' and 'defence of the Fatherland'. We were told that we were reliving the achievements of the heroes of the Great Patriotic War against the Nazis, and who was I to doubt it? It was continually hammered into us that we were the best of the best, so why should I question whether what we were doing was right? Later, when I began to see things differently, my army mates said, 'Either you've gone mad or you want to go mad.' And yet, as I said, I was too fatalistic to try to change anything. (I was brought up by my mother, who was a powerful and dominant woman.)

At training-camp veterans from the Special Forces described to us how they'd stormed villages and slaughtered all the inhabitants. It seemed romantic. We wanted to be as strong and fearless as they were. I love music and books but I also wanted to storm villages, cut throats and boast about it afterwards. I've probably got an inferiority complex.

My actual memories, though, are very different... My first attack of sheer panic, for example. We were driving in the APC when the shelling started. The APCs came to a halt. 'Take defensive positions!' someone shouted. We started jumping off. I stood up, ready to jump, but another lad took my place and was killed by a direct hit from a grenade. I felt I was falling, slowly, horizontally, like in a cartoon... with bits of someone else's body raining down on me. It's fixed in my memory for ever, that's what's so terrible. I guess that's how you experience your own death, from a distance. Strange. I managed to crawl into an irrigation-ditch, stretched out and lifted my wounded arm. After a bit I realised I wasn't seriously injured, but I cradled my arm and didn't move.

No, I didn't turn into one of those supermen who storm villages and cut throats. Within the year I was in hospital, suffering from dystrophy. I was the only 'new boy' in our unit, the other ten, nearing the end of their tour of duty, were known as 'grandads'. I was forced to do all their washing, chop all the wood, and clean the whole camp – I never got more than three hours' sleep a night. One of the things I had to do was fetch water from the stream. One morning I had a strong instinct not to go – I had a strong feeling the mujahedin had been about that night, planting mines, but I was so scared I'd be beaten again, and there was no water for washing. So off I went, and duly stepped on a mine. It was only a signal mine, thank God, so a rocket went up and illuminated the whole area. I fell, crawled on . . . 'must get at least a bucket of water, for them to clean their teeth with. They won't care what's happened, they'll just beat me up again . . . '

That was typical of camp life. It took just one year to turn me from a normal, healthy lad into a dystrophic who couldn't walk through the ward without the help of a nurse. I eventually went back to my unit and got beaten up again, until one day my leg was broken and I had to have an operation. The battalion commander came to see me in hospital.

'Who did this?' he asked.

It had happened at night but I knew perfectly well who'd done it. But I wasn't going to grass. You just didn't grass – that was the iron law of camp life.

'Why keep quiet? Give me his name and I'll have the bastard court-martialled.'

I kept quiet. The authorities were powerless against the unwritten rules of army life, which were literally life and death to us. If you tried to fight against them you always lost in the end. Near the end of my two years I even tried to beat up someone myself. I didn't manage it, though. The 'rule of the grandads' doesn't depend on individuals – it's a product of the herd instinct. First you get beaten up, then you beat up others. I had to hide the fact that I couldn't do it from my fellow *dembels*. I would have been despised by them as well as by the victims.

When you get home for demob you have to report to the local recruiting office. A coffin was brought in while I was there – our 1st lieutenant, by sheer chance. 'He died in the execution of his international duty,' I read on the little brass plate, and remembered how he used to stumble along the corridor, blind drunk, and smash the sentry's jaw in. It happened regularly once a week. If you didn't keep out of the way you'd end up spitting your teeth out. There's not much humanity in a human being – that's what war taught me. If a man's hungry, or ill, he'll be cruel – and that's just about all humanity amounts to.

I only went to the cemetery once. 'He died a hero.' 'He displayed courage and valour.' 'He fulfilled his military duty.' That's what the gravestones said. There were heroes, of course there were, in the particular sense in which the word is used in war; like when a man throws himself over his friend to protect him, or carries his wounded commander to safety. But I know that one of those heroes in that cemetery deliberately overdosed, and another was shot dead by a sentry who caught him breaking into the food store (we'd all climbed in there at some time or other . . . I longed for biscuits and condensed milk). Forget what I said about the cemetery, please, tear it up. No one can say what's true about them and what isn't, now. Let the living have their medals and the dead their legends – keep everyone happy!

The war and life back home have one thing in common: neither are anything like the way they're described in books! I've created a world of my own for myself, thank God, a world of books and music which has cut me off from all that and been my salvation. It was only here at home that I began to sort out who I really was and what had happened to me. I prefer to sort it out alone, I don't like going to the Afgantsi clubs, and I can't see myself going to schools to give speeches about war, and telling the kids how I was turned from an immature boy into a killer, no, not even a killer, into a machine that just needed food and sleep and nothing else. I hate those Afgantsi. Their clubs are just like the army itself, and they have the same army mentality. 'We don't like the heavy metal fans, do we, lads? OK, let's go and smash their teeth in!' That's a part of my life I want to leave behind for ever. Our society is a very cruel one, which is a fact I never noticed before.

When I was in hospital over there we stole some Phenazipam – it's used to treat mental breakdown and the dose is one or two tablets per day. One night a couple of the boys took 30 between them, and at three in the morning went to the kitchen to wash the dishes (which were all clean). A few others and I sat there grimly, playing cards. Someone else pissed on his pillow. A totally absurd scene, until a nurse rushed out in horror and called the guards.

That's how I mainly remember the war – as totally absurd.

A Mother

I had twins, two boys, but only Kolya survived. He was on the 'Special Care' register of the Maternity Institute until he was eighteen, when his call-up papers arrived. Was it necessary to send boys like him to Afghanistan? My neighbour kept getting at me – and perhaps she was right. 'Couldn't you scrape a couple of thousand roubles together and bribe someone?' We knew a woman who did exactly that, and kept her son out. And my son had to go instead. I didn't realise that I could save my son with money. I'd thought the best gift I could give him was a decent upbringing.

I went to visit him for the oath-taking ceremony. I could see he wasn't ready for war. He was quite lost. I'd always been honest with him.

'You're not ready, Kolya. I'm going to appeal . . . '

'Don't appeal, Mum, and don't let them humiliate you. Do you really think it bothers them if I'm "not ready". They don't give a damn!'

All the same I made an appointment with the battalion commander.

'He's my only son. If something happened to him I couldn't go on living. And he's not ready, I can see he's not ready.'

He was sympathetic. 'Go back to your local recruiting office. If you can get them to send me an official request I'll have him transferred back home.'

I took a night flight home and got to the enlistment office at nine o'clock. Our Military Commissar is Comrade Goryachev. He was sitting there talking to someone on the phone.

'What d'you want?'

I told him. The phone rang and he picked up the receiver, looked at me and said, 'I won't do it.'

I begged him. I went on my knees. I was prepared to kiss his hand. 'He's my only child.' He didn't even get up from his desk. 'Please, at least write his name down!' I begged as I left. I still hoped he might reconsider, if he didn't have a heart of stone.

Four months went by. They were put through an accelerated

intensive three-month training course and suddenly I got a letter from my son in Afghanistan. Just four months . . . A single summer.

One morning I left the flat to go to work. They met me as I was going down the stairs. Three soldiers and a woman. The men were in front, carrying their caps in their left hands. Somehow I knew that this was a sign of mourning. I turned round and ran upstairs. They realised I must be the mother so they followed me upstairs. I went down in the lift – I wanted to rush into the street and run away, escape, put my hands over my ears and block everything out. By the time I reached the ground floor – the lift had stopped to let people get in – they were standing there waiting for me. I pressed the button and went up again . . . I got to my floor and ran to the flat, but in my shock forgot to slam the door shut. I heard them coming in. I hid in the bedroom, they came after me, with their caps in their left hands.

One of them was Goryachev, the Military Commissar. With what little strength I had left I threw myself at him like a cat.

'You are dripping with my son's blood!' I screamed. 'You are dripping with my son's blood!'

He said nothing. I tried to hit him. I can't remember what happened after that.

It was over a year before I felt I could face people again. Before that I was totally alone. I blamed everyone for my son's death – my friend who worked in the bakery, a taxi-driver I'd never seen before in my life, Commissar Goryachev. I realise that was wrong. Then I wanted to be with the only people who could know what I was going through.

We got to know each other at the cemetery, by the gravesides. You'll see one mother hurrying from the bus in the evening after work; another already sitting by her gravestone, crying; a third painting the railing round her son's grave. We talk about only one thing – our children, as if they were still alive. I know some of their stories off by heart.

'I went out on to the balcony, looked down and saw two officers and a doctor. Back in the flat I looked through the peep-hole to see where they were going. They stopped in our hallway and turned right. Was it to the neighbours? They had a son in the army, too. The bell . . . I open the door:

'"Has my son been killed?"

'"Be brave, Mother . . ." "Mother", they called me.'

'It wasn't like that for me. They just said: "The coffin's outside, Mother. Where shall we put it?" My husband and I were getting ready to go to work, the eggs were frying, the kettle was boiling . . . '

'Mine was called up, had his hair shaved off . . . and five months later they brought him back in a coffin.'

'Mine too . . . '

'Mine – nine months . . . '

'"Is there anything in there?" I asked the soldier accompanying the coffin.

'I saw him being laid in the coffin. He is there.' I stared at him and he lowered his eyes. 'Something's in there . . . '

'Did it smell? Ours did . . . '

'And ours. We even had little white worms dropping on to the floor . . . '

'Mine smelt only of fresh timber.'

'If the helicopter is blown up they collect the pieces. They find an arm, or a leg, and identify them by the watch, or the socks . . . '

'Our coffin had to wait outside for an hour. Our son was six foot six tall, he was a para. It was like a sarcophagus, a wooden coffin inside a zinc one. It took six men to get it up the stairs . . . '

'It took them eighteen days to bring mine home. They wait until the plane is full, the black tulip . . . They flew to the Urals first, then to Leningrad, and only then to Minsk . . . '

'They didn't send back a single one of his belongings . . . If only we had something to remember him by . . . He smoked – if only we had his lighter . . . '

'I'm glad they don't open the coffins, so that we don't see what has happened to our sons. I'll always remember him alive and in one piece . . . '

How can we survive? We won't live long with this pain and these wounds in our hearts.

'We're going to give you a new flat,' I was promised by the local authority. 'You can choose any empty flat in the area.'

I found one in the city centre, built of proper brick, not prefab concrete, with a nice modern layout. I went back to the town hall with the address.

'Are you out of your mind? That block's strictly for Central Committee members.'

'Is my son's blood that much cheaper than theirs?'

The local Party secretary at the institute where I work is a good man, and honest. I don't know how he managed to get access to the Central Committee on my behalf. All he said to me was this: 'You should have heard how they spoke to me. "All right, she's grief-stricken – but what's wrong with you?" That's what they asked me. I was almost thrown out of the Party.'

Perhaps I should have gone myself to get an answer from them?

'I'm going to the grave today. My son is there, with his friends, and mine.'

Private, Tank Crew

There's something wrong with my memory and I may have to drop out of my second year at college. Words and faces, even my own feelings, seem to escape me. All that's left are fragments, bits and pieces, as if there's something missing inside . . .

I remember these words from the military oath:

'I stand ready to defend my Motherland, the Union of Soviet Socialist Republics, when ordered to do so by the Soviet Government, and, as a soldier of the armed forces of the USSR, I swear to defend it with courage, skill, dignity and honour, not sparing my blood and even my life for the achievement of total victory over our foes . . . '

From my first days in Afghan . . .

I thought I was in paradise. For the first time I saw oranges growing on trees. I hadn't yet seen mines hanging like oranges from those same trees (the tank-aerial touches the trip-wire and triggers the bomb). When the 'Afghan wind' blows, your porridge is full of sand, the sun is blotted out and it gets so dark you can't see your hand in front of your face. A few hours later the sun comes out and you see the mountains again. Not a sign of war. Then – a burst of machine-gun fire, a mortar attack, the crack of a sniper's bullet, and two of your mates are dead. Sun, mountains, and the gleam of a snake in the sand.

You can't imagine what death is like even with the bullets whistling overhead. A body lies in the dust and you call out to it, because you can't take in what's happened, although a voice inside you says, 'That's what death is.' I was wounded in the leg, but not as badly as I thought. 'I seem to be injured,' I thought. I felt surprised but calm. My leg was hurting, but I couldn't quite believe that this had happened to me personally. I was still a new boy – I wanted a chance to fight and go home a hero.

Someone cut away the top of my boot and applied a tourniquet to my vein, which was severed. I was in pain but it would have been cowardly to show it so I kept quiet. Running from tank to tank means crossing an open space up to a hundred metres wide. There were shells flying about and rocks flying in all directions but I wasn't about to admit I couldn't run and crawl with the rest of them . . . I'd've looked like a coward. I crossed myself and ran, covered with blood. The battle lasted for another hour or more. We'd started out at 4 a.m., fighting didn't stop until 4 p.m., when we had something to eat. I remember my bloody hands tearing at the white bread. Later I found out that my friend had died in hospital from a bullet in the head. I kept waiting for his name to be mentioned at evening roll-call: 'Igor Dashko was killed while fulfilling his international duty.' He was a quiet boy and no 'Hero of the Soviet Union', but all the same, he shouldn't have been forgotten so immediately and completely, and just wiped off the lists . . .

Who was I talking about? Oh yes, Igor Dashko . . . I saw him laid out in his coffin. I wasn't even sad any more, but I looked at him for a long while so I wouldn't forget . . .

From my time back home:

We flew to Tashkent and went to the station, but couldn't buy tickets. That evening four of us slipped 50 roubles each to two conductors, who – lo and behold – found us seats in their train. They got 100 roubles each, nice work if you can get it, but we didn't care. We were laughing like madmen and thinking, 'We're alive, we're alive!!'

When I got home I opened the door, picked up a bucket and crossed the yard to fetch some water. Ecstasy!

I was presented with a medal at my college. Next day there was an article in the paper, with the headline: 'A Medal Finds Its Hero'. I laughed, they made it sound as though the Frontier Scouts had been searching for me for forty years. And I certainly never said that we 'went to Afghanistan dedicated to the dawn of the April revolution on Afghan soil'. But that's what they wrote.

I loved hunting before I went into the army. I planned to go to Siberia after I was discharged and become a professional hunter. Well, one day I went hunting with a friend of mine. He shot one goose, then we saw another, injured. He was trying to shoot it and I was racing after it, trying to save it. I was sick of killing and I still am.

There's something wrong with my memory. Just fragments, bits and pieces, as if there's something missing inside . . .

A Soldier

What was happening to my body didn't show on the outside, and my parents refused to let me be obsessed with something I couldn't do a thing about.

I went to Afghanistan with my dog Chara. If you shout, 'Die!', she falls to the ground. 'Shut your eyes!' she covers her face with her paws. If I was upset she'd sit herself next to me and cry.

I was bursting with pride my first few days over there. I've been seriously ill since I was a child and the army had turned me down. 'Why isn't this lad in the army?' people asked. I was ashamed, and hated the idea of people laughing at me. The army is the school of life and makes a man of you. Well, I got into the army and started applying to be sent to Afghanistan.

'You'll kick the bucket before the week's out,' they warned me.

'I still want to go.' I needed to prove I was the same as everyone else.

I didn't tell my parents where I was stationed. I've had cancer of the lymph glands since I was aged twelve and they've devoted their lives to me. I told them only the Forces Post Box Number, and that I was 'attached to a secret unit in a location that cannot be disclosed'.

I took my dog and guitar with me.

'How did you manage to end up here?' I was asked by the army security department.

'Well . . . ,' and I told them about all my applications.

'You actually volunteered? You must be mad!'

I've never smoked but I nearly took it up over there.

I fainted the first time I saw casualties, some of them with their legs torn off at the groin or with huge holes in their heads. Everything inside me was shouting, 'I want to be alive!'

One night someone stole a dead soldier's submachine-gun. The thief was one of our soldiers too. He sold it for 80,000 afoshki, and showed off what he'd bought with the money: two cassette-recorders and some denims. If he hadn't been arrested we'd have torn him to pieces ourselves. In court he sat quietly, crying.

When we read articles in the Soviet press about our 'achievements' we laughed, got angry and used them as toilet paper, but the strange thing is this: now I'm home, after my two years out there, I search through the papers to find articles about 'achievements' and actually believe them.

I thought I'd be happy when I got home, and planned big changes in my life. A lot of soldiers go home, get divorced, remarry and go off somewhere new. Some take off to Siberia to work on the oil pipe-line; others go to Chernobyl, or join the fire brigade. Somewhere where there's risk and danger. They have a craving for real life instead of mere existence. Some of our boys had terrible burns. First they go all yellow, then they shed their skin and turn pink.

Mountain operations? Well, you carry your gun, obviously, and a double issue of ammo, about 10 kilos of it, plus a mine, that's another 10 kilos, plus grenades, flak-jacket, dry rations. It comes to at least 40 kilos. I've seen men so wet with sweat they look as though they've been standing in torrential rain. I've seen the orange crust on the frozen faces of dead men. Yes, orange, for some reason. I've seen friendship and cowardice . . . What we did had to be done. No, don't start on that subject, please! There are a lot of clever dicks around now, but why didn't they tear up their Party cards, or shoot themselves in protest, while we were over there?

When I got home my mother undressed me and patted me all over. 'All in one piece, you're fine!' she kept saying. Yes, I was fine on the surface, but inside I was on fire. Everything irritates me now – even sunshine, or cheerful songs, or someone laughing. My old books, my tape-recorder, photos and guitar are all in my bedroom as before – but I've changed. I can't walk through the park without looking behind me. If a waiter in a café stands behind me to take my order I want to jump up and rush out – I can't stand anyone standing at my back. If someone provokes me my immediate reaction is, 'Shoot the little shit!' In war we had to do the exact opposite of what we'd been taught in normal life, and now we're meant to unlearn all the skills we learnt in war. I'm an excellent shot and my grenades always hit their target. Who needs all that now?

We believed we were there to defend something, namely the Motherland and our way of life. Yet back home, what do I find? My friend can't lend me a fiver because his wife wouldn't like it. What kind of a friend is that? I soon realised we were surplus to requirements. We might just as well not have made it – we're unwanted, an embarrassment. After Afghanistan I got a job as a car mechanic. Then I worked for the Komsomol at regional level in the ideology department, but I left there too, even though it was a cushy job. Life here is one big swamp where all people care about is their wages, dachas, cars and how to find a bit of smoked sausage. No one gives a damn about us. If we didn't stand up for our rights ourselves nobody would know a thing about this war. If there weren't so many of us, 100,000 in fact, they'd have shut us up, like they did after Vietnam and Egypt . . . Out there we all hated the enemy together. But I need someone to hate now, so that I can find some friends again. But who?

I went to the recruiting office and applied to go back to Afghanistan but I was refused. The war would soon be over, they said.

A lot more like me will be home soon. Yes, there'll be a lot more of us one day.

You wake up in the morning and you're glad you can't remember your dreams. I never tell my dreams to anyone. There is something that really happened that I can't talk about either . . .

I dream I'm asleep and see a great sea of people, near where I live. I look round and feel very cramped, but for some reason I can't stand up. Then I realise I'm lying in a coffin, a wooden coffin. I see that so clearly, but I'm alive, and I know I'm alive, even though I'm in a coffin. A gate opens and all the people pass through the gate on to the road, carrying me along with them. The faces of the crowd are full of grief but also a kind of mysterious ecstasy I can't understand. What's happened? Why am I in this coffin? Suddenly the procession comes to a halt. 'Give me a hammer!' I hear someone say. I suddenly realise I'm dreaming. 'Give me a hammer!' I hear again. The lid is hammered down, then I hear hammer-blows and one nail goes through my finger. I beat my head and legs against the lid. Bang – the lid flies off. The people watch as I sit up straight. 'I'm in pain!' I want to shout. 'Why are you nailing me down? I can't breathe in here.' They're crying but they can't, or won't, speak to me. And I don't know how to get them to hear me. I think I'm shouting, but my lips are glued together and I can't open them. So I lie back in the coffin. 'If they want me to be dead perhaps I *am* dead and must keep quiet.' Again someone says, 'Give me a hammer!'

The Third Day

Author: 'In the beginning God created the heaven and the earth . . .

And God called the light Day, and the darkness he called Night.

And the evening and the morning were the first day.

And God said, Let there be a firmament in the midst of the waters, and let it divide the waters from the waters . . .

And God called the firmament Heaven. And the evening and the morning were the second day.

And God said, Let the waters under the heaven be gathered together unto one place, and let the dry land appear; and it was so . . .

And the earth brought forth grass, the herb yielding seed after his kind, and the tree yielding fruit, whose seed was in itself, after his kind . . .

And the evening and the morning were the third day.'

What am I looking for in the scriptures? Questions, or answers? Which questions and which answers? How much humanity is there in man? A great deal, according to some; very little, say others.

Perhaps my Leading Character will be able to help me. I wait by the phone all day, but it is evening before he calls.

Leading character: 'So the whole thing was a stupid mistake, was it? Do you realise what that means to me and the rest of us? I went over there an ordinary Soviet bloke, sure the Motherland wouldn't betray us or lie to us. You can't stop a madman going mad. Some people say we went through a form of purgatory, others call it a cesspit. A plague on both your houses, is what I say! I want to live! I love life! I'll soon have a baby son and I'm going to call him Alyoshka, in memory of my friend. To my dying day I won't forget how I carried him, his head, and his legs, and his arms, all separate, and his flayed skin . . . If it's a girl I'll still call her Alyoshka . . .

So it was all just a stupid mistake, was it? But we weren't cowards, and we didn't betray you, did we? I won't phone again, I can't go on living in the past. I've forgotten everything, forgotten it all. You can't stop a madman going mad . . . No, I won't shoot myself. I'm going to have a baby son . . . Alyoskha . . . I want to live! That's it! Goodbye! . . .

Author: He put down the receiver, but I went on talking to him for a long time. Hello, I'm listening . . .

'And the evening and the morning . . . '

Major commanding a Mountain Infantry Company

A lot of people now claim it was all a waste of time. I suppose they want to carve 'It Was All In Vain' on the gravestones.

We did our killing over there but we're being condemned for it at home. Casualties were flown back to Soviet airports and unloaded in secret so the public wouldn't find out. You say that's all in the past now, do you? But your 'past' is very recent. I came home on leave in 1986. 'So you get a nice suntan, go fishing and earn fantastic amounts of money, do you?' people asked me. How could they be expected to know the truth, when the media kept quiet.

Even the air is different over there. I still smell it in my dreams. 'We were an occupying force' – that's what the newspapers claim now. If so, why did we give them food and medicine? We'd arrive in a village, and they'd all be happy to see us. We'd leave, and they'd be equally happy to see us go. I never understood why they were always so happy.

Once we stopped a bus for a security check. I heard the dry click of a pistol and one of my men fell to the ground. We turned

him on his back and saw a bullet had gone through his heart . . .
I felt like mortaring the lot of them. We searched the bus but
didn't find the pistol or anything else, except copper kettles and
baskets full of fruit being taken to market. The passengers were
all women, but someone killed my man . . .

Go on! Carve 'It Was All In Vain!' on the gravestones . . .

We were on foot, on a routine patrol. I tried to shout 'Halt!'
but for some reason I was struck dumb. We carried on and bang!
Some moments later I lost consciousness; then I realised I was at
the bottom of the crater. I tried to crawl but I didn't have the
strength and the others overtook me. I wasn't in pain, though. I
managed to crawl 40 yards or so, until I heard someone say, 'Sit!
It's safe now.' I tried to sit like the others, then I saw my legs
were gone. I dragged my gun towards me to shoot myself but
someone snatched it out of my hand. 'The major's lost his legs!'
I heard him say, and then, 'I'm sorry for the major.' When I heard
that word 'sorry' pain raced through my whole body, such a
dreadful pain that I began to howl.

Even now, here at home, I never take the path through the
forest – I stick to asphalt and concrete. I'm scared of grass.
There's a soft, springy lawn by our house but it still frightens me.

In hospital we men who'd lost both legs asked to be put together
in one ward. There were four of us. Two wooden legs stood by
each bed, eight wooden legs in total. On 23 February, Soviet
Army Day, some schoolgirls came with their teacher to give us
flowers. They stood there crying. None of us ate a thing or said
a word for two days afterwards.

Some stupid relative or other came to visit and brought a cake.

'It was all a waste of time, boys!' he said. 'Don't worry, though,
you'll get a nice pension and sit and watch television all day long!'

'Get out!' Four crutches flew at his head.

Some time after that one of the four tried to hang himself in
the toilet. He wound one end of a sheet round his neck and tied
the other to a window-handle. He'd received a letter from his
girlfriend: 'You know, Afgantsi are out of fashion now,' she'd
written. And he'd lost both his legs . . .

Go on! Carve 'It Was All In Vain!' on the gravestones.

A Nurse

When I got back home all I felt like doing was sitting in front of the mirror, brushing my hair. I wanted to have a baby, wash nappies and listen to baby-talk. The doctors advised against it. 'Your heart can't take the strain,' they said – and my baby girl was born by Caesarean section because I did actually have a heart attack. 'No one accepts our poor health is the result of Afghanistan,' a friend wrote to me. 'They think that if we weren't wounded we weren't affected.'

The way I was recruited was quite incredible. In 1982 I was in my third year of a correspondence course in the university philology faculty. I was summoned to the enlistment office:

'We need nurses in Afghanistan. How do you feel about volunteering? You'd get one and a half times your normal salary, plus foreign currency vouchers.'

'But I'm a student now.' After my training I'd worked as a nurse while studying to become a teacher, which was what I discovered I really wanted to be.

'You're a member of the Komsomol,* aren't you?'

'Yes.'

'Think it over.'

'I don't need to. I want to go on studying.'

'I advise you to think it over a bit longer than that. If you don't, we'll give the university a call and tell them what kind of Komsomolka you really are. The Motherland demands . . . '

My neighbour on the flight from Tashkent to Kabul was a girl returning from leave. 'Have you brought an iron and a hot-plate with you?' she asked.

'I thought I was going to a war . . . '

'Oh God! Another romantic idiot! I suppose you like reading war-stories?'

'I hate them.'

'Why are you here, then?'

That bloody 'Why?' followed me for my whole two years out there.

* Communist Union of Youth. Until recently, membership was almost unavoidable.

The clearing-centre was a long row of tents. In the canteen tent they served buckwheat porridge and handed out vitamin tablets you couldn't buy for love or money in the Soviet Union.

'You're a pretty little thing. What are you doing here?' a middle-aged officer asked me.

I burst into tears.

'Who's been upsetting you?'

'You!'

'Me?'

'You're the fourth person today to ask me what I'm doing here.'

I flew from Kabul to Kunduz by plane, and from Kunduz to Faizabad by helicopter. Whenever I mentioned Faizabad the reaction was, 'What? It's all shooting and killing there – you're a dead duck!' I saw Afghanistan from the air. It's a big and beautiful country, with mountains, and mountain rivers, which reminded me of the Caucasus, and vast open spaces like so much of our own country. I fell in love with it.

In Faizabad I was the theatre sister and also put in charge of the surgical ward. The field-hospital consisted entirely of tents. My very first operation there was on an old Afghan woman with a damaged subclavian artery. When I looked for surgical clamps I discovered there weren't any, so we had to hold the wound together with our fingers. When you touched the surgical thread it crumbled into dust – it hadn't been replaced since the end of the last war in 1945.

All the same, we saved the old woman. That evening I looked into the post-op ward with the surgeon to find out how she was feeling. She was lying there with her eyes open, and when she saw us her lips started moving. I thought she was trying to say something – until she spat a gob of phlegm at us. I couldn't understand what right she had to hate us. I went rigid with shock: we'd saved her life and she . . .

The wounded were brought in by helicopter. You heard it and started running.

The temperature in the operating theatre rose to 40° Celsius. It was so hot you could hardly breathe; the cloth you wiped away the surgeons' sweat with was itself dripping into the open wound. A non-sterile orderly gave them drinks through a straw inserted through the mask. There was a shortage of plasma, so a soldier was called to donate some. He lay down right there in the theatre and gave blood. The medical orderlies knew nothing about sterile conditions. Once I was racing back and forth between two tables when the lamp over one of them suddenly flickered off. An orderly changed the bulb with his sterile gloves and started to put his hands back into the wound.

'Get out!'

'What's the problem?'

'Out! This patient has an open rib-cage! Out!'

Sometimes we were operating for 24 or even 48 hours at a stretch. If it wasn't the war-wounded, it was the self-mutilators, soldiers who shot themselves in the knee or fingers. A sea of blood and a shortage of cotton-wool . . .

Such men were generally despised, even by us medics. 'There are lads getting killed out there, and you want to go home to Mummy? You think you'll be sent back home? Why didn't you shoot yourself in the head? I would, if I were you!' That was the sort of thing I used to say, I promise you. At the time they seemed the most contemptible of cowards; now I'm beginning to realise that perhaps it was a protest as well, and an unwillingness to kill other people.

I came home in 1984.

'Do you think we should be out there?' I was asked, rather hesitantly, by a boy I knew.

'If we weren't, the Americans would be!' I answered furiously. As if that proved anything!

At the time we thought about such questions amazingly little. We kept our eyes shut. Or rather, all we saw were our wounded, mutilated and horribly burnt patients, and we learnt how to hate, but not to think. I'd look out of the helicopter and see the mountain-sides covered with red poppies and other flowers whose names I never found out, and I realised I no longer loved all that beauty. In May, with its scorching heat, I'd look at the empty, dry earth with a kind of spiteful pleasure. 'That's what you deserve! We're suffering and being killed because of you!' I thought I hated it.

Injuries from fire-arms, mines . . . The helicopters never stopped coming, or the boys being carried in on stretchers, some covered with a sheet.

'Dead or wounded?'

'Well, not wounded . . . '

'What, then?' I turn down the edge of the sheet and see a skeleton held together by skin. We often had such cases from the remote outposts.

'What happened to you?'

'I gave him his tea and it had a fly in it.'

'Who's "him"?'

'I took a "grandad" his tea, and a fly flew out of it. They beat me up and didn't let me eat for a fortnight.'

Christ! So much blood being spilt, and they do this to a young soldier far from home.

In Kunduz two 'grandads' forced a new recruit to dig a hole one night and stand in it. They buried him up to his neck, with only his head sticking out of the ground, and urinated over him all night long. When they dug him out in the morning he shot them both dead. The case was the subject of a special Order of the Day, which was published throughout the army.

Christ! So much blood, and they do this.

The things I'm telling you are all horrible, but I wonder why it's only the horror I seem to remember? There was a lot of friendship and mutual support out there, and heroism too. Do you think I was too prejudiced by that old Afghan woman who spat at us? There's more to that story, in fact . . . She was brought in from a village which our Spetsnaz had dealt with. She was the only one left alive. And if you want to go right back to the beginning, it all started when two of our helicopters were destroyed by machine-gunfire from that same village, and the pilots were finished off with pitch-forks. Who started it, and why, and when? We didn't try and work it all out, we were just so sorry for our own people.

One of our doctors was sent into action, to actually fight. The first time he came back he was crying. 'All my life I've been trained to heal people, but today I killed them. How could I do that?' Within a month he was analysing his feelings quite calmly:

'You start firing and suddenly it's exciting. Take that, and that, and that!'

Rats used to drop on to us at night, so we put muslin netting round our beds. The flies were as big as tea-spoons but we got used to them. Man is the most adaptable creature on earth.

The girls used to dry out scorpions and use them as jewellery. They chose big fat ones, and either stuck them on a pin or threaded them on to cotton. I spent my spare time 'weaving', as I called it, unravelling the thread from parachute shroud-lines and sterilising it ready for stitching up wounds. When I came back from leave I brought with me a suitcase full of surgical needles, clamps and thread. Crazy! And this time I remembered to bring a hot-plate and my iron – so I wouldn't have to dry my wet gown with my body-heat.

At night we'd sit together, preparing cotton-wool balls and washing and drying the used gauze bandages. We were one big family and we guessed, even then, that when we got home we'd be a lost and unwanted generation. There was the eternal question, for example, of why so many women were drafted into Afghanistan for the duration? To begin with we were just a bit puzzled when dozens of 'cleaners', 'librarians' and 'hotel workers' started arriving, often one cleaner for two or three prefabs, or one librarian for a few shelves of shabby old books? Well, why do you think? We professionals kept away from such women, although they didn't bother us personally.

I fell in love with a man there and we became lovers. He's still alive, although I've lied to my husband and told him he was killed.

'Did you ever meet a live muj?' my younger brother asked me when I got home. 'Did he look like a bandit and have a dagger between his teeth?'

'I did. But he was a good-looking boy with a degree from Moscow University.' My brother imagined a mixture of a *basmach* and a mountain tribesman straight out of Tolstoy's 'Hadji-Murat'.*

---

* Basmach: A Central Asian partisan fighting for independence in the Civil War after the Revolution. Tolstoy's story deals with a similar war of resistance to Tsarist rule in the Caucasus.

Another question: 'But why *did* you work two or three days and nights at a stretch? You were earning good pay for your eight hours' work. Why didn't you just go off duty?'

'You don't understand a thing!' I'd say.

They didn't. But I know I'll never be needed the way I was needed there.

I saw the most incredible rainbows there, great high columns of colour all over the sky. I'll never see rainbows like those again, covering the whole sky.

A Mother

I was a happy young woman with two lovely boys. Yura was twelve years old when Sasha went into the army at eighteen.

'I wonder where you'll be sent, Sasha?'

'I'll go wherever the Motherland needs me.'

'You see what a fine boy your brother is, Yura!' I said proudly.

When Sasha's call-up papers came Yura ran to me:

'Will Sasha be going to the war, Mum?'

'Wars kill, my love,' I told him.

'Just you see, Mum, he'll come back with a medal, the one "For Valour",' and off he went to play with his friends, 'fighting the mujahedin'. Rat-ta-ta-tat . . . Rat-ta-ta-tat . . . That evening he came home. 'Do you think the war will be over before I'm eighteen, Mum?'

'I hope so.'

'Our Sasha's lucky – he'll be a hero. You should have had me first and then him.'

When we got Sasha's suitcase back all it had in it was a pair of blue underpants, a toothbrush, half a bar of soap and a soap-dish. We were given a certificate of identification.

'Your son died in hospital.'

One phrase goes round and round in my brain like a gramophone record: 'I'll go wherever the Motherland needs me.'

They carried the coffin in and then out again as if it were empty.

When they were little, whether I called 'Sasha!' or 'Yura!' they'd both come running. Now I called: 'Sasha!', but the coffin was silent. 'Where have you been, Yurochka?'

'When you call him like that, Mum, I want to run to the other end of the world.'

He ran away from the cemetery, too, and we had a job finding him.

They sent us Sasha's four decorations, including his medal 'For Valour'.

'Look at this medal, Yura!'

'I see it, Mum, but our Sasha can't.'

It's three years now since my son died and I haven't dreamt about him once. I go to sleep with his vest and trousers under my pillow. 'Come to me in my dreams, Sasha. Come and see me!'

But he never does. I wonder what I've done to offend him.

I can see the school and the playground from my window, and Yura playing with his friends, fighting the mujahedin. But all I can hear is: Rat-ta-ta-tat . . . rat-ta-ta-tat . . .

1st Lieutenant, Interpreter

Two years were enough . . . I just want to forget the whole stupid nightmare. I never went there.

But the truth is, I did.

In 1986 I graduated from the military academy, took my accumulated leave and that summer went to Moscow to report for duty at the HQ of a certain important military organisation. It wasn't easy to locate. I eventually found the reception desk and dialled the three-figure number I'd been given.

'Hello? Colonel Sazonov speaking.'

'Good morning, Comrade Colonel! I am at your disposal. At the moment I'm down at reception.'

'Ah, yes, I know . . . Do you know where you're being posted?'

'To the DRA [Democratic Republic of Afghanistan]. Kabul.'

'Didn't expect it, eh?'

'On the contrary, Comrade Colonel!' And I was being completely honest, because for the previous five years it had been drummed into us that we *would* be going over there.

You know the movie image of an officer departing for war? The hurried preparations after an urgent phone call, the stiff-upper-lip farewell to his wife and children before he strides to the waiting aeroplane, its engines roaring in the pre-dawn shadows? Well, it wasn't quite like that. My road to war was paved with bureaucratic documents. First I had to get my orders, my gun and my dry rations. Then, in addition to a certificate that said I had a 'correct understanding of Party and Government policy', I required a service passport, visa, testimonials, instructions, vaccination certificates, customs declarations and ration cards. Eventually, however, I boarded my plane, settled down in my seat and heard a drunken major exclaim, 'Forward! To the mines!'

The newspapers informed us that the 'military and political situation in the DRA remains complex and contradictory'. Military opinion maintained that the withdrawal of the first six regiments was pure propaganda – there was no question of a total withdrawal of Soviet forces in the foreseeable future, and none of my fellow-passengers doubted that the war would last out our tour of duty. 'Forward! To the mines!' as the drunken major, already asleep, shouted again.

Well, I was a paratrooper and the army, as I soon found out, was divided into paras and the rest, known as *solyari* (a term whose etymology I never discovered). Many of our soldiers and NCOs, as well as some officers, had their arms tattooed. These tattoos were mostly rather similar, usually featuring an Ilyushin-76 with a parachute beneath it, but there were some variations: one I saw was a romantic scene with clouds, birds, a para hanging from his 'chute and the touching inscription 'Love the sky!' Among the unwritten rules of the paras was the following: 'A para kneels for two reasons only – to drink water with his hands, and to pay his respects to his dead friend.'

My war . . .

'Atten-shun! Your route will take you from your camp here, via the district party offices in Bagram, to the village of Shevan. Speed of the convoy will be dictated by the leading vehicle. Distance between vehicles to be dependent on speed. Code-words: I'll be known as Freza, the rest of you by the numbers on the sides of your vehicles. Stand at ease!' This was the normal routine before the departure of one of our agitprop expeditions. The CO might add, 'You are forbidden to remove your helmets or flak-jackets. Keep your gun in your hands at all times.'

I jump into my vehicle, a small, lightly armoured and easily manoeuvrable affair known over there as a *bali-bali*. *'Bali'* is Afghani for 'Yes'; when Afghans test their microphones they always say 'bali-bali' instead of our 'One two three four testing'. As an interpreter I'm interested in anything to do with language.

'Salto, Salto, this is Freza. Let's get this show on the road!'

Behind a low stone wall we find a single-storey building of brick and plaster. A red sign proclaims, 'District Party Committee'. There to greet us on the porch stands Comrade Lagmaan, dressed in Soviet khaki.

'Salaam Alekum, raik Lagmaan!'

'Salaam Alekum. Tchetour asti! Khud asti! Dzhor asti! Khair asti?' He intones the familiar phrases of traditional Afghan welcome, thereby indicating his intense concern with our state of health. No reply to these questions is required, although the identical phrases may be repeated.

The CO doesn't miss the opportunity to utter his favourite phrase: *'Tchetour asti? Khub asti?* Afghan's nasty.'

Comrade Lagmaan doesn't understand and, bewildered, looks at me. 'It's a Russian proverb,' I explain.

We are invited into his study. Tea is brought in metal teapots on a tray. Tea is an indispensable aspect of Afghan hospitality. Without tea work cannot begin and discussion is unthinkable. To decline a cup of tea is no less a snub than to refuse to shake hands on meeting.

In the village we are met by the elders and the eternally dirty kids (the youngest are never washed at all, in accordance with the Sheriat, their faith, which maintains that a layer of dirt protects them from evil influences). They are dressed in whatever rags they can find. Since I speak Farsi they all insist on testing my knowledge of the language. The test, as ever, is in the form of the question, 'What's the time?' My reply evokes a storm of pleasure: I really do speak Farsi, after all!

'Are you a Muslim?'

'I am,' I lie.

Proof is required. 'Do you know the *kalema?*' The *kalema* is the special formulation one utters to become a Muslim. '*La ilyakh illya miakh va Mukhamed rasul allakh*', I declare. 'There is no God but Allah and Muhammad is his Prophet.' '*Dost! Dost!* (A friend!),' the kids mutter, stretching out their skinny hands as a sign of acceptance.

They often ask me to repeat these words, and bring their friends, who also admiringly whisper, 'He knows the *kalema!*' Afghan songs blare out from the loudspeakers, which even the Afghans call 'Alla Pugacheva' [a universally popular Russian singer]. We soldiers hang out visual propaganda materials from our vehicles – flags, posters, slogans – and unfurl a screen for the film show. The medics put up tables and unpack their crates of medicines.

The meeting opens. A mullah in a long white robe and a white turban comes forward to read a *sura* from the Koran. Then he turns to Allah, begging him to protect believers from all the evils of the universe. Bending his arm at the elbow he raises his palms to Allah and we all copy his movements. Now Comrade Lagmaan begins to speak. His is a very long speech, a characteristic feature of Afghan life. They are all capable of making speeches and love to do so. There's a phenomenon known in linguistic jargon as 'emotional colour'. Well, an Afghan speech is not only coloured but highly decorated – with metaphors, epithets and elaborate comparisons . . .

(Afghan officers frequently expressed their surprise that our political workers used notes in their talks and discussions. At party meetings and political seminars our lecturers and propagandists relied on the same stiff and tired old phraseology and vocabulary learnt from countless books and pamphlets; for example, 'in the avant-garde of the wider communist movement', 'the importance of setting an example at all times', 'ceaselessly to put into practice', 'as well as successes there will be setbacks' and even the sinister 'some Comrades do not understand'.)

Long before I arrived in Afghanistan such meetings as ours in the village had become meaningless obligations; the villagers came for their medical check-ups and a free packet of flour each. The ovations and friendly shouts of '*zaido bod!*' – 'Hail to the April

Revolution' – were a thing of the past, as were the raised fists which invariably accompanied every speech in the early days, when the people still believed in our aims – the splendid ideals of the April Revolution and the brilliant future that it seemed to promise.

The children do not listen to the speech – they're waiting for the film. As usual, we have cartoons in English followed by two documentaries in Farsi and Pushtu. Their favourite movies are sentimental Indian love stories and adventures with lots of guns and violence.

After the film-show we distribute presents – today, toys and bags of flour. In fact we hand them over to the village headman who is meant to share them out among the poor and the families of war-victims. As he swears publicly that all will be done honestly and properly his son begins to carry the gifts to their house.

'Do you think he'll share things out fairly?' the CO worries.

'I doubt it. The locals have already warned us he's a grafter. Tomorrow it'll all be for sale in the shops.'

Command: 'Prepare to move off!'

'Vehicle number 112 ready, 305 ready, 307, 308 . . . ' The children see us off with a hail of stones. One hits me. '"From the grateful Afghan people", as they say,' I observe.

We return to our unit via Kabul. The shop-windows are hung with signs in Russian: 'Cheapest vodka'; 'Any goods at any price' and 'Russian Friends, Come to Bratishka [brother] for All Your Purchases!' The merchants call out in Russian: 'T-shirts!', 'Jeans!', 'A Grey Count dinner service for six places!', 'Trainers with velcro!', 'Lurex with blue and white stripes!' We pass barrows laden with our condensed milk, cans of peas, thermoses, electric kettles, mattresses, blankets . . . It's all so utterly, totally different from home.

Private

I don't recall any particular scenes from my life in Afghanistan. There were 200 of us in the plane; 200, all men. A person on his own and the same person in a group are two different people.

During the flight I wondered what I'd have to go through in the months to come.

I remember a piece of advice from our CO's farewell talk. 'If you're in the mountains and have a fall, don't shout! Fall as silently as a stone. It's the only way to protect your comrades.'

When you look up at the sky from a high crag the sun seems so close you could catch it in your hands.

Before I went into the army I read a book by Aleksandr Fersman called *My Memories of Stone*. I remember being struck by some of the expressions he used, such as 'the life of stone', 'the memory of stone', 'the voice of stone', 'the soul of stone', 'the body of stone', 'the name of stone'. I'd never realised that you could speak about stone as though it were alive. Over there I learnt that stone was as fascinating to look at as water or fire.

One of our instructions:

'When shooting an animal you should fire slightly in front of it so that it runs into your bullet. The same applies to a running man.'

We are in the mountains from early morning until late at night. You literally vomit from tiredness. First your legs, then your arms turn to lead, then they start to shake at the joints.

One of the lads had a fall. 'Shoot me! I can't walk!'

Three of us grab him and drag him with us.

'Leave me, you guys! Shoot me!'

'We'd shoot you all right, you fucker, but you've got your Mum waiting at home.'

'Shoot me!'

Thirst was a torture. You drink your water-bottle dry before you're half-way to wherever you're meant to be going. Your tongue is so swollen it sticks out of your mouth and won't go back – but you still manage to smoke. You get to the snow-line and look for melted water. You drink from a puddle, crunching the muddy ice between your teeth, forgetting about all those chlorine tablets and manganese ampoules you're supposed to take, oblivious of anything but crawling and licking the snow. A machine-gun's clattering away behind you but you go on lapping up your puddle. You gulp it down so as not to die thirsty! There's a body, lying face down in the water – it looks as though it's drinking too.

Now I look at the whole thing from a distance. What sort of person was I over there? I never answered your first question: how did I come to be in Afghanistan? I volunteered to 'go to the aid of the Afghan people'. Radio, TV and the press kept telling us about the Revolution, and that it was our duty to help. I got myself ready for war by learning karate – it's not easy, the first time you hit someone in the face, and hear the bone crunch. You have to step over a certain boundary inside yourself – then smash!

The first body I saw was an Afghan boy aged about seven. He was lying there with his arms out as though asleep. Next to him was his horse, completely frozen and with its stomach split wide open. What had the kid done – or the animal, for that matter – to deserve that?

A couple of lines from one of our Afgantsi songs:

'Why, and for whom, did they give their lives
Cut down by bullets and mines and knives?'

Two years after I got home I was still dreaming I was at my own funeral . . . or else waking up in a panic because I had no ammo to shoot myself with.

'Any medals? Were you wounded?' my friends asked. 'Did you kill anyone?' I tried to explain what I'd been through but no one was interested in that. I started drinking, on my own, to 'absent friends,' to Yarka, for example. I might have saved him. We were together in hospital in Kabul. I had a shoulder wound and shell-shock, but he'd lost both legs. There were a lot of lads there with legs and arms missing. They'd smoke and crack jokes. They were OK there, but they didn't want to go home. They'd beg to stay until the last possible moment. Going home was the hardest thing of all, starting a new life. The day he was due to fly home Yurka cut his wrists in the toilet . . .

I'd tried to cheer him up a bit while we played chess of an evening.

'Look on the bright side, Yurka,' I'd say. 'What about Alexei Meresyev in "A True Story"?* You've read it, haven't you?'

* Meresyev was a World War II pilot who lost both his legs in action but, equipped with artificial limbs, returned to the front to perform further acts of heroism.

'I've got a beautiful girl waiting for me,' he'd say.

Some days I just hate everyone I meet in the street or see through the window. I can hardly stop myself... well, let's say it's just as well those customs officers confiscated our guns and grenades. We did what we had to do, and are we now going to be forgotten about? Yurka, too?

I wake up at night and don't know whether I'm here or back there. Who was it described the insane as 'those whom life has taken by surprise'? I see my own life with an objective eye now. I've got a wife and a kid. I used to love pigeons, and early morning. Yeah, an objective eye. But I'd do anything to find happiness again.

NCO in the Security Service

My daughter comes home from school and said, 'Mama, no one believes me when I tell them you were in Afghanistan.'

'Why?'

'They're just amazed. They ask me who sent you there.'

I'm still not used to this sense of safety and I'm enjoying it. I'm not used to not being shot at and bombed, to being able to turn on a tap and drink a glass of water which doesn't stink of chlorine. Over there everything – bread, macaroni, porridge, meat, stewed fruit – tastes of chlorine.

I can hardly recall a thing about these two years I've been home. I do remember meeting my daughter again, but the rest just escapes me. It all seems so petty and trivial and irrelevant compared with what I went through there. OK, so someone bought a new kitchen table and a TV, so what? But that's the height of excitement here.

My daughter's growing up. She wrote to the CO of my unit in Afghanistan. 'Please send my Mummy back to me as soon as possible, I miss her very much.' Apart from her I can't get interested in anything now.

The rivers there are incredibly blue. I never realised water could be such a heavenly colour. Red poppies grow there like daisies do here, the mountainsides are like bonfires. Big camels gaze at everything like old men, and they never get frightened. A donkey got blown up by an anti-personnel mine – I used to see him in the market, pulling a cart full of oranges.

Damn you, Afghanistan!

I can't live at peace with myself any more. I feel different from everyone else. When I came home my friends and neighbours – all women – were forever inviting themselves over. 'Valya, we'll only pop in for a moment,' they'd say. 'Tell us, what kind of china can you buy there? What about carpets? Are there really lots of clothes and videos available? What did you bring back? Anything you want to sell?'

More coffins came over than cassette-recorders, I can tell you, but that's all been forgotten about . . .

Damn you, Afghanistan!

My daughter's growing up. We share a single room in a communal flat, although I was promised that when I got home we'd get a place of our own. I went to the housing committee with my documents.

'Were you wounded?' they asked.

'No, I came home in one piece. I may look OK, but that doesn't mean I'm not damaged inside.'

'Aren't we all? It wasn't us that sent you there.'

I was queuing for sugar one day and heard someone say, 'They brought suitcases full of stuff back with them and now they want special privileges . . . '

Once I saw six coffins laid side by side: Major Yashenko, his lieutenant and soldiers. The coffins were open, and they lay there with sheets over them; you couldn't see their faces. I never thought to hear men cry, even howl, the way they did there.

Big stone obelisks were put up where men were killed in action, with their names engraved on them, but the mujahedin threw them into the ravines or blew them up to wipe out every last trace.

Damn you Afghanistan!

My daughter's grown up without me. She spent those two years at boarding-school. When I went there her teacher complained about her bad marks. She wasn't doing well for her age.

'What did you do over there, Mummy?'

The women helped the men, I told her. There was a woman

who told a man, 'You're going to live.' And he did. 'You're going to walk.' And he did. She wouldn't let him send a letter he'd written to his wife. 'Who needs me, now I've lost my legs?' he'd written. 'Forget about me!'

'I'll tell you what to write,' she said. 'My dearest wife, my dearest Alenka and Alyosha . . . '

You want to know how I came to be there? The CO called me in. 'You're needed over there,' he told me. 'It's your duty!' We were brought up on that word, it's second nature to us.

At the clearing centre I came across a young girl lying on a bare mattress, crying. 'I've got everything I could possibly want at home – a four-room flat, a fiancé and loving parents.'

'Why are you here, then?'

'I was told things were going badly here, that it was my duty.'

I didn't take anything home with me – except my memories. Damn you, Afghanistan.

This war will never be finished – our children will go on fighting it.

'Mummy, no one believes you were in Afghanistan,' my daughter said to me again last night.

Private

Don't try and tell me we were *victims* of a *mistake*. I can't stand those two words and I won't hear them spoken.

We fought well and bravely. Why are we being treated like this? I knelt to kiss the flag and took the military oath. We were brought up to believe these things were sacred, to love and trust the Motherland. And I *do* trust her, in spite of everything. I'm still at war, really, although it's thousands of miles away. If a car exhaust goes off outside my window or I hear the sound of breaking glass I'll go through a moment of animal terror. My head is a complete void, a great ringing emptiness, like the long-distance telephone*

* In the Soviet Union a trunk call is signalled by a longer and harsher ringing tone than that of a local call.

or a burst of automatic fire. I can't and I won't just stamp out all that part of my life, or my sleepless nights, or my horrors.

Sometimes we'd drive around singing at the tops of our voices, calling out to the girls and teasing them. From the back of a lorry they all look great! That was fun!

There were a few cowards. 'I won't go!' they'd say. 'Even prison's better than war.'

'Take that!' We'd make their lives a misery and beat them up. Some of them deserted.

My first fatality was a chap we pulled out of a tank. 'I want to live!' he said – and died. It's unbearable to look at anything beautiful, like the mountains, or a lilac-covered canyon, straight after you've been in battle. You just want to blow it all up. Or else you go all soft and quiet. Another lad had a slow death. He lay on the ground and started to name everything he could see, and repeat it, like a child who's just learning to talk: 'Mountains . . . tree . . . bird . . . sky . . . ' Until the end.

A young Tsarandui (that's Afghani for policeman) said to me once, 'Allah will take me to heaven when I die, but where will you end up?'

Where I ended up was hospital. My father came to see me there in Tashkent.

'You've got the right to stay in the Soviet Union if you've been wounded,' he told me.

'How can I stay here when my friends are over there?'

He's a communist, a party member, but he went to church and lit a candle.

'What did you do that for, Dad?'

'I need something to put my faith in. Who else can I pray to for your safe return?'

The lad in the bed next to mine was from Dushanbe [Soviet Tadjikistan]. His mother came to visit him with cognac and baskets of fruit.

'I want you home, son. Who do I have to go and see?'

'Look, Mum, let's just drink to our health and leave it at that.'

Perhaps she's alive, my daughter, somewhere far away from here . . . I'd be happy wherever she was, just as long as she's alive. I want it so much it's all I ever think of.

I dreamt she came home, took a chair and sat in the middle of the room. She had lovely long hair falling to her shoulders. She pushed it out of her face. 'Mama, why do you keep calling me over and over again, you know I can't come to you. I have a husband now, and two children . . . I have a family.'

Even in my dream I remembered that about a month after we buried her I started thinking she'd been kidnapped, not killed. Whenever we went for a walk people used to turn round and look at her, she was so tall and lovely, and her hair just poured. Anyway, no one took me seriously, but I had a sign that she was alive . . .

I'm a medic and I've always thought of it as a sacred profession. I loved my daughter and pushed her in the same direction. Now I blame myself – if she'd been in some other line of work she'd have stayed at home and be alive now. It's just the two of us now, my husband and I, no other children. It's a completely empty existence. We sit at home in the evening and watch television. Sometimes we don't say a word to each other all night. When I start singing, and crying, my husband groans and goes out for a walk. You can't imagine the pain in my heart. In the morning I don't want to get up but I have to go to work. Sometimes I think I'll just stay in bed and wait until they come and take me to her.

I've got a dreadfully vivid imagination. I feel I'm constantly with her and she's changing all the time. We even read together although now I prefer books about plants and animals, anything but people.

I thought nature would help me, and springtime . . . We went for walks, my husband and I, saw the violets in bloom and the tiny leaves unfurling on the trees, but I began to cry. The beauty of nature and the joy of life hit me so hard. I was frightened by the passing of time. I knew it would take her, and the memory of her, away from me. Some things about her are receding already, the things she used to say, the way she smiled. I collected the stray hairs from her suit and kept them in a matchbox.

'What are you doing that for?' my husband wanted to know.

'Let me do it. It's all there is left of her.'

I'll be sitting at home sometimes and I'll hear her voice, suddenly and clearly: 'Don't cry, Mama.' I look round but there's no one there. So I go on thinking about her. I see her lying there, the grave already dug and the earth ready to receive her. I kneel next to her: 'My darling little girl, my darling little girl. What's happened to you? Where are you? Where have you gone?' But we're still together, as if I were lying in the coffin with her.

I remember that day so well. She came home from work and told me, 'The medical director called me in today.'

'And?' Even before she answered I knew something was wrong.

'He's had an order to send one member of staff to Afghanistan.'

'And?'

'What they actually want is a theatre sister.' She was theatre sister on the cardiology ward.

'And?' I couldn't think of anything to say, I just repeated that one word.

'I said I'd go.'

'And?'

'Someone's got to. And I'd like to be somewhere I'm really needed.'

We knew there was a war on, blood was being spilt, and nurses were needed. I burst into tears, but I couldn't say no to her. She looked at me sternly. 'We've both taken the Hippocratic oath, Mama,' she said.

It took her several months to get her papers ready. She came and showed me her references, including one which proclaimed she had a 'correct understanding of Party and Government policy', but I still didn't believe she was going.

Talking to you like this makes me feel better, as though she's here with us, and I'm going to bury her tomorrow. The coffin's here in the room. She's still with me. Perhaps she's still alive . . . All I want to know is – where is she now? Does she still have her long hair? And what blouse is she wearing? I need to know everything.

To tell you the honest truth, I don't want to see anyone. I prefer to be alone with Svetochka and talk to her. If someone comes in it spoils everything. I don't want to let anyone into this world of mine. I don't want to share her with anyone. One woman did come to see me once, from work. I wouldn't let her go, we sat together until it was so late we thought she'd miss the last bus; her husband phoned, he was worried about her too. Her son had been in Afghanistan, but he'd come back totally different from the boy they'd known. 'I'll stay home and help you with the baking, Mum,' or 'I'll go with you to the launderette, Mum.' He was scared of men and only got on with girls. She asked the doctor about it and he told her to be patient and everything would get better. I feel closer to people like her now. I understand them. I could have made friends with her, but she never came to see me again. She saw Svetochka's picture on the wall and cried the whole evening . . .

But I was trying to remember something . . . What was I going to tell you . . . ? Oh yes, the first time she came home on leave? No, how we saw her off when she first left? Her school-friends and colleagues came to the station to say goodbye, and an old surgeon bowed and kissed her hands. 'I'll never come across hands like these again,' he said.

She did come home on leave. She was thin and small and slept for three days. Got up, ate and slept. And again. And again.

'How are you getting on out there, Svetochka?'

'Fine, Mama. Everything's fine.' She sat quietly smiling to herself.

'What's happened to your hands, Svetochka?' I hardly recognised them, they were like a fifty-year-old's.

'There's too much work out there for me to worry about my hands, Mama. Before an operation I wash my hands with antacid. "Aren't you worried about your kidneys?" one doctor asked me. Men dying, and he's worrying about his kidneys. But don't you worry, I'm happy there, it's where I'm really needed.'

She went back three days early:

'Forgive me, Mama, but there are only two nurses left for the whole field-hospital. Enough doctors but a shortage of nurses. The girls are exhausted. I've just got to go.'

She was terribly fond of her grandmother, who was nearly ninety. We went to see her in the country. She was standing by a big rose-bush and Svetochka told her, 'Don't go and die on me, Grandma. Wait for me!' Grandma cut all the roses and gave them to her . . .

We had to get up at five in the morning. 'I haven't had enough sleep, Mama,' she said when I woke her. 'I don't think I'll have enough sleep again.' In the taxi she opened her bag and gasped. 'I've forgotten the key to the flat. What happens if I get home and you're not here?' I found her key in an old skirt and was going to send it to her, so she wouldn't worry about opening the door.

Suddenly she's alive. She's walking somewhere, laughing, enjoying the flowers – she loved roses. I still go to Grandma's, she's still alive. "Don't go and die on me. Wait till I get home!" Grandma still remembers that. Once I got up at night. On the table was a bunch of roses she'd cut that evening, and two cups of tea . . .

'Why aren't you asleep?'

'I'm having a cup of tea with Svetlanka'. She always called her Svetlanka.

I dream about her and in my dream I tell myself, 'I'll go and kiss her now. If she's warm it means she's alive.' I go to her, kiss her, she's warm – she's alive!

Suddenly she's alive, in another place.

Once I was sitting by her grave in the cemetery and two soldiers passed by. One of them stopped. 'Oh! That's our Sveta. Look!' He noticed me. 'Are you her mother?'

I threw myself at him. 'Did you know Svetochka?'

He turned to his friend. 'She had both her legs blown off during a bombardment, and died.'

I burst into tears. He was shocked: 'Didn't you know? Forgive me.' And he ran away.

I never saw him again. Or tried to find him.

Another time I was sitting near the grave and a mother came by with her children. 'What kind of a mother would let her only daughter go off to war at a time like this?' I heard her tell them.

'Just give away her daughter?' The gravestone had 'To My Only Daughter' carved on it.

How dare they. How can they? She took the Hippocratic Oath. She was a nurse whose hands were kissed by a surgeon. She went to save their sons' lives.

'People!' I cry inside me. 'Don't turn away from me! Stand by the grave with me for a little while. Don't leave me alone . . .'

Sergeant, Intelligence Corps

I assumed people would become kinder and gentler after all the bloodshed. Surely they wouldn't want even more killing?

But this friend of mine picks up the paper. 'They have returned from captivity,' he reads, and starts swearing.

'What's up with you?' I ask.

'I'd put 'em all up against the wall and shoot them myself!'

'Haven't you seen enough blood already.'

'They make me sick, those traitors. We were getting our arms and legs blown off while they were going round New York looking at skyscrapers.'*

Over there we were so close I never wanted to be away from him. Now I'd rather be alone. Loneliness is my salvation. I enjoy talking to myself.

'I hate that man. I hate him.'

'Who?'

'Me!'

I'm scared to go out of the house. I'm scared to touch a woman. I'd be better off dead, then they'd have put up a memorial plaque at my old school and make a hero out of me . . .

How we do go on about heroes and heroism! Everyone wants to be a hero. Well, I didn't. I didn't even know there *were* Soviet forces in Afghanistan. I wasn't interested – I was in love for the first time. Now I'm scared to touch a woman, even when I'm

---

* A reference to a few well-publicised cases of Soviet Army deserters who were taken from Afghanistan to the USA and other Western countries (where they were much fêted) but who later returned voluntarily to the USSR.

jammed against one in a crowded trolley-bus. I've never admitted that to anyone. I can't relate to women now. My wife left me. It was strange, the way that happened. I burnt the kettle. It was smouldering away on the gas and I sat and watched it getting blacker and blacker. My wife came home from work.

'What have you burnt this time?' she asked.

'The kettle.'

'That's the third one . . .'

'I like the smell of burning.'

She slammed the door and left, two years ago now, which is when I started being afraid of women. A man should never let a woman know too much about him. They'll listen kindly to what you have to say and condemn you later, behind your back . . .

'What a night! You were shouting again, killing someone all night long.' That's what my wife used to say.

I never got round to telling her about the sheer joy of our helicopter pilots when they were dropping their bombs. It was ecstasy in the presence of death.

'What a night! You were shouting again . . .'

I never told her how our lieutenant was killed. On patrol one day we came to a stretch of water and stopped the vehicles.

'Halt!' he shouted and pointed to a dirty bundle lying near the water-line. 'Is it a mine?'

The sappers came and picked it up: the 'mine' began to cry. It was a baby.

What to do with it? Leave it? Take it with us? 'We can't abandon him,' the lieutenant decided. 'He'll die of cold. I'll take him to the village. It's just nearby.'

We waited an hour. The village was 20 minutes away there and back.

We found them lying in the village square. The lieutenant and his driver. The women had killed them with their hoes . . .

'What a night! You were shouting and killing someone all night long!'

Sometimes I even forget my name and address, or what I'm meant to be doing. You pull yourself together, try and start living again . . .

I leave home and immediately start worrying. Have I locked

156

the door or haven't I? Did I turn the gas off? I go to sleep and wake up wondering if I set the alarm-clock. When I go to work in the morning and meet my neighbour, I can't remember if I've said Good Morning to him or not?

As Kipling said:

'Oh, East is East and West is West, and never the twain
shall meet
Till Earth and Sky stand presently at God's great Judg-
ment Seat
But there is neither East nor West, Border, nor Breed,
nor Birth,
When two strong men stand face to face, though they
come from the ends of the earth!'

When she married me my wife said: 'You've come back from Hell, from Purgatory, I shall save you.' In fact I'd crawled out of a dung-heap. And now I'm afraid to touch a woman. When I went to Afghanistan the girls here were in long dresses – now they're all in short ones. I can't get used to it. I asked her to wear a long dress, but first she laughed, then she got angry. That's when I began hating myself.

What was I talking about? Oh yes. About my wife's long dresses. They're still hanging in the cupboard. She never bothered to come and fetch them.

And I still haven't told her about . . .

Major, Battalion Commander

I've been an army man all my life. True soldiers think in a particular way, which doesn't include asking questions like whether this or that war is just or unjust. If we were sent to fight, that in itself meant it was both just and necessary. I always made a point of personally explaining to my men how important the defence of our southern borders was. I gave them my own ideo-logical grounding, you could say, in addition to their twice-weekly political education lectures. How could I admit to doubts? The army won't tolerate free-thinking; once you're in harness you live by command. From morning to night.

I never once saw a portrait of Tsiolkovsky [a Russian philosopher, scientist, and pioneer of the Soviet space programme], for example, or Tolstoy, on the barracks walls. What you'd find were pictures of people like Nikolai Gastrello and Alexandr Matrosov, heroes of our Great Patriotic War against the Nazis. Once, when I was a young lieutenant I hung up a picture of Romain Rolland in my room – I'd cut it out of some magazine or other. The CO came round.

'Who's that?' he said.

'Romain Rolland, a French writer, Comrade Colonel.'

'Well, take your Frenchman down, and be quick about it! Haven't we got enough heroes of our own?'

'But Comrade Colonel . . . '

'Dismiss! You'll go straight to the depot and come back with Karl Marx.'

'But he was a German.'

'Silence! 48 hours' arrest!'

Who cares about Marx? I myself used to point out to my men how useless foreign machinery was. 'What good is this foreign car? It'll fall to bits on our roads! *Our* industry and *our* cars and *our* people are the best!' It's only now – and I'm in my fifties – I'm beginning to realise that Japan might make a higher-quality machine-tool, the French might be better at producing nylon stockings, and Taiwan has the prettiest girls.

I dream I've killed a man. He's down on all fours, he won't lift his head. I can't see his face (and yet, however often I have this dream he always has the same face). Calmly I shoot him. I see his blood. I shout out, wake up and remember the dream . . .

The war is now being described as a 'political mistake', a 'crime', and 'Brezhnevite adventurism'. That doesn't alter the fact that we had to fight, kill and be killed. '*Judge not, that ye be not judged!*' What were we there to defend? Was it the April Revolution? No, even at the time I didn't think so, although I was terribly torn inside. So I tried to convince myself we were defending our garrisons and our own people there.

I remember paddy-fields on fire – war is the ally of fire – and peasants running away. You never see Afghan children crying. They're skinny and small and you can never guess how old they are, with their little legs sticking out of those wide trousers they wear.

You always had the feeling that someone was trying to kill you. It's something you never get used to like the melons and watermelons, which are enormous there, and so ripe they burst if you poke them with a bayonet. Dying is simple, killing is much harder. We never spoke of our dead. That was one of the rules of the game, if I can put it like that.

I always put a letter to my wife in my pocket before I went into action. A goodbye letter. 'Drill a hole in my revolver and give it to our son,' I wrote. And I had to take letters out of the pockets of my lads, and photos: Tanya from Chernigov, or Mashenka from Pskov, taken in provincial studios, all very similar, with those well-worn phrases painstakingly written on them: 'Write soon, my love, to your waiting dove', or 'Sent with a kiss for the darling I miss'. Sometimes they lay on my desk like playing-cards, the faces of those simple Russian girls . . .

I can't adjust to this world. I tried, but it didn't work. My blood pressure shot up – I need the stress, the edge, that contempt for life which sends the adrenalin racing round my veins. I need that fast pace, the excitement of going into attack . . . The doctors diagnosed clogged-up arteries.

I'd like to go back there, but I don't know how I'd feel about it all now. The broken-down and burnt-out old tanks and APCs – is that really all that's left of us there now?

I went to the cemetery, to walk round the Afgantsi graves. I met one of the mothers there.

Go away, major! You're old and grey. You're alive. My son's lying here, he died too young to shave.'

A friend of mine died not long ago. He'd served in Ethiopia and the heat ruined his kidneys. All his experiences over there died with him, but another friend told me what went on in Vietnam, and I knew others who served in Angola, Egypt, Hungary in 1956, Czechoslovakia in 1968. Now we go fishing, look after our gardens and live comfortably on our pensions . . .

I had one lung removed in Kabul. Near Khmelnitsky, though,

there's a hospital for long-term casualties who've been rejected by their families or who just can't face going home. One of them still writes to me. I had a letter from him not long ago. 'I'm lying here with my arms and legs gone. When I wake up in the morning I don't know if I'm a man or an animal. Sometimes I want to mew or bark. I have to bite my tongue.'

I need that pace, the excitement of going into battle. But who's the enemy now? I couldn't stand up in front of my lads nowadays and lecture them about how we're the finest and fairest in the world. But I still maintain that that was what we were aiming at. We failed. But why?

Private, Artillery Regiment

We didn't betray our Motherland. I did my duty as a soldier as honestly as I could. Nowadays it's called a 'dirty war', but how does that fit in with ideas like Patriotism, the People and Duty? Is the word 'Motherland' just a meaningless term to you? We did what the Motherland asked of us.

Nowadays they say we were an occupying force. But what did we take away with us, except for our comrades' coffins? What did we get out of it, apart from hepatitis and cholera, injuries and lives crippled in all senses of the word? I've got nothing to apologise for: I came to the aid of our brothers, the Afghan people. And I mean that. The lads out there with me were sincere and honest. They believed they'd gone to do good – they didn't see themselves as 'misguided fighters in a misguided war', as I saw it described recently. And what good does it do, trying to make out we were simply naïve idiots and cannon-fodder? Who does that help? The so-called 'truth-seekers'? Well, remember what Jesus said when he was examined by Pontius Pilate:

'"To this end was I born, and for this cause I came into the world, that I should bear witness unto the truth."'

'Pilate asked, "What is truth?"'

A question which is still waiting for an answer.

I have my own truth and it's this: that we were innocent, however naïve our faith may have been. We thought the new

government would give the land they had taken from the old
feudal barons to the peasants, and the peasants would accept it
with joy – but they never did accept it! We thought the tractors,
combines and mowers we gave them would change their lives, but
they destroyed the lot! We thought that in the space age it was
absurd to think about God – we even sent an Afghan lad into
space: 'Look, there he is, up there where your Allah lives!' we
said.

But Islam was totally unshaken by our modern civilisation. It
was all illusion, but that's the way it was, and it was a special part
of our lives which I treasure and don't want destroyed or tarnished.

We protected each other in battle, threw ourselves between our
friend and the mortar coming straight at him. You don't forget
something like that.

I wanted my homecoming to be a 'surprise' but worried about
the shock to my mother, so I phoned: 'Mum, I'm alive, I'm at the
airport!', and heard the receiver crash to the ground.

Who says we lost the war? Here's where we lost it, here, back
home, in our own country. We could have won a great victory
here too. We came back as strong as steel forged in the fire, but
we weren't given the chance – or the power. Every day someone
or other scrawls the same protest over the war memorial: 'Put it
in your Army HQ where it belongs!' And my eighteen-year-old
cousin doesn't want to go into the army 'to obey a lot of stupid
or criminal orders'.

What is truth?

There's an old woman doctor living in our block of flats. She's
seventy. As a result of all these articles nowadays, the revelations,
exposés, speeches, the avalanche of truth crashing down on us,
she's gone mad. She opens her ground-floor window and shouts:
'Long live Stalin! Long live communism – the glorious future of
all Mankind!' I see her every morning, no one bothers her because
she's quite harmless, but sometimes I'm terrified.

Still, we didn't betray the Motherland . . .

A Mother

The door-bell rings. I rush to open it but there's no one there. I'd thought it might be my son, home unexpectedly . . .

Two days later there's a knock at the door. Two soldiers.

'Is my son with you?'

'Well, no . . . '

It got very quiet. I fell to my knees in the hall, by the mirror. 'My God! My God! Oh my God!' I cried.

There was an unfinished letter on the table:

'My dearest son, I read your last letter and was very pleased with it. There's not a single grammatical error, but two punctuation mistakes, like last time. "I think" and "I did" are subsidiary clauses which are not followed by a comma. You should have written: "I think you'll be proud of me" and "I did what Dad told me". Now, don't be cross with your old Mum!

'It's hot in Afghanistan, dear, so do be careful. You catch cold so easily.'

A lot of people came to the funeral but they kept silent. I stood there with a screw-driver and wouldn't let anyone take it away from me. 'Let me see my son! Let me see my son!' I demanded. I wanted to open the zinc coffin.

My husband tried to commit suicide. 'I can't go on. Forgive me, mother, but I can't go on living.'

I tried to talk him out of it. 'We must put up a gravestone to him,' I said.

He couldn't sleep: 'The boy comes to me when I go to bed. He kisses me, puts his arms round me . . . '

By tradition we keep a loaf of bread for forty days after the funeral. It crumbled into little pieces within three weeks. That was a sign that the family would crumble away, too . . .

We hung our son's photographs everywhere in the flat. It helped me, but made it worse for my husband:

'Take them down. He's looking at me,' he would say.

We put up the stone, a good one, of expensive marble, and spent all the money we'd been saving for his wedding on the memorial. We adorned the grave with red tiles and planted red flowers. Dahlias. My husband painted the railings round the grave. 'I've done all I can. The boy will be pleased with it.' The next morning he took me to work. He said goodbye. When I came back from my shift I found him hanging from a towel in the kitchen, opposite a photograph of our beloved son.

'My God! My God! Oh my God!'

You tell me – were they heroes or not? Why must I bear all this grief? Sometimes I think, yes, he is a hero, and there are so many of them lying there in the cemetery, and at other times I curse the Government and the Party. And yet I myself taught him that 'duty is duty, my dear. We must do our duty.' At night I curse the lot of them, but in the morning I run to the cemetery and kneel by his grave and beg him to forgive me.

'Forgive me, dearest, for talking like that. Forgive me,' I say.

A Widow

I got a letter. 'Don't worry if you don't get any letters for a while. Write to the old address,' it said. Then I heard nothing for two months. It didn't occur to me that he might be in Afghanistan. In fact I was getting ready to go and visit him at his new posting.

In his next letter he didn't say a word about war, just that he was getting a tan and going fishing. He sent a photograph of himself on a donkey kneeling in the sand. I didn't realise they were being killed out there.

He'd never bothered much with our little daughter. He didn't seem to have any fatherly feelings, perhaps because she was too little. Then he came home on leave and spent hours sitting and watching her, but there was a sadness in his eyes which terrified me. Every morning he got up and took her to nursery school – he loved to carry her on his shoulders – and picked her up in the afternoon. We went to the cinema and theatre but most of all he enjoyed staying at home.

He was greedy for love. He resented me going to work, or even into the kitchen to do some cooking. 'Stay with me', he would say. 'Go and ask them for leave while I'm here. And we can do without stew today.' On his last day he deliberately missed the plane so we could have another two days together.

That last night . . . it was so good I burst into tears. I was crying, and he wasn't saying a word, just looking, looking . . . Then he said:

'Tamarka, if you have another man, don't forget this.'

'You must be mad! You're not going to be killed! I love you so much you'll never be killed.'

He laughed.

He didn't want me to get pregnant. 'When, if, I come back, we'll have another baby,' he said. 'How would you manage with two of them on your own?'

I learnt to wait. But I felt ill if I saw a hearse go by, and wanted to scream. I'd go home and wish we had an icon. I would have gone down on my knees and prayed, 'Keep him safe for me! Keep him safe!'

The day it happened I'd gone to the cinema, for some reason. I stared at the screen but saw nothing. I felt very agitated inside but without understanding why; I had a strong sense that people were waiting for me, that there was somewhere I had to go. I could hardly sit the film out. Later I learnt that it was then the battle was at its height.

I heard nothing for a week, and even had two letters from him. Usually I was overjoyed and kissed them, but this time I felt angry and frustrated. How much longer do I have to wait for you? I thought.

On the ninth day a telegram was pushed under the door. It was from his parents: 'Come. Petya dead.' I started screaming, which woke the child. What to do? Where to go? I had no money. Petya's salary cheque wasn't due until tomorrow. I wrapped my little girl in a red blanket, I remember, and went out. The buses weren't running yet.

I stopped a taxi. 'The airport.'

'I'm going to the park.'

'My husband has been killed in Afghanistan.'

Without a word he got out of the car and helped me in. First I went to my friend to borrow money. At the airport I couldn't get tickets for Moscow and I was frightened to show them the telegram. Suppose it was a mistake? If I believed he was alive he *would* be alive. I was crying, everyone was looking at me. Eventually they found us two seats in an old cargo plane.

That night I flew to Minsk. I had to get to the Stariye Dorogy district but the taxis didn't want to do the 150 kilometre journey. I begged and pleaded until one finally agreed: 'Give me 50 roubles and I'll take you.'

I got to the house at two in the morning. Everyone was in tears. 'It's true, Tamara. It's true.'

In the morning we went to the local enlistment office and got a typical military explanation: 'You will be informed when it arrives.'

We waited for two days and then phoned Minsk. 'You can come and fetch it yourselves,' they told us. We got to the district office. 'It's been taken to Baranovichi by mistake,' they told us there. That was another 100 kilometres away, and we hadn't enough petrol for the minibus we'd hired. By the time we got to Baranovichi Airport it was the end of the day and there was no one about. Eventually we found a watchman sitting in a hut.

'We've come to . . . '

'There's a crate of some sort over there. Go and have a look at it. If it's yours you can take it.'

We found a dirty box lying on the airfield, with '1st Lieutenant Dovnar' scrawled over it in chalk. I tore open a board where the little window was let into the side of the coffin. His face was uninjured but he was unshaven, he hadn't been washed and the coffin was too short. And the smell . . . I couldn't bend down and kiss him. That's how my husband was returned to me.

I knelt by the man who had been my love.

This was the first Afghan coffin to come to Yazyl, his parents' village. I saw the horror in everyone's eyes. No one had any idea what was going on out there. The coffin was still being lowered into the grave when a tremendous hailstorm began. The hailstones, like white gravel thrown over the budding lilac, crunched underfoot as we stood there. Nature itself was protesting.

I could hardly bear to be in his parents' home because his presence was so strong there, with his mother and father.

We talked very little. I felt his mother hating me because I was alive and he was dead: I would get married again but she had lost her son for ever. Nowadays she tells me, 'Tamara, get married.' But at the time I couldn't look her in the eyes. His father almost went mad. 'Such a wonderful boy . . . dead,' he said, over and over again. We tried to rally him, Petya's mother and I, saying Petya had won medals, that Afghanistan had needed him, he'd died defending our southern borders, and so on. He didn't listen. 'Bastards!' he shouted. 'Bastards! Bastards!'

For me the worst time came later. The most terrible thing was getting used to the thought that I must stop waiting, because there was no one to wait for. I'd wake up wet with horror: Petya was coming home and little Olesha and I were living somewhere else. It took me a long time to realise that I was and would be alone now. I looked at the post-box after every delivery. All 'Addressee is a casualty'. I hated holidays and special occasions, and stopped going out. I had only my memories . . . and of course you only remember what was good.

We went dancing the first time we met. Next day we walked in the park. On the third day he asked me to marry him. I was already engaged – we'd even applied for the licence. When I told my fiancé he went away and wrote me a letter in huge capitals covering the whole page: 'A-A-A-A-A-A!!' Petya decided he'd come home on leave in January and we'd get married. I didn't want to get married in January: I fancied a spring wedding! In the Minsk Palace of Weddings, with music and flowers.

Well, we had a winter wedding, in my home village. It was funny and quick. At Epiphany, when they say that your dreams foretell the future, I had a dream and told my mother about it.

'There was this handsome boy in soldier's uniform, Mum, standing on a bridge calling to me. But as I went towards him he moved further and further away until he'd disappeared altogether.'

'If you marry a soldier you'll be left on your own,' she said.

Two days afterwards he turned up.

'Let's go to the registry office!' he said on the doorstep.

There they took one look at us and said, 'Why bother to wait the two months? Go and fetch a bottle of cognac and we'll do it for you now!'

We were man and wife within the hour. There was a snowstorm outside.

'Where's the taxi you ordered to carry your young bride home?' I demanded.

'Here it is!' He raised his hand and stopped a passing tractor.

For years I went on dreaming of those early days, that old tractor . . . He's been dead for eight years now and I still dream about him often.

'Marry me again!' I beg him.

But he pushes me away. 'No! No!'

I grieve for him not just because he was my husband but because he was a real man, with a big strong body. I'm so sorry I never gave him a son. The last time he came home on leave I wasn't at home. He hadn't sent a telegram and I wasn't expecting him; in fact, I was at my girl-friend's birthday party next door. He opened the door there, heard the loud music and laughter, sat down on a kitchen stool and started crying.

Every day he met me from work. 'When I'm walking to meet you my legs start shaking, as though we're going to say goodbye.'

Once, when we went swimming, we sat on the riverbank and lit a bonfire. 'I hate the idea of dying on foreign soil,' he said.

'Don't get married again, Tamarka,' he begged me that night.

'Why do you say such things?'

'Because I love you so much. I just don't want to think of you with someone else.'

Sometimes I feel I've been alive for ever, and yet my memories are so few.

Once, when my daughter was still tiny, she came home from nursery school. 'We had to tell about our Daddies today and I said mine was a soldier.'

'Why?'

'The teacher didn't ask if he was alive, just what his job was.'

She's growing up now. 'Get married again, Mum,' she advises me when I'm irritable with her.

'What kind of Dad would you prefer?'

'I'd prefer my own Daddy.'

'And if you can't have him?'

'Someone like him.'

I became a widow at twenty-four. In those first few months I'd have married the first man who came along. I was going out of my mind and had no idea how to look after myself. All around me life was going on as usual: someone was building himself a *dacha*, or buying a car, or had a new flat and was looking for a carpet or some nice red tiles for the kitchen. Other people's normal lives simply showed up the fact that I had none. It's only very recently that I've begun to buy a bit of furniture or bake a cake. How could we celebrate any special occasion in this flat?

In the last war everyone was in mourning, there wasn't a family in the land that hadn't lost some loved one. Women wept together then. There's a staff of 100 in the catering college where I work, and I'm the only one who had a husband killed in a war which all the rest have only read about in the papers. I wanted to smash the screen the first time I heard someone on television say that Afghanistan was our shame. That was the day I buried my husband a second time.

Private, Intelligence Corps

We arrived at the Samarkand conscript reception-centre. There were two tents: in one we had to get out of our civvies (those of us with any sense had already sold our jackets and sweater and bought a bottle of wine with the proceeds); in the other we were issued with well-used uniforms, including shirts dating from 1945, *kirzachi* and foot-bindings.* Show those *kirzachi* to an African, who's lived with heat all his life, and he'd faint! Yes, even in Third World African countries soldiers are issued with lightweight boots, trousers and caps, but we were expected to do heavy building work – and sing as we worked! – in 40 degrees Celsius while our feet were literally cooking.

The first week we worked in a refrigeration plant, loading and unloading bottles of lemonade. Then we were sent to work on officers' homes – I did all the bricklaying for one of them. We

* *Kirzachi*: heavy, multi-layered waterproof boots of substitute leather. Foot-bindings are used in the Soviet Army instead of socks.

spent a fortnight putting a roof on a pigsty. For every three slates we used we exchanged two others for vodka; the timber we sold by length, at a rouble a metre.

In that Samarkand training-camp we had just two periods on the firing-range: the first time, we were issued with nine rounds, the second, we got to throw a grenade each. Then we were lined up on the parade-ground and read the Order of the Day: we were being sent to the DRA 'in the execution of our international duty'. Anybody who doesn't wish to go – two paces forward – march! Three boys stepped out, but the CO kicked them back again. 'I was just testing your battle-readiness,' he said. We were issued with two days' dry rations and a leather belt – and off we went, all of us.

The flight seemed long, and we were subdued. I looked out of the window and saw those beautiful mountains. I'd never seen mountains before – I'm from Pskov, which is all meadows and forest. We landed at Shindantai I still remember the date: 19 December 1980.

They looked me up and down: 'Six foot four, eh? Reconnaissance can do with boys like you.'

From Shindanta we drove to Gerat. We were put to work building again. We built a firing-range from scratch, digging the earth and clearing it of rocks. I built a slate roof and did some carpentry. Some of the boys never got to fire a weapon before their first taste of action.

We were hungry every minute of the day. There were two 20-gallon drums in the kitchen, one for the first course, a watery cabbage-soup without a scrap of meat, and one for the second course, a gooey paste of dried potato mash or pearl barley, also without meat. Oh, and canned mackerel, one tin between four of us. The label said: 'Year of manufacture: 1956. Consume within 18 months.' In my year and a half in Afghanistan I stopped being hungry only once, when I was wounded. You were looking for ways to get or steal food the whole time. We climbed into the Afghans' orchards and gardens, even though they shot at us and laid mines to blow us up with. We were desperate for apples, pears, fruit of any kind. I asked my parents to send me citric acid, which they did. We dissolved it in water and drank it. It was nice and sour and burnt your stomach.

We sang the Soviet national anthem before we went into action for the first time. I was a speed-cyclist before the army, and built up such big muscles that people were scared of me and left me alone. I'd never even *seen* a fight, or a knife used in anger, or blood. Suddenly there we were, going into battle in an APC. We'd driven from Shindanta to Gerat by bus, and been out of barracks once, in a truck. Now, riding on top of this armoured carrier, weapon in hand, sleeves rolled up to the elbow, well, it was a completely new and strange feeling. A sense of power and strength, and a certainty that no one and nothing could hurt us.

The villages seemed so low, the irrigation canals looked tiny, the trees few and far between. In half an hour we were so confident we felt like tourists. It all seemed so exotic – the birds, the trees, the flowers. I saw those thornbushes for the first time in my life. We forgot all about war.

We crossed a canal by a mud bridge which I was amazed could take all those tons of metal. Suddenly – BANG! The leading APC had caught a direct hit from a grenade-launcher. Pals of mine were being carried away, their heads blown off like cardboard targets, hands hanging down lifelessly. My mind couldn't take in this new and terrible world.

Command: 'Deploy mortars!' – with their 120 shells a minute. We fired every one of them into the village where the attack had come from, which meant several into every single house. After it was all over we collected up our boys in bits and pieces, even scraping them from the sides of the APC. We spread out a tarpaulin, their common grave, to try and sort out which leg or fragment of skull belonged to whom. We weren't issued with identification tags because of the 'danger' of them falling into enemy hands. This was an undeclared war, you see – we were fighting a war which wasn't happening.

We were very quiet on the way home from this new world. We had something to eat and cleaned our weapons.

'Want a joint?' one of the older guys asked me.

'No thanks.'

I didn't want to start on all that in case I didn't have the will-power to give it up. After a while, though, we all smoked – it was the only way to keep going. They should have let us have a quarter of a pint of vodka a day, like in World War II, but this was a 'dry' country. Somehow or other you had to unwind, to blot it all out. We'd put it in the rice or porridge. Your pupils got as big as saucers, you could see like a cat in the dark and you felt as light as a bat.

Recce men kill at close quarters rather than in set-piece battles, and silently, with a stiletto or bayonet, almost never a gun. I soon got used to it.

My first? You mean the first guy I killed close up? We'd approached a village, I looked through the night-vision binoculars and saw a little lantern, and a rifle, and this guy digging something up. I handed my gun to my mate and got up close enough to jump him to the ground. I stuffed his turban in his mouth to stop him shouting out. The only knife I had on me was a pen-knife I used to cut bread and open cans with, an ordinary little knife. As he lay there on the ground I grabbed him by the beard, pulled it up and slit his throat. The skin of his neck went taut, which made it a lot easier. There was a lot of blood.

I was usually put in charge of our night raids. We'd crouch behind a tree, knives at the ready, watching as they went past, with a scout in front. It was our job to kill him. We took turns to do it. If it was my turn I'd let him get a little bit past me and then jump him from behind. The main thing is to grab the throat with your left hand and throttle him to keep him quiet as you stick the knife into him with your right. Right through, under his liver. I used a knife I picked up from one of them, a Japanese job with a blade over a foot long which cut like it was going through butter. There'd be a quick twitch and he'd be dead without a squeak.

You soon got used to it. It was less a psychological problem than the technical challenge of actually finding the upper vertebrae, heart or liver. We learnt karate, immobilisation techniques and how to kill with our bare hands.

Only once something snapped inside me and I was struck by the horror of what we were doing. We were combing through a village. You fling open the door and throw in a grenade in case there's a machine-gun waiting for you. Why take a risk if a grenade can sort it out for you? I threw the grenade, went in and saw women, two little boys and a baby in some kind of box making do for a cot.

You have to find some kind of justification to stop yourself going mad. Suppose it's true that the souls of the dead look down on us from above?

I got back home and tried to be good, but sometimes I have a desire to cut the odd throat. I came home blind. A bullet went in one temple, came out the other and destroyed both retinas. I can only distinguish light and dark but that doesn't stop me recognising the people whose throats I'd like to cut: the ones who won't pay for gravestones for our lads, the ones who won't give us flats ('It wasn't us who sent you to Afghanistan'), the ones who try and wash their hands of us. What happened to me is still boiling inside. Do I want to have my past taken away from me? No! It's what I live by.

I learnt to walk without my eyes. I get around the city, using the metro and the pedestrian crossings, on my own. I do the cooking – in fact my wife admits I cook better than she does. I've never seen my wife but I know what she looks like, the colour of her hair, the shape of her nose and her lips. I feel everything with my hands and body, which see everything. I know what my son looks like. I used to change his nappies, did his washing, and now I carry him around on my shoulders.

Sometimes I think we don't need our eyes – after all, you close them anyhow when the most important things are going on, and when you're feeling really good. A painter needs his eyes because that's the way he earns his living, but I've learnt to live without them. I *sense* my world now, and words mean more to me than they do to you sighted people.

A lot of people seem to think I'm a man with a great future behind me. 'You've had it, boy!' Like Yuri Gagarin after that first space flight. But they're wrong: the most important part of my life is still to come. I'm convinced of it.

Your body is no more important than a bicycle, say, and I should know – I was a professional cyclist. Your body's an instrument, a machine to work with, that's all. I realise now I can find happiness and freedom without my eyes. Look how many sighted people can't see. I was more blind when I had my sight.

I'd like to cleanse myself of everything that's happened, of all the dirt they shoved us into. It's only our mothers who can understand and protect us now.

You don't know how terrified I get at night, jumping a man with my knife, over and over again. And yet it's only in my dreams I can be a child again, a child who isn't afraid of blood because he doesn't know what it means and thinks it's just red water. Children are natural experimenters, they want to take everything to bits to find out how it's made. But blood frightens me, even in my dreams.

A Mother

I rush to the cemetery as though I'm meeting someone here – and I am, I'm going to meet my son. I spent the first few nights here on my own and never felt a moment's fear. I know all the birds' little habits, and how the grass moves in the wind. In spring I wait for his flowers to grow up, out of the earth, towards me. I planted snowdrops, so that I'd have an early hello from my son to look forward to. They come to me from down there, from him . . .

I sit with him until nightfall. Sometimes I give a sort of scream, which I don't hear until the birds fly up around me. A storm of crows swirls and flaps over my head until I fall silent. I've come here every day for four years, morning or evening, except when I had my heart attack and couldn't come for eleven days. I wasn't allowed to get up, but eventually I did anyway. I managed to get to the toilet on my own, which meant I could escape to my son, even if I collapsed on his grave. I ran away in my hospital nightie.

Before that I had a dream in which Valera said to me, 'Don't come to the cemetery tomorrow, Mama. It isn't necessary.'

But I raced here and found the grave as silent as if he weren't here. He'd gone, I felt in my heart. The crows sat quietly on the gravestone and railing instead of flying away from me as they usually did. I got up from the bench and they flew up in front of me, agitated, stopping me from going to the grave. What was going on? What were they trying to warn me about? They settled down and flew up to the trees; only then did I feel myself drawn to the graveside once again. A sense of deep peace descended and the turbulence left my soul. His spirit had returned. 'Thank you, my little birds, for telling me not to go away. I waited until he came back.'

I feel ill at ease and alone when I'm with other people. I don't belong any more. People talk to me and pester me with this and that. I feel better here with my son. If I'm not at work I'm usually here. To me it's not a grave but his home.

I worked out where his head is; I sit nearby and tell him everything about my everyday life. We share our memories. I look at his photograph. If I stare at it deep and long he either smiles at me or frowns a little bit crossly. We're still together, you see. If I buy a new dress it's only for me to come and see him in and for him to see me in. He used to kneel in front of me and now I kneel in front of him.

I always open this little gate in the railing here and get down on my knees. 'Good morning, my dear . . . Good evening, dear . . . ' I say. I'm always with him.

I wanted to adopt a little boy from the children's home, someone like Valera, but my heart isn't strong enough.

I force myself to keep busy; it's like pushing myself into a dark tunnel. I'd go mad if I let myself sit in the kitchen and gaze out of the window. Only my own suffering can save me from madness. I haven't been to the cinema once in these four years. I sold the colour television and spent the money on the gravestone. I haven't switched the radio on. When my son was killed everything changed, my face, my eyes, even my hands.

I fell madly in love with my husband and just leapt into marriage! He was a pilot, tall and handsome in his leather jacket and flying boots. Was this beautiful bear of a man really my husband? The other girls sighed with envy! I was so tiny next to him, and I got so cross that our great shoe industry couldn't produce a smart pair of high-heels to fit me! I used to long for him to get a cough or cold so I could have him at home and look after him all day.

I desperately wanted a son, a son like him, with the same eyes, the same ears and the same nose. And heaven must have heard my prayer – the baby was the spitting image of his father. I couldn't believe I had two such wonderful men, I just couldn't believe it. I loved my home, even the washing and ironing. I was so in love with everything that I wouldn't step on a spider or a ladybird or a fly, but carry them gently to the window and let them fly away. I wanted everything to live and love as joyfully as I did. When I came home from work I'd ring the bell and turn the light on in the hall so that Valera could see my happiness.

'Lerunka!' I'd call. (That was my name for him when he was a boy.) 'I'm home! I've miiiissed youououou!' Out of breath from running back from work or the shops.

I loved my son to distraction, just as I do now. I was brought photographs of the funeral but I wouldn't take them, I couldn't believe it. I was like a faithful dog, dying on his master's grave. I always was a loyal friend.

One time I remember, when I was still breast-feeding him, my breasts were bursting with milk, but I'd arranged to meet a friend of mine to give her a book she wanted. I waited for an hour and a half in the snow but she never came. Something must have happened, I thought, you don't just promise to come and simply not turn up. I ran to her home and found her asleep. She couldn't understand why I burst into tears. I loved her, too – I gave her my favourite dress, the light blue. That's the way I am.

I was very shy when I was young and never believed anyone could love me, and if a boy said I was beautiful I didn't believe that either. But when I did finally launch myself into life I brimmed over with excitement and enthusiasm. After Yuri Gagarin made that first flight into space Lerunka and I were shouting and jumping for sheer joy in the street. I was ready to love and embrace everyone on earth at that moment . . .

I loved my son to distraction. And he loved me back the same way. His grave draws me as though I hear him calling.

'Have you got a girlfriend?' his army pals asked him.

'Yes,' he said, and showed them my old student card with a photo of me in long, long curls.

He loved waltzing. He asked me to dance the first waltz at his graduation ball. I didn't even know he could dance – he'd had lessons without telling me. We went round and round and round . . .

I used to sit by the window in the evening, knitting and waiting for him. I'd hear steps . . . no, not him. Then more steps, yes, 'mine' this time, my son was home. I never guessed wrong, not once. We'd sit down in the kitchen and chat until four in the morning. What did we talk about? About everything people do talk about when they're happy, serious matters and nonsense too. We'd laugh and he'd sing and play the piano for me.

I'd look at the clock.

'Time for bed, Valera.'

'Let's sit here a bit longer, mother of mine,' he'd say. That's what he called me, 'mother of mine', or 'golden mother of mine'.

'Well, mother of mine, your son has got in to the Smolensk Military Academy. Are you pleased?' he told me one day.

He'd sit at the piano and sing:

'My fellow officers – my lords!
I shan't be the first or the last
To perish on enemy swords.'

My father was a professional officer who was killed in the siege of Leningrad, and my grandfather was an officer, too, so in his height, strength and bearing my son was born to be a soldier. He'd have made a wonderful hussar, playing bridge in his white gloves. 'My old soldier' I used to call him. If only I'd had the tiniest hint from heaven . . .

Everyone copied him, me included. I'd sit at the piano just like him, sometimes I even caught myself walking like him, especially after his death. I so desperately wanted him to live on inside me.

'Well, mother of mine, your son will soon be off!'

'Where to?' He said nothing. I started to cry. 'Where are you being sent, my darling?'

'What do you mean "where"? We know very well where. Now then, golden mother of mine, to work! Into the kitchen – the guests'll soon be here!'

I guessed immediately: 'Afghanistan?'

'Correct,' he said, and his look warned me to go no further. An iron curtain fell between us.

His friend Kolka Romanov rushed in soon after. Kolka, who could never keep anything to himself, told me that they'd applied to be posted to Afghanistan even though they were only in their third year.

The first toast: 'Nothing venture, nothing gain!'

All evening Valera sang my favourite song:

> 'My fellow officers – my lords!
> I shan't be the first or the last
> To perish on enemy swords.'

There were four weeks left. Every morning I'd go to his room and sit and watch him while he slept. Even asleep he was beautiful.

I had a dream, a warning as clear as a knock at the door. I was in a long black dress, holding on to a black cross carried by an angel. I began to lose my grip and looked down to see whether I would fall into the sea or on to dry land, and saw a sunlit crater.

I waited for him to come home on leave. For a long time he didn't write, then one day the phone rang at work.

'I'm back, mother of mine! Don't be late home! I've made some soup.'

'My darling boy!' I shouted. 'You're not phoning from Tashkent, are you? You're home? Your favourite bortsch is in the fridge!'

'Oh no! I saw the saucepan but didn't lift the lid.'

'What soup have you made, then?'

'It's called "idiot's delight"! Come home now and I'll meet you at the bus stop!'

He'd gone grey. He wouldn't admit that he was home on hospital leave. 'I just wanted to see that golden mother of mine for a couple of days,' he insisted. My daughter told me later how she'd seen him rolling on the carpet, sobbing with pain. He had malaria, hepatitis and other things, too, but he ordered his sister not to say a word to me.

I started going to his room in the morning again, to watch him sleeping.

Once he opened his eyes: 'What's up, mother of mine?'

'Go back to sleep, darling, it's still early.'

'I had a nightmare.'

'Just turn over, go back to sleep, and you'll have a good dream. And if you never tell your bad ones they won't come true.'

When his leave was over we went with him as far as Moscow. They were lovely sunny days with the marigolds in bloom.

'What's it like out there, Valera?'

'Afghanistan, mother of mine, is something we should definitely not be doing.' He looked at me and at no one else as he said it. He wiped the sweat from his brow and embraced me. 'I don't want to go back to that hell, I really don't,' he said, and moved away. He looked round one last time. 'That's all, Mama.'

He had never, ever called me 'Mama', always 'mother of mine'. As I say, it was a beautiful sunny day and the marigolds were in bloom. The girl at the airport desk was watching us and started crying.

On the 7th of July I woke up dry-eyed. I stared sightlessly at the ceiling. He'd woken me, he'd come to say goodbye. It was eight o'clock and I had to go to work. I wandered round the flat, I couldn't find my white dress for some reason. I felt dizzy and couldn't see a thing. It wasn't until lunchtime that I calmed down.

On the 7th of July . . . Seven cigarettes and seven matches in my pocket, seven pictures taken on the film in my camera. He'd written seven letters to me, and seven to his fiancée. The book on my bedside table, open at page seven, was Kobo Abe's *Containers of Death* . . .

He had three or four seconds to save his life as his APC was crashing into a ravine: 'Out you jump, boys! I'll go last'. He could never have put himself first.

'From Major S. R. Sinelnikov: In execution of my military duty I am obliged to inform you that 1st Lieutenant Valery Gennadevich Volovich was killed today at 10.45 a.m. . . . '

The whole town knew. His photograph in the Officers' Club was already hung with black crêpe, and the aeroplane would soon be landing with his coffin. But no one told me, no one dared . . . At work everyone around me seemed to be in tears and gave me various excuses when I asked what was wrong. My friend looked in at me through my door. Then our doctor came in.

It was like suddenly waking from a deep sleep. 'Are you mad, all of you? Boys like him don't get killed!' I protested. I started hitting the table with my hand, then ran to the window and beat the glass. They gave me an injection. 'Are you mad, all of you? Have you gone crazy?'

Another injection. Neither of them had any effect. Apparently I shouted, 'I want to see him. Take me to my son!'

'Take her, take her, or she won't survive the shock.'

It was a long coffin, with VOLOVICH painted in yellow on the rough wood. I tried to lift the coffin to take it home with me. My bladder ruptured.

I wanted a good dry plot in the cemetery. Fifty roubles? I'll pay the 50 roubles. Just make sure it's a nice dry plot. I knew it was a swindle but I couldn't object. I spent the first few nights here with him. I was taken home but came back again. It was harvest-time and I remember the whole town, and the cemetery too, smelt of hay.

In the morning a soldier came up to me. 'Good morning, mother.' Yes, he called me 'mother'. 'Your son was my commanding officer. I would like to tell you about him.'

'Come home, with me, son.'

He sat in Valera's chair, opened his mouth and changed his mind. 'I can't, mother.'

When I come to the grave I always bow to him, and I bow to him again when I leave. I'm only home if people are coming. I feel fine here with my son. Ice and snow don't bother me. I write letters here. I go home when it's dark. I like the street-lights and the car headlights. I'm not frightened of man or beast. I feel strong.

'I don't want to go back to that hell.' I can't get those words of his out of my mind. Who is to answer for all this? Should anyone be made to? I'm going to do my best to live as long as possible. There's nothing more vulnerable about a person than his grave. It's his name. I shall protect my son for ever . . .

His comrades come to visit him. One of them went on his knees. 'Valera, I'm covered in blood. I killed with my bare hands. Is it better to be alive or dead? I don't know any more . . . '

I want to know who is to answer for all this. Why do they keep silent? Why don't they name names and take them to court?

> 'My fellow officers – my lords!
> I shan't be the first or the last
> To perish on enemy swords'

I went to church to speak to the priest. 'My son has been killed. He was unique and I loved him. What should I do now? Tell me our old Russian traditions. We've forgotten them and now I need to know.'

'Was he baptised?'

'I so much wish I could say he was, Father, but I cannot. I was a young officer's wife. We were stationed in Kamchatka, surrounded by snow all year round – our home was a snow dug-out. Here the snow is white, but there it's blue and green and mother-of-pearl. Endless empty space where every sound travels for miles. Do you understand me, Father?'

'It is not good that he wasn't baptised, mother Victoria. Our prayers will not reach him.'

'Then I'll baptise him now!' I burst out. 'With my love and my pain. Yes, I'll baptise him in pain.'

He took my shaking hand.

'You must not upset yourself, mother Victoria. How often do you go to your son?'

'Every day. Why not? If he were alive we'd see each other every day.'

'Mother Victoria, you must not disturb him after five o'clock in the afternoon. They go to their rest at that time.'

'But I'm at work until five, and after that I have a part-time job. I had to borrow 2,500 roubles for a new gravestone and I've got to pay it back.'

'Listen to me, mother Victoria. You must go to him every day at noon, for the midday service. Then he will hear your prayers.'

Send me the worst imaginable pain and torture, only let my prayers reach my dearest love. I greet every little flower, every tiny stem growing from his grave: 'Are you from there? Are you from him? Are you from my son?'

Postscript:
Notes from my Diary

I perceive the world through the medium of human voices. They never cease to hypnotise, deafen and bewitch me at one and the same time. I have great faith in life itself – I suppose I'm an optimist by nature. At first I feared that the experience of my first two books [about World War II] in this 'voice genre' as I call it, might actually get in the way of this third venture. I needn't have worried, for this was a totally different war with much more powerful and merciless weaponry: take, for example, the 'Grad' rocket-launcher, which is capable of dislodging a mountain-side. The bitter psychology of this conflict was also very different from the positive mood of the nation as a whole during World War II: Afghanistan wrenched boys from their daily life of school and college, music and discos, and hurled them into a hell of filth. These were eighteen-year-olds, mere school-leavers who could be induced to believe anything. It was only much later that we began to hear such thoughts expressed as, 'We went to fight a Great Patriotic War, namely World War II, but found something totally different.' Or, 'I wanted to be a hero but now I don't know what kind of a person they've turned me into.' Such insights will come, but not soon and not to everyone.

'There are two things necessary for a country to love bullfighting. One is that the bulls must be raised in that country, and the other, that the people must have an interest in death.' (From *Death in the Afternoon* by Ernest Hemingway.)

After excerpts from this book were published in various newspapers and Belorussian magazines a storm of queries and opi-
nions, judgments, convictions and prejudice, broke about my head,
together with the political rhetoric inseparable from 'intellectual'
life in our country. There was a deluge of telephone calls, letters
and personal encounters which left me feeling that the book was
still in the process of being put together . . .

From some of those letters:

I find your book impossible to read. It makes me want to cry out
loud, perhaps because it is only now that I begin to understand
what kind of war this was. Those poor boys – we all stand guilty
before them! What did we know about the war? We should
embrace every one of them and ask his forgiveness. I didn't fight
in this war, but I was part of it.

Here are some of the things I felt, thought and heard at the
time.

I read a book by Larissa Reissner, a Bolshevik writer of the
1920s, describing Afghanistan as full of half-naked tribesmen
dancing and chanting, 'Long live the Russian magicians who
helped us drive out the British.'

The April Revolution gave us the immense satisfaction of
believing that socialism had triumphed in yet another country. All
the same . . .

'Just a few more parasites hanging round our neck,' whispered
a man sitting next to me in the train.

At a seminar at city Communist Party HQ the following question was posed: why did we allow Amin to kill Taraki?* The
seminar leader, a Moscow functionary whose job it was to lay
down the Party line, replied: 'The strong had to be replaced by
the weak.' This left an unpleasant taste in the mouth.

At the time, the official justification for the Soviet invasion of

* Nur Mohammed Taraki (1917–79) led a new government set up in 1978 by the
Marxist People's Democratic Party, only to become the victim of a coup in the
following year.

Afghanistan was that 'the Americans were on the brink of an airborne invasion which we anticipated and thus prevented by less than one hour.'

Afghan sheepskins were suddenly all the rage. Women envied their friends whose husbands were in Afghanistan. The press reported that our soldiers were planting trees and rebuilding bridges and roads.

Leaving Moscow by train I found myself sharing a compartment with a young couple. We began talking about Afghanistan and I more or less spouted the official line, which they ridiculed. They were doctors who'd spent two years in Kabul. They strongly defended soldiers who bought goods there to resell in the Soviet Union. They said life out there was very expensive and the pay was inadequate. In Smolensk I helped them down with their luggage, which consisted of a large amount of Western-made articles, such as radios, videos and sophisticated kitchen equipment.

When I got home my wife told me the following story about a neighbour of ours. This woman had no husband and her only son had been posted to Afghanistan. She went to whoever it was she had to go to, went down on her knees to beg him, kissed his boots, and returned satisfied. 'I've got my boy out!' she said. She also coolly described how 'the top brass are buying their own sons out'.

My son came home from school and told us that some Green Berets, the parachute force, had been to the school to give a talk. 'You should have seen their Japanese watches!' he said wonderingly. I later asked one such veteran how much his watch had cost and how he could afford it. After some umming and aahing he admitted, 'We stole a truckload of fruit and sold it.' He told me that everyone particularly envied soldiers on petrol-tanker duty. 'They're all millionaires!'

I can't forget the harassment of Andrei Sakharov. I certainly agree with one thing he said: 'We always prefer dead heroes to living men and women who may have made a few mistakes.'

I heard recently that some rank-and-file soldiers and a couple of officers were studying for the priesthood at the seminary at Zagorsk [a famous monastery not far from Moscow]. What, I wonder, drove them to it? Was it repentance, or a desire to escape from the cruel realities of life, or a thirst for some kind of spirituality? For them, apparently, the privileges their war veterans' cards bought them – the extra food, the flashy foreign clothes and the private land – were not enough to keep their mouths and eyes shut.

(N. Goncharov)

That was from a man who did not experience Afghanistan at first hand. The following is from a woman, a civilian employee, who did:

I'm one of those who went out there, although with every year that goes by I find it harder to answer the inevitable question: 'You're not a soldier, so what did you go there for?' What business had a woman going out there? The more the war is condemned, the more we women are disapproved of and the less we are understood.

People like me were victims of blind faith. We believed all the talk about the April Revolution and accepted everything we'd been taught since our earliest schooldays. But we came home different people. We wanted the truth to be known. I waited and waited for it to start coming out.

If I could live my life again I wouldn't go to Afghanistan. 'Be done with the whole thing! And try and make everyone forget you were there!' my friend wrote to me. No, I don't want to just wash it away, but I would like to sort things out. My life might have turned out differently if I hadn't gone – but to be absolutely honest, I don't regret it. I still remember that sense of sharing our troubles and aiming at higher things. We realised we'd been deceived, and wondered why we were so gullible.

I was amazed when I saw how many women there were there. I'd thought I was the only little fool and somehow assumed I wasn't quite normal. There were thousands of us! We all had some practical reason for going, of course, whether to earn money, or carve out a career, or solve some personal problem, but inside all of us there was still that . . . *faith*. We wanted to be needed and we wanted to help. I personally felt that there ought to be women wherever wars were being fought. Perhaps I was naïve to think that every war was like our Great Patriotic War against the Nazis, but how could a hospital, for example, function without women? Those defenceless, mutilated men needed them, even if only for the comforting touch of a soft hand. It was simple charity and a woman's proper work. I met boys there who actually volunteered for dangerous action. They showed true heroism and didn't stop to think they were going to their deaths.

I'm sorry these thoughts of mine are coming out in such a jumble. I'm upset and there's so much I want to say . . .

The myth about brotherhood at the front was dreamed up here at home. It didn't exist. Everything was for sale, including women. Yes, it's true! But that wasn't the most important thing. In spite of all that we were still idealists. We had our faith. The worst came later. We were sent to Afghanistan by a nation which sanctioned the war and returned to find that same nation had rejected it. What Afchnan mu is the way wi.'ve simply been erased from the public mind. What was only recently described as one's 'international duty' is now considered stupidity. When was that frontier crossed? That's the most important question of all.

I'm trying to think of a comparison. It's like . . . a mountaineer, climbing up very high . . . then he falls, breaks his leg, but for the rest of his life he still longs for the mountains. That's the nostalgia we feel – especially the men. They risked their lives and became killers – and because of that they think they're somehow special. They've been touched by something unique. Perhaps it's some kind of illness within us. Or perhaps we still haven't come home?

(G. Khaliulina, civilian employee)

My son had just left schoool to enter a military academy when the war in Afghanistan began. Throughout those ten years, when other mothers' sons found themselves in a foreign land with guns in their hands, I was sick with worry. I knew my son might be there one day. It's not true that the public didn't know what was going on. Everyone could see parents opening their doors to those zinc coffins or having their sons returned to them broken and crippled. Such things weren't mentioned on radio or television, of course, or in the newspapers (until you recently dared to), but it was plain for all to see. And what did our 'humane' society, and we ourselves, do about it? Well, we handed out medals to the 'great' old men, Brezhnev, Andropov and the rest, at every conceivable opportunity.

We fulfilled, and over-fulfilled, one five-year plan after the other (while the shelves of our shops stayed as empty as ever), built our dachas and amused ourselves while eighteen- and twenty-year-olds were being shot and killed on foreign soil. What kind of people are we, and what right have we to ask our children to do the things they had to do there? How can we, who stayed at home, claim that our hands are cleaner than theirs? And although their suffering, their torture, has cleansed *them* of their sins, we have not yet been cleansed of ours. The machine-gunned and abandoned villages and ruined land are not on their consciences but on ours. We were the real murderers, not they, and we murdered our own children as well as others.

These boys were heroes! They weren't fighting for any so-called 'mistaken policy'. They fought because they put their faith in us. We should kneel before every one of them. If we truly faced up to the comparison of what we did here with what befell them there, we might go mad.

(A. Golubnichaya, construction engineer)

Today, of course, Afghanistan is a profitable and fashionable subject. That will no doubt please you, Comrade Alexievich, because your book will be all the rage. Nowadays in this country a lot of people are crawling out of the woodwork who are fascinated by any opportunity to smear the good name of their Motherland, including some Afgantsi. And it's people like you who give them the ammunition they need to defend themselves with. 'Look what we were forced to do,' they say. Decent people don't *need* to defend themselves – they stay decent whatever circumstances they find themselves in – and there are plenty of such veterans of Afghanistan, but they weren't the ones you sought out.

Although I wasn't in Afghanistan, I fought all through World War II and I know there was plenty of dirt in that war too; but I don't intend to bring it all up and I won't allow others to either. It's not just that that war was different. We all know that we have to eat in order to live, and that eating also implies going to the toilet (if you'll pardon the expression), but we just don't mention such things.

So why couldn't you and those like you observe the same taboo in your books about these wars? If Afgantsi themselves protest against the 'revelations' in books like yours we should respect their wishes. And I know what makes them object so violently: it's a normal human emotion called shame. They're ashamed. You picked up that emotion accurately enough, but you had to go further, and take it before the court of public opinion. In telling us that they shot camels and killed civilians you wanted to demonstrate the futility and wickedness of war, but you don't realise that in doing so you insult those who took part in it, including a lot of innocent boys.

(N. Druzhinin, Tula)

Then there were the phone calls:

'OK, we aren't heroes, maybe, but now we're murderers, according to you. We murdered women, children and their animals. Maybe in thirty years I'll be ready to tell my son that not everything was as heroic as the books say it was. But I'll tell him myself, in my own words and in thirty years' time. Now it's still an open wound which is only just beginning to heal and form a scab. Don't pick it! Leave it alone! It's still very painful.'

'How could you? How dare you cover our boys' graves with such dirt? They did their duty by the Motherland to the bitter end and now you want them to be forgotten . . .

'Hundreds of little museums and memorial corners have been set up in schools all over the country. I took my son's exercise books and his army overcoat to his old school to serve as an example.

'Who needs your dreadful truth? I don't want to know it!!! You want to buy your own glory at the expense of our sons' blood. They were heroes, heroes, heroes! They should have beautiful books written about them, and you're turning them into mince-meat.'

'I had my son's stone engraved with these words: "Remember, friends, he died that the living might live." I know, now, that that was not true – he did not die for the sake of the living. I was lied to when I was young and continued the process with him. We were so good at believing. "Love the Motherland, son, she'll never betray you and love you always." I used to repeat to him. Now I would like to write something different on his grave: "Why?" ' (A mother)

'My neighbour brought me a newspaper with the excerpt from your book. "Forgive me," she said, "but this is the war you told us about." I couldn't believe my eyes. I didn't think it possible to write such things and have them printed. We've got so used to living on two levels, one according to what we read in books and the press, and the other – totally different – according to our own experience. It's more shocking than comforting, when newspapers actually start to describe life as it really is. Everything you wrote is true, except that the reality was even more terrible. I would like to meet you and talk to you.' (A woman)

'I see my son leave the flat every morning but I still can't believe he's home. When he was over there I'd tell myself, if they send him back in a coffin I'll do one of two things: go on a protest march or go to church. I was invited to his old school. "Come and tell us about your son and how he won the Red Star twice over," they begged. But I didn't go. I'm forty-five. I call ours the "obedient generation" and the Afghan war the acme of our tragedy. You've hit a nerve by daring to ask us and our children this question: "Who are we? And why can they do what they want with us?"' (A mother)

' "Oh, they're dreadful people!" I heard someone say at work, talking about the Afgantsi. But so are we all. The war didn't make them any worse than they were before. In fact I sometimes think the war must have been a cleaner experience for them than our day-to-day life was for us here at home. That is why they long to go back.' (A woman)

'How much longer are you going to go on describing us as mentally ill, or rapists, or junkies? We were told the opposite over there. "When you get home you'll be in the vanguard of *perestroika*. You'll clean up the whole stagnant mess!" they said. We thought we'd be restoring order to society but they won't let us get on with the job. "Study!" they keep telling us. "Settle down and have a family!"

'It was quite a shock for me, the black marketeers, the mafia and the apathy – but they won't let us get on and do something serious about it. I felt utterly bewildered until some clever guy said to me, "What can you actually do, apart from shooting? Do you really think that justice comes out of the barrel of a gun?" That was when I began to think, to hell with my gun. I'll have to stop thinking it's still hanging over my shoulder, I told myself.'

'I cried when I read your article, but I shan't read the whole book, because of an elementary sense of self-preservation. I'm not sure whether we ought to know so much about ourselves. Perhaps it's just too frightening. It leaves a great void in my soul. You begin to lose faith in your fellow-man and fear him instead.' (A woman)

'Now you just listen to me! I'm fed up with the whole damn thing! Why is it that whenever you write about girls who went to Afghanistan you always make us out to be prostitutes? I don't deny that some of them were, but not all. It makes me want to scream! Why should we all be tarred with the same brush? Take the trouble to look inside us and you'll find some very tormented souls.

'For a year and a half after I got home I couldn't sleep at night; if I did doze off my dreams were full of bodies and shelling, and I woke up in a panic. I went to see a psychiatrist, not to ask for sick leave, just for some tablets or even a bit of advice. His response was, "Did you really see a lot of corpses?" God, I wanted to slap his silly young face! I haven't bothered with any more doctors.

'This feeling that I don't want to go on living gets stronger with every passing day. I have no desire to meet anyone or see anything but because of our wretched housing shortage there's nowhere to escape to. I don't want or need anything for myself, but do try to do something for the ones asking for your help.

'The same thing's happening to all the people I've kept in touch with from my time over there. All the same, I don't trust what you're saying. You're trying to convince us that we were cruel – but do you realise how cruel you yourself, and your society, have been?

'I won't mention my name. Take it that I'm already dead.'

'You want me to accept that it was a sick generation that came back from the war, but I prefer to see it as the generation whose eyes were opened. At least we found out who our real friends were. Yes, of course young boys were killed, but who knows how many of them might have died in drunken brawls and knife-fights anyway? I read somewhere (I can't remember the exact statistics) that more people die in car accidents every year in this country than were killed in ten years of war. The army hadn't had a real war to fight for a long time and this was a chance to test ourselves and our latest weapons. Those boys were heroes, every one of them, but it's because of people like you that we're now in retreat on all fronts. We've lost Poland, Germany, Czechoslovakia. What's happened to our Empire? Is this what I fought all through the war for, right up to Berlin in 1945?'

'We want justice for ourselves. Just recently I've begun to wonder how we've developed this acute sense of justice after coming back from a war where there was none. Don't mention my surname if you print this – I don't want any funny looks from the people round me.'

'Why all this talk of mistakes? And do you really think all these exposés and revelations in the press are a help? You're depriving our youth of their heroic heritage. People are killed out there and you go on talking about mistakes. I suppose the real heroes aren't the boys being pushed around in wheelchairs by their mothers or wearing artificial legs under their jeans, but the ones who broke their legs in motorbike crashes so as not to go into the army, or deserted to the enemy?'

'I was on holiday by the Black Sea and saw a few young lads crawling over the sand to get to the water. I didn't go to the beach any more, I'd just have started crying. They were laughing and trying to flirt with us girls but we all ran away from them. Yes, I did, too. I want those boys to be happy, to know that we value them even the way they are. They want to live! I love them because they're alive!'

'My only son was killed there. The only comfort I had was that I'd raised a hero, but according to you he wasn't a hero at all, but a murderer and aggressor. Then how would you describe our sons' courage? They shot themselves when they were fatally wounded rather than surrender and dishonour themselves as Soviet soldiers, and threw themselves on grenades to save their comrades' lives. Do you think that was all a gigantic lie?
'Why? Why do you continually pick up what is black in man, rather than what is fine and noble? Remember Gorky's phrase: "Man – the very word is proud!"' (A father)

'Of course there were criminals, addicts and thugs. Where aren't there? Those who fought in Afghanistan must, absolutely, must be seen as victims who need psychological rehabilitation.
'Somewhere I read the confession of an American Vietnam veteran. He said a terrible thing. "In the eight years since the war the number of suicides – officers as well as other ranks – is about the same as the number of fatalities in the war itself." We must urgently consider the souls of our Afgantsi.'

'They say up to a million "enemy" lives were lost fighting for their own interests and their own freedom. However heroically the aggressors may themselves have died, that onslaught on basic human rights was no act of heroism, even though we try and dress it up as such today. The most important question is this: in whose name was all this done? There's been enough hero-worship now,

Afgantsi. We sympathise with you. That's the paradox! We know that oppressed and demoralised young men were forced to take part in the war, but the fact remains that, even while you yourselves were dying, you were bringing death and destruction to another people. That was a crime rather than heroism. Only repentance can bring relief to you who partook in a shameful episode.

'Please publish my opinion. I'm curious to know what dirt these "heroes of our time" will throw at me.'

'I don't know what my son did in Afghanistan. Why was he there? We began asking such questions even while the war was still on, and I almost got thrown out of the Party for it. And I would have been, but for the fact that my son was brought home in a zinc coffin. I couldn't even give him a Christian funeral.' (A father)

'This is still a very painful memory. We were in a train, and a woman in our compartment told us she was the mother of an officer killed in Afghanistan. I understood – she was the mother, she was crying, but I told her, "Your son died in an unjust war. The mujahedin were defending their homeland."'

'They took young kids to fight and destroyed them . . . and for what? To defend the Motherland and our southern borders?

'They rehoused me after, but I sit here alone, crying. Three years later I go to the cemetery every day, and imagine the weddings and grandchildren that will never be.

'They phoned me from HQ. "Come, Mamasha," – that's what they called me – "come and receive the medal on your son's behalf." They presented me with his Red Star. "Say a few words, Mamasha,' they asked. So I did. I held up the medal. "Look!" I said. "This is my son's blood."'

'It won't be long before they call on us to put the country to rights and give us the weapons to do it with. I think there's going to have to be a reckoning pretty soon. Just publish their names! Don't let them hide behind pseudonyms.'

'Some people are stupid enough to blame those eighteen-year-old boys for everything and it's your book that is responsible for that. We must distinguish the war from those who took part in it. The war was criminal and has been condemned as such, but the boys must be defended and protected.'

'I'm a Russian literature teacher. For many years I taught my pupils some words of Karl Marx: "The death of a hero is not like that of the frog in the fable, who inflated himself until he burst. It resembles, rather, the setting of the sun." What does your book have to teach us?'

'They want to transform us from a lost generation into reliable defenders of the status quo (we've already proved our faith in it, after all). Nowadays they're sending us to Chernobyl, Tbilisi or Baku, wherever there's danger.'

'I don't want to have children, I'm frightened of what they might say about me and about the war when they grow up. Because I was there. It was a filthy war and we should admit that it was so. But because we stay silent our children will have to do it for us.

'I'm ashamed to admit this but when I got back I was sorry I didn't win a medal, not even a minor one. Now I'm glad I didn't kill anyone.'

'We are forced to suppress so much of ourselves in this country, and we know so little about ourselves. How much do we know, for example, about the cruelty of our own teenagers? There's so little written about this question and hardly any research done. Until very recently, of course, there was no call for it – weren't our Soviet teenagers the finest in the world? Just as we had no drug addicts, rapists or robbers! Well, it turned out we have more than our fair share of all of them. Then these adolescent boys were handed out guns and had a simple message hammered into them: "All mujahedin are bandits and all bandits are mujahedin!" Now they come home and tell us all about how they lobbed grenades into villages. For them this is the norm. "Forgive them, Father, for they know not what they do . . ."'

Arthur Koestler asked this question: 'Why, when we tell the truth, does it always sound like a lie? Why, when we proclaim the New Age, do we cover the ground with corpses? And why do we accompany our paeans to the glorious future of socialism with threats?'

In shelling those quiet little villages and bombing the ancient mountain-paths we were shelling and bombing our own ideals. This cruel truth is something we must face up to and survive. Our children are already playing games called 'Mujahedin' and 'Limited Contingent' [as the first Soviet forces were euphemistically described].

It will take great courage to recognise the truth about ourselves. I know – I've tried it. I still remember the way a twenty-year-old shouted, 'I don't want to hear about any political mistakes! I just don't want to! Give me my two legs back if it was all a mistake.' And I also remember what the boy in the next bed said: 'They put the blame on a few men who were already dead.* And everyone else was innocent – apart from us! Yes, we used our weapons to kill. That's what you handed them out for. Did you expect us to come home angels?'

There are only two ways forward from all this: to become aware of the truth, or to shield ourselves from it. Are we to hide ourselves away yet again?

In *The Black Obelisk* Erich Maria Remarque wrote:

> 'Shortly after the truce was called a strange process began to occur, and it continues to this day. The war, which until 1918 had been hated almost without exception by the soldiers involved, was gradually transformed into the great event of their lives. They returned to an everyday existence which had seemed, as they lay in the trenches and cursed the war, a kind of paradise. Now, faced with the frustrations and problems of ordinary life, they recalled the war as a vague memory of another time and another place; and quite against their wishes and

* Presumably he had in mind Brezhnev, Andropov, Chernenko etc.

even without their active participation, it took on a different aspect, like a retouched painting. The mass slaughter was seen as an adventure from which they had fortunately emerged unharmed. Suffering was forgotten, grief assuaged; and death, which had spared us, became what it always does become for the living, something abstract, even unreal, which takes on reality only when it strikes the man next to us or threatens us directly. In 1918 the Veterans' Society was intensely pacifist; now it has taken on a sharply nationalistic character. Memories of the war, and the sense of soldierly comradeship so strongly alive in nearly all the members, have been cunningly transformed by Volkenstein into pride in the war itself. Those who lack this nationalist fervour are held to besmirch the memory of those cruelly betrayed heroes who wanted so passionately to live.'

I must admit I'm bewildered when I see those young men pinning on their Afgantsi uniforms, pinning their medals to their chests, and going off to schools to talk to the children. I can't understand how a mother can be forced to give ten or twenty speeches about her dead son, to the point where she's almost too exhausted to drag herself home.

We've worshipped many gods. Some have been consigned to the scrapheap, others to museums. Let us make Truth into a god! A god before whom each of us shall answer according to his own conscience, and not as a class, or a university year, or a collective, or a people ... Let us be charitable to those who have paid a greater price for insight than we ourselves. Remember: 'I brought my friend, and my own truth, back with me from a raid ... Head, arms and legs, all severed, and his skin flayed ... '

Our lives are forever tied to those red gravestones, with their inscriptions in memory, not only of the dead, but also of our naïve and trusting faith:

Tatarchenko Igor Leonidovich
(1962–1981)
In the execution of his duty and true to his military
oath. He showed courage and steadfastness and died on

active service in Afghanistan.
Dearest Igor, You left this life without having known it.

Mama, Papa

Ladutko Aleksandr Viktorovich
(1964–1984)
Died while fulfilling his international duty
You died an honourable death
You did not spare yourself
You died a hero's death on Afghan soil
That we might live in peace.

To my dear son, from Mama

Bartashevich Yuri Frantsevich
(1967–1986)
Died in the execution of his international duty
We love, remember and mourn.

His family

Bobkov Leonid Ivanovich
(1964–1984)
Died in the execution of his international duty
Sun and moon are extinguished without you, dearest son.

Mama, Papa

Zilfigarov Oleg Nikolayevich
(1964–1984)
Died true to his military oath.
You did not fulfil your dreams and ambitions
Your dear eyes were closed too soon
Dear Oleg, dearest son and brother
We cannot express the pain of your loss.

Mama, Papa, your brothers and sisters

Kozlov Andrei Ivanovich
(1961–1982)
Died in Afghanistan
My only son.

Mama

Bogush Viktor Konstantinovich
(1960–1980)
Died defending his country
The earth is a desert without you . . .